UPWARDS

UPWARDS

*The story of the first woman to solo thru-paddle
the Northern Forest Canoe Trail*

Laurie Apgar Chandler

Laurie Apgar Chandler

Cover design by Megan Chandler
Author photograph by Jacob Melton
Cover photograph (Deadwater North Campsite, Allagash River) by Laurie Chandler
Map by Katina Daanen/Indigo Design

Interior design and production by
Maine Authors Publishing
12 High Street
Thomaston, Maine 04861

Printed in the United States of America

For my parents, George and Joan Apgar, with love

CONTENTS

THE
NORTHERN FOREST
CANOE TRAIL

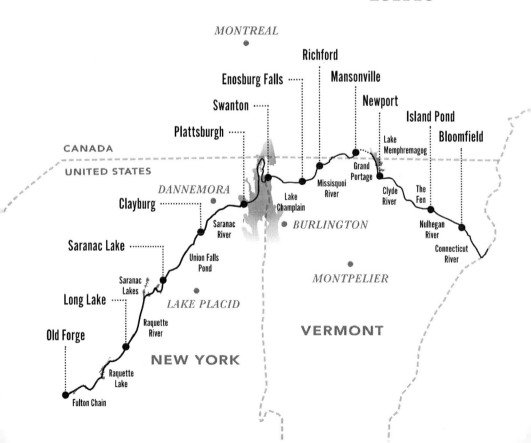

Fort Kent

Allagash
Village

QUÉBEC CITY

St. John
River

Churchill Dam

Allagash
River

Round
Pond

Mud Pond
Carry

Umsaskis Lake

Chase Rapids

Eagle Lake

Northeast
Carry

Chamberlain Lake

The
Birches

Chesuncook
Lake

Jackman

West Branch
Penobscot
River

Stratton

Moose
River

Moosehead
Lake

Rangeley

Long Pond

MAINE

Spencer and Little Spencer
Streams

Flagstaff Lake

BANGOR

South Branch
Dead River

Errol

Mooselookmeguntic
Lake

Groveton

The
Richardsons

Androscoggin
River

AUGUSTA

Upper
Ammonoosuc
River

NEW
HAMPSHIRE

PORTLAND

CONCORD

PROLOGUE

The most difficult thing is the decision to act; the rest is merely tenacity.

—Amelia Earhart

This book came so close to never being written—to blowing gently into the tumbling river of life. Perhaps it would have drifted silently for a time, then slipped quietly beneath the water, lost forever. Five months had passed since my return home. Several weeks even since my January 2016 recognition as the first woman to solo paddle the entire Northern Forest Canoe Trail without help.

It was too early, really, to be awake on that quiet Saturday, but so worth it. The Maine woods had been transformed. I followed the wandering path of a black Lab, her tracks the first on the newly christened snow. The moon was just half of a brilliant sphere, but still it cast faint shadows in the hushed and reverent woods. A hint of dawn's colors tinged the eastern sky, and moonlight touched the snow-capped branches. I breathed softly so as not to break the spell. Awe, tranquility, and a growing purpose filled my soul. God felt so very close. I longed to write, to hold this moment forever, to share its power.

Months had slipped by under the smothering blanket of procrastination, my writing energy gone after the frantic blogging of the summer. But this was my gift, I mused, a promise I had made to myself, perhaps even a calling. In those woods, I made a vow. Whether my writing was enough for others, it would be enough for me. Its destiny, be it for a hundred friends or many more strangers, was a mystery, just as the question of whether I could truly paddle and portage a solo boat for 740 miles once had been.

Amelia Earhart said it well: "Just go get started." For within each of us there abides this place, this spring of dreams, where we glimpse the possibility of many things. We call this daydreaming. Although, if you're like me, it often happens in the depths of the night and fades away by the light of day. While a dream is confined to our hearts and minds, it stays safe. Exploring it, voicing it, committing to it, takes courage. And yet, when once it's freed, it blossoms. So it was with my dream.

This is the story of that dream, the tale of an improbable mustard seed of faith that flourished into the adventure of a lifetime. I invite you to journey with me, discovering an inner strength that I only hoped was there. Finding the wilderness of centuries past on remote lakes, but also in the nooks and crannies of busy, developed places. Encountering the abiding goodness of people. Experiencing solo travel, not as a longing for the companionship of others, but as the gift of listening to and knowing yourself. And gazing in wonder at the drama, intricacy, and awesome glory of the natural world.

Journey with me and perhaps you, too, will emerge a different person.

The Northern Forest Canoe Trail (NFCT) is the longest mapped inland paddling route in the country. Much newer than its hiking counterpart, the Appalachian Trail, the NFCT celebrated its 15th birthday in 2015, the year of my journey. Stewardship of the trail is provided by a membership-based nonprofit headquartered in Waitsfield, Vermont.

The NFCT's mission encompasses past, present, and future. The organization works to preserve and share the historical and cultural stories from a time when rivers were the highways of life. They promote inspiring outdoor experiences in the Northern Forest and build partnerships, continually improving trail infrastructure and protecting the waterway for future generations. The NFCT does its job well, thanks to the down-to-earth people who are its staff, volunteers, and paddlers.

Wilderness paddling was for me even newer. It all began in the summer of 2005, when Chris and I got married. We hauled my dad's impossibly heavy square-sterned guide boat to the Allagash for our honeymoon. We did an easy part, one without large lakes, long portages, or scary rapids, but still I cried when it was time to come home. In 2009, I went back. This time it was in Chris's old blue canoe, just months after we had lost him to a sudden, massive, surreal heart attack. Dad went with me. It was a bittersweet journey, as we followed the same route as four years before.

We went slowly, absorbing the late summer solitude. At the end, I vividly remember my wondering question to the ranger at Michaud Farm, "So if I came here by myself, you would let me paddle the Allagash?" His answer in the affirmative simply amazed me. Was it that day that the mustard seed was planted?

Or was it two years later, in 2011, the summer of Paddle for Hope? That journey was my first expedition. Cancer had touched my heart through the death of a student, a beautiful, vibrant soul who danced through life with a smile, even through the osteosarcoma and the gradual surrendering of a myriad of dreams. If I was angry and perplexed, how must her family feel? From the pain, the compassion, the needlessness of it all came Paddle for Hope, a 350-mile solo kayak trip to raise money for the Maine Children's Cancer Program.

For 30 days, often alone, I paddled from the Magalloway River, just across the border in New Hampshire, to Fort Kent, Maine. That was the easier half of the Northern Forest Canoe Trail, those miles in Maine. We raised $10,681, from a multitude of friends and even some generous strangers, and the mustard seed was growing. By the time I finished Paddle for Hope, I was wondering if a woman alone could complete the entire trail, without help. The first half is much more difficult. There are long upstream rivers, many portages that must be carried, and the crossing of windy Lake Champlain. Could a woman in her fifties do it? Could I do it?

Financially, several things had to happen first. I needed a two-month block of time without working, and I needed a new boat. Now that my children, Megan and Taylor, were grown, I was simplifying my life and selling my house, much as I loved it. The house had gone on the market in 2013, sold in 2014, and by 2015 I was ready. In my basement bedroom at Mom and Dad's, cozy by the wood stove, the planning began. That winter and spring were spent training and gearing up, and in March I started a blog.

Because journaling captures the spirit of the moment, thoughts before you know the outcome, I will be sharing some of my favorites along the way. On June 1, three weeks before departure, I wrote this post, trying to answer the eternal question, "Why are you doing this?"

May You Find Fireplace Birds

We christened them the "fireplace birds," but of course they had another name. In those shortening days toward the end of August 2009, the Allagash was a quiet place. As Dad and I canoed from Umsaskis Bridge to Michaud Farm, the cool mornings and chilly swimming were more than compensated for, by moose heavy with antlers and the beautiful solitude of the river.

Our cheeky friends first visited us at Lock Dam. Hopping contentedly among the ashes of the fire pit, focused on pecking who knows what, they were surprisingly tame. The colorful male and his drab partner were a species new

*Dad cooking dinner at Long Lake Dam in 2009 at the
camp where we first met the fireplace birds*

*to us. Dad and I love our birds, especially new ones, and felt their presence
yet another gift of the late summer wilderness. Imagine our surprise, the next
evening, when we discovered two more in the Outlet campsite on Round Pond.*

*Dad and I will never forget those birds, or the midnight stampede of a
moose through our campsite and down into the river with a mighty splash, or
our first otter family in the Musquacook Deadwater. A journey is so much more
than the destination. One of my hopes for this summer is to absorb the experience, to treasure the moments. And which parts will live on in my stories, in
the memories of my heart? I don't know, of course. But if you ask me why I will
live on tuna and granola, portaging in the pouring rain and paddling into
the wind, with sweat and bugs my closest friends, I go because of the fireplace
birds, whatever they will be.*

And those birds? They were white-winged crossbills, *Loxia leucop-
tera*, a finch that feeds almost exclusively on spruce and tamarack seeds,
eating up to 3,000 in a single day!

CHAPTER 1

A LOOK OVER MY SHOULDER

In the bulb there is a flower, in the seed, an apple tree;
in cocoons a hidden promise: butterflies will soon be free!
In the cold and snow of winter there's a spring that waits to be,
unrevealed until its season, something God alone can see.

—Natalie Sleeth, "Hymn of Promise"

The boat simply wouldn't budge, held by the relentless and surprisingly powerful current. The deeper channel, which minutes ago had been a welcome ally, now seemed a sinister opponent. It didn't matter that I was desperate, that the day of solid rain and cold was moving toward darkness. That no one knew where I was, miles from where I had planned to end my day. The tree, dark and ugly, uncaring, pinned the kayak tightly.

I had come around the bend with such a sense of confidence, too. Finally, the South Branch of the Dead River had been gaining momentum, moving me toward my destination, the Kennebago Road bridge. It was the fifth day of Paddle for Hope, June 23, 2011.

The morning had begun as mornings will, with tranquility and wonder, and the promise of all the day before me. A gentle current, cedar waxwings flitting among the twisted alder, and the splash and scramble of a spotted fawn up the muddy bank. Casting a gray Rooster Tail in the first of the riffles, I caught a trout. Its speckled sides flashed brightly as I brought it in. There were more, quick to take the lure, but I had to go or my early start would be long gone.

By late morning, mist had turned to drizzle and then to driving rain. The second portage of the day followed the cracked pavement of old Route 16, where I wheeled my loaded boat along on its trusty kayak cart. I had already walked about five miles that day. More than three to reach the river in the first place and another couple to scout this road out and back, only at the far end finding a sign to confirm I was going the right way.

A cluster of cabins (we call them "camps" in Maine) overlooked the rushing water. I wandered through one yard, curious for a peek at what I was missing on the river below. According to the *AMC River Guide: Maine*, the gorge the portage bypassed had four Class III or IV ledge drops. They were runnable, by a "solid Class III boater," something that I was not.

An unlocked back porch on the nearest cabin looked so tempting. And not too much like trespassing, as the room's only entrance was from the outside. *Would its owner mind a stranger's brief, respectful visit?*

Inside, it was dry, blessedly dry. A simple table, chairs to sit on, a cocoon of peace and comfort for a little while. The rain beat a steady rhythm overhead. I made a mug of hot chocolate and ate a snack. The temperature that afternoon would never rise above the low 50s, with constant rain. Thankfully, the extra miles of portaging had brought some feeling back into my numb feet, at least for now. I cupped the warm mug and my spirits lifted.

From the cozy porch, it wasn't far to the put-in. The boat slid easily down the grassy bank and into the river. Now my progress slowed, as the river threw it all at me…shallow areas, Class II rapids, rocks, rocks, and more rocks. I was in and out of the boat many times. At some point, a bad slip gave me the worst of the more than twenty bruises that would eventually cover my legs. On this stretch, there were no campsites, official or otherwise, and I began to doubt that I would reach the bridge that day. It was there that I had planned to meet my parents for a shuttle to their campsite for the night.

Gradually, though, the river deepened and I was moving once again. Relaxing, I began hoping to make the rendezvous after all.

Until now, my appreciation of river danger had been largely academic. Sitting by the wood stove reading about first descents or year-long paddling voyages across Canada was as close as I'd been to potential disaster. On the Allagash, my father had been very careful of "strainers." These fallen trees are extremely dangerous and can trap, submerge, and pin boats and people as river current sweeps through them. I had listened with half an ear, thinking he was overly cautious, overly dramatic.

Some four miles past the portage, the river curved left around a rather large sand and gravel beach. It was a bend like any other bend. Until, without warning, the current grabbed me. There was no thought of danger, no reaction time. In a breath, the boat was pulled with force into an ancient blowdown. It tipped toward the beach, and began to fill with water. Luckily, I could hop out and stand. My own safety was never threatened.

It was at this moment that I made a fateful decision. Some of my loose clothing and other items were floating away. It's amazing how you get lazier and lazier about tying in items like a soaking wet shirt or the water bottle you are drinking from.

So, off I went to grab my stuff and deposit it on the beach. A bad decision? The river used the time well. My boat was now upside down, fully under water, a tremendous force pushing it into the tree. My large green dry bag, still clipped to the boat, floated near the surface like a giant balloon. The kayak wouldn't budge, and I shuddered, imagining myself trapped underwater by that relentless power, a churning force that nothing could stop.

Without the boat, I was stuck. Though not far from the state highway in miles, I was in truth totally isolated. I later learned that Dad tried to walk in, to find me there, only to meet an impenetrable swamp. I was soaked and had been for hours, the chill gradually stealing my body's warmth. The atmosphere of this dismal place seemed evil, and my prospects hopeless.

Thankfully, I was carrying a small orange SPOT satellite transponder, capable of several functions. Every day, I sent a check-in/ OK message to a group of friends and family, giving the time and coordinates of my position, with a link to Google maps. And, although I never had, I could also send a HELP message to my small support team.

In desperate straits, there was a third option. Pushing the SOS button would send a full-fledged 911 far and wide, to wardens and emergency services and who knows who else. I most definitely did not want to have to do that!

The prayer I lifted up came from the very center of my being, faith and desperation mingling in a heartfelt plea. I felt God there, beside me on that lonely river.

God had been a quiet presence in my life for a long time, forever really. Our Presbyterian church was as much a part of my growing-up years in Pennsylvania as school, friends, and our small but close family. There was my brother Greg, seven years younger than me, my mom and dad, and the blessing of having all four grandparents, and even great-grandparents, in my life. We spent our time together, often in the outdoors.

My best friend Pamela, outgoing and dramatic, was good for quiet, bookish me. She was an organizer, of adventures and even what we'd join in high school: French Club and Model United Nations, and we'd play field hockey, too. Later, field hockey brought me a wonderful group of friends as I continued playing in college. A master's degree in forestry from Duke followed my degree in biology from Albright College. And woven through the years was my relationship with God, calm and steady and not often tested by anything difficult.

Adulthood changed all that. First a divorce and later widowhood, in a second marriage that had sadly been heading in the same direction as the first. If my life had been mostly a journey across serene lakes and gently flowing rivers, those were the first tough rapids.

My first marriage, to Howard, took me to a farm in Tidewater Virginia, where I embraced country living. We had pick-your-own strawberries and, on summer weekends, we drove our pickup to the local farmers' market, brimming with bushel baskets full of vegetables.

After Megan came along in 1991 and Taylor in 1993, there would be a baby bundled up in a little carrier amid a mound of pumpkins or a cute kid in overalls helping to sell the produce. The Methodist church, where generations of Howard's family rested in a shaded cemetery, became our new church home. For work, I did forestry research at a tree nursery—academically stimulating and outdoors—the perfect job for me.

By 1999, when I discovered we wouldn't be staying married, I had moved on from the Virginia Department of Forestry to work for a local paper mill. The kids and I were on our own, and it wasn't long until we moved to Pennsylvania to live with my parents, while I went back to college. I was going to become a teacher and try a new career.

We began to talk again about moving to Maine, a dream that was rekindled with each vacation there. Inexplicably, we finally chose to move in the middle of a very snowy winter, in late January 2003. Until our furniture arrived, we camped around the wood stove in the log cabin that I had bought, thawing icy chunks of firewood to burn the next day. Soon, both my grandmothers and my aunt and uncle were in Maine, too. People here often work a mix of jobs just to make a living. I worked at my kids' school, in special education, and at our lighthouse in the summers, later adding youth minister at the United Church of Christ to my busy schedule.

My second marriage, to Chris, had a lot going for it. Another set of wonderful in-laws, our shared love of outdoor adventure, two pairs of children spanning ages nine to thirteen. And Chris and I had met at church. How perfect is that? But it wasn't perfect, sadly, although parts were very, very good. Blending the families, sharing a life that we had both had to ourselves for quite a while, was not easy. So we floated on the high points and wallowed in the low points and, in March 2008, after less than three years of marriage, Chris found an apartment of his own.

We tried counseling and even traveled to Honduras in January 2009, on a mission trip. There we worked together to build a house, among the coffee and bananas, where lofty mountains seemed to reach the clouds above. In church at night, the lively music touched our souls as the people had our hearts. Chris said it was the most meaningful thing he'd ever done.

We both loved college basketball, and I am, of course, a loyal Duke fan. A couple of months after we returned home from Honduras, Chris called one evening to invite me over to watch a game. It was the NCAA playoffs against Texas, Duke's bid to make the Sweet Sixteen. I couldn't, though. I already had plans.

"Well, how about going to L.L. Bean tomorrow for their spring fly-fishing weekend?" he offered instead.

I wouldn't commit, then called back later that evening to say, "Sure, let's go." In many ways, Chris and I were still good friends, still there for each other. Traveling a rocky road, yet planning a spring of fly-fishing together. We agreed to leave right after church.

You're probably familiar with the International Scale of River Difficulty, even if you don't know it by that name. The U.S. version of this worldwide whitewater rating system is maintained by the organization American Whitewater. Class I rapids are the easiest, just quick moving water with riffles, small waves, and few obstructions. Class II are harder, but still straightforward. Their larger waves and numerous rocks have clear channels for maneuvering through in safety. Class III may require scouting in advance. Paddlers will encounter strong current, with some challenging combination of waves and eddies, ledges and rocks, requiring higher skills.

At the far end of the scale is Class VI, Extreme and Exploratory Rapids: *"These runs have almost never been attempted and often exemplify the extremes of difficulty, unpredictability, and danger. The consequences of errors are very severe and rescue may be impossible."*

March 22, 2009 was my first Class VI rapid, the Sunday I became a widow. There was simply nothing anyone could have done, the doctor said.

Afterward, the hospital gave me a plain brown envelope. In it was a piece of paper, the printout of a heartbeat. The jagged tortured ups and downs and then…just a straight line. The rest is a blur. At the memorial service, which was just the farewell we'd hoped for, I stood with Chris's parents and his children, hugging and thanking so many loved ones. Later, with his ashes in a wooden box carved with a ship, we laid him to rest.

Chris had died in church. Not ours, but visiting another place of worship, alone.

Later, their pastor had called me on the phone.

Usually, on Sunday mornings, she stands at the door greeting people, she began. That morning, though, she had felt an urgent need to be in prayer. No reason why, just a pull from God for heartfelt conversation. That somewhere there was a need. For twenty minutes, up until the start of worship, she had been praying for Chris and what would happen just minutes into the service. And for her congregation, whose quick and expert CPR never had a chance. Everything about this was unexplored territory, mysterious and confusing.

Chris's last words, amazingly, had been those of the Apostle's Creed.

"I believe in God, the Father almighty, Creator of heaven and earth," he had begun. The earth that Chris had loved so much. The lakes where he paddled, the mountains where he hiked, and the oceans where he sailed. The earth where his children, who had been the center of his life, would finish growing up without his yummy home-cooked meals and enthusiastic celebration of every holiday.

"And in Jesus Christ, his only Son, our Lord." Chris had still been working on his walk with Jesus, perhaps just truly wanting one in this past year. I believe he came the closest in a village far away, through the building of a home and the spirit of a simple church.

And last of all, *"I believe in the Holy Spirit, the holy catholic Church, the communion of saints, the forgiveness of sins, the resurrection of the body, and life everlasting."* The resurrection of the body, and life everlasting, the final words before he left us, for a journey that only God could see.

His last words before the line that had beat for fifty-five years went flat. How can anyone understand that, come to terms with it?

Where did my strength come from that afternoon on the Dead River? Where did I get the courage to journey alone through the wilderness? My strength and courage came from God and my family and from surviving what had already come my way. From a great loss and enduring the guilt that went with it. From accepting God's forgiveness and forgiving myself, for all that I might have done differently. And from discovering that life, like a river, has only one direction to go and that is forward.

Standing hip deep in the water, I pushed away the horrifying, paralyzing image of me caught in that tree instead of my boat. The prayer just naturally welled up from a place deep inside. More than words, it was a plea for understanding, for God to show some compassion on this mess that I had just made of my carefully planned journey.

As the cold and dismal rain beat down, I forced myself to be logical, not to panic, although panic would certainly be warranted. From all that winter reading about wilderness adventures, I knew that calm and clarity were what would save me. I gave myself one hour to free the boat. If I couldn't, I would try to walk out to Route 16 and send a HELP message.

The first step was to unhook my various bags. Numb fingers, a bloodless white, struggled to obey my simple wishes. The dry bag clips needed a forceful squeeze to open and my fingers weren't cooperating. Finally, though, they came free, one by one. Seeing the colorful pile grow on the damp sand was encouraging. Then I found my small folding saw and tried to remove the limbs downstream of the boat. It was very slow going and I rethought my strategy.

"Please, God, grant me the strength to free my boat," I prayed again. "Please, please, don't make someone have to come and rescue me."

Finally, out of options, I tried pulling upstream, straight into the current. There was the slightest movement and hope returned. Adrenaline kicked in. I planted my feet, my battered body gave a mighty effort and slowly, ever so slowly, the unyielding river yielded. The strong push of the current against my legs was a constant reminder of how much worse it could have been. Inch by inch, the boat moved upstream, until a true miracle had occurred and my boat was free.

There was no way, though, that I could go any farther tonight. Shivering and numb, I sent an OK message and then took stock of the situation. The rain had let up, thankfully. I dragged the boat to the highest point on the gravel beach, then discovered my GPS was gone, as well as one water bottle, one sock, and my Tevas. The foam in the bow of the boat was ripped out, but could easily be wedged back into place. With a sad heart, I searched for the GPS without success...all my waypoints, the track of my trip so far, all gone.

But the bigger picture said I should be very, very grateful to have my boat on dry land. To be setting up a damp tent with an almost-dry sleeping bag. To be putting on warm clothes that had been well-packed deep inside a dry bag. Supper was an apple, some cheese, and the least soggy of my bagels. There being no place to hang my food, I tucked it under the spray skirt and flipped the boat, hoping for the best. Well before dark, I was huddled in my sleeping bag, wool hat and hood sealing me in. I burrowed deeper, wanting to forget this day of challenge and loss, and fell into a restless sleep.

Those two dark days were now a part of me. They had changed me in ways I only partly understood. I was tougher but also far more humble. More respectful of nature's power and of my own. The blessing of each new day, whatever it brought, was a gift not to be wasted.

In the early days of grief, there was a song I clung to, entitled "Hymn

Fateful tree on the South Branch of the Dead River in 2011

of Promise." Written by Natalie Sleeth after the death of a friend, it spoke so strongly to me of the contradictions of life. I would vacuum blindly, the mechanical roar muting my quavering voice, and sing the words, again and again. *"There's a dawn in every darkness, bringing hope to you and me. From the past will come the future, what it holds, a mystery, unrevealed until its season, something God alone can see."*

From winter's icy snows there does come the rebirth of spring. From darkness, the dawn. From our past, inevitably, must come our future. Perhaps a far different one than we had hoped for and dreamed of, but it is the one we get.

After death, our faith tells us, comes new life and a resurrection in Christ. For me, though, what waited after death still felt like such a mystery. A life of faith on earth, though, I could understand, for I was living it. The presence of God in my life was giving me courage, hope, and a purpose when life seemed darkest.

Perhaps, for now, that understanding was enough to go forward with. To provide the foundation for a new dream, a surprising new future: my attempt to thru-paddle the Northern Forest Canoe Trail unassisted, in a solo canoe. Often alone and yet never really.

CHAPTER 2

WHAT FAITH CAN SEE

If you have faith as small as a mustard seed... nothing will be impossible for you.

—Matthew 17:20

With a satisfying snap, I clipped in the last of my dry bags, a bright rainbow against the subdued yellow of the Kevlar hull. Those bags held my world, my life, for the coming summer, each item carefully chosen during the long snowy winter. Luckily, everything fit.

The canoe and I had been together just one month. Essentially, we were strangers, wary, awkward, without the trust of long acquaintance. I was in awe of how light she felt and how well she handled, but there was still so much we hadn't faced together. On her hull was just a single scratch.

So I reflected, my house was gone, long gone now. In its place, thirteen feet of marvelous canoe floated snugly at the edge of a small Adirondack pond. The water sparkled in the brilliant summer morning. Nearby stood the kiosk marking the western end of the Northern Forest Canoe Trail—my beginning. Last evening, I had signed in, the 23rd aspiring thru-paddler of 2015. On this morning of raw nerves, the trail's eastern terminus, in Fort Kent, Maine, seemed an infinite distance away.

As Dad finished arranging his gear, I remembered to send the morning message from my new SPOT Gen3. After a few minutes, a green light let me know that it had worked. Family and friends would know that, at last, I was starting. Next, I turned on the tracking feature, something I hadn't had in 2011. It would continuously transmit my position every ten minutes, all day long, vastly reassuring the small group with access to the data. A different message would go out each evening, once I had safely arrived in camp.

For the first time that morning, I reclaimed a bit of the confidence that had brought me to the threshold of the grandest adventure of my life, so far.

The day had not started well. Dad and I had both woken in the gray dawn, anticipation our alarm clock. Our canoes were out back, locked to a picnic table on the motel's dewy lawn. In our small room, everything else lay in random piles, wherever it had landed during yesterday's final flurry of sorting and packing.

More gear and my first resupply box waited in Dad's truck, a week's paddling ahead. Yesterday, we had first driven here to drop off our stuff, then moved the truck to a municipal parking lot in the town of Saranac Lake. My friend Dan Brown, a 2014 NFCT thru-paddler, had kindly shuttled us back. Hopefully we had kept what we would need.

Clumsily, we searched for the breakfast bag and started coffee on the tiny patio.

In the bathroom, trying to get awake, I happened to glance in the mirror. At first, my mind refused to believe what I was seeing. Two red and swollen eyes, with all the signs of pinkeye. *No,* I thought, *how many obstacles do I have to overcome before I even get on the water?* Within minutes, I was almost crying and definitely coming unglued, with good reason.

After planning this expedition for months, I had almost had to quit before I began. Five weeks before, in mid-May, I had developed a severe case of viral conjunctivitis with complications. Much of the last month or so had been spent with a parade of doctors and medications. There'd been pain and swelling, extreme light sensitivity, and, ultimately, the loss of all clear vision in my right eye.

It had required much trust to continue preparations as best I could and not just give up.

Only in the past three weeks had the light sensitivity improved, and it was only days since my vision had returned. Now, this morning, I had woken again to red, runny, swollen eyes. It was a nightmare.

Fathers are great, though. They help us keep life in perspective.

"It's probably just allergies," Dad said calmly. "There's probably something in this room you're sensitive to—cleaning products, mold…"

Now whether he could truly believe that, I have no idea. I seriously doubt it. But he sounded convincing enough to quiet me down. My panic gradually subsided and I thought of what had been keeping me going for weeks. Having faith and just taking the next step forward, a lesson that I would continue to practice over the coming months.

Thinking back, I remembered the training days on McCurdy Pond, where our friends Ed and Carol had shared their dock with me. After my brand-new boat arrived, but before I could clearly see. That's where the scratch came from, hitting a rock while squinting through just one eye. Swathed in dark glasses and hat, seeing only the outline of the shore, but still paddling. After all that, of course, there was no direction to go but forward.

So, at 7:30 a.m. on June 20, 2015, I officially began my thru-paddle. It was a moment filled with determination and joy that overcame the uncertainty of what lay ahead. Fittingly, Dad would share that beginning, as he had shared so much else throughout my life.

There's an old photo of me in a hoodie. It's a light color, maybe pink. I'm camping on a windswept beach on the coast of Maine, many years before we lived there. On a blue-and-white-checked tablecloth sits an old-fashioned lantern, and above is a sturdy canvas tarp. In the background, beach grass bows in the wind. You can almost feel the brisk air, hear the surf roar, taste the salt in that fading photo, and I look so happy. I was seven months old, I think, and on my father's shoulders. He was grinning, too.

Around the house, Mom's the one you hear. You never need to guess what mood she's in. You'll know. She'll be humming, or sighing, or sharing something interesting from a magazine. For many years, she taught preschool at our church, handling two large classes every day, back when no one ever had a classroom aide. The kids must have loved her enthusiasm for all the little things of life.

Mom's helped me most in recent years by what she hasn't done. Never once, although she could have, did she say, "Please don't go. Take someone with you." Or, "Not again!"

Dad is quieter, but it is the deep quiet of a strong river. When Dad was seven, his family bought an old mill in New Jersey, full of chickens. There was still a sluiceway and millstones in the basement and a lot of chicken poop. He was the oldest and he learned a lot in those years, about carpentry and gardening and making do with less. There was only money for a year of college, but he simply taught himself—enough chemistry to become the technical manager for a plastics company. When he retired, they hired a Ph.D. to take his place.

In our family, Dad's known as the man of a hundred hobbies. He loves learning and can remember an incredible amount of what he reads. As the years passed by, his hobbies came and went. Some were athletic, like running and biking, karate and golf. Some were creative, like pewter and woodworking, the trombone and the bells. There was learning Morse code for amateur radio and French for business travel. In recent years, though, boating looked like it was here to stay. As an officer in the U.S. Power Squadrons, Dad even taught courses in navigation, weather, and boating safety.

Dad was 76 now, with a long history of cardiovascular issues. The walking this week would be a stretch for him. Luckily, there was the miracle of modern medicine, in the shape of a long, carefully packed plastic box, filled with a rainbow of pills for the week ahead. He would make it. After all, last summer he had paddled 200 miles up in Maine, part of his own quest to solo paddle the Northern Forest Canoe Trail in sections. So off we went, his grin no different from that long-ago photo.

Those first miles, we were both aware of every shifting breath of wind. Wind, more than any other element, defines the character of a day on the water. There are the daily constants, as morning stillness often gives way to afternoon frenzy. Then there are the variables of strength and direction, which change from day to day. In the Adirondacks, the prevailing westerlies would push us, we hoped, as we traveled generally northeast toward Lake Champlain. Unless they decided not to.

On First Lake, the start of the eight-lake Fulton Chain, a doe carefully licked her dappled fawn on the edge of a lakeside lawn. It was a welcome touch of wildness just minutes into our trip. Otherwise, it would turn out to be more a day of powerboats and people.

On Third Lake, I spotted the fire tower mentioned on NFCT Map 1, which lay close at hand. In all, thirteen maps cover the long length of the trail. Finishing each would be a milestone along the way. These maps are well worth having, even for the casual paddler. Waterproof and durable, their navigational information is supplemented by geological, historical and ecological tidbits.

For paddlers tackling the entire trail from west to east, there is a second essential resource, *The Northern Forest Canoe Trail Through-Paddler's Companion* (referenced in this book as *The Companion*). Author Katina Daanen and I became friends when she donated to Paddle for Hope and I discovered her blog. Her plan was to canoe the entire trail that summer of 2011 with a series of partners—friends and family who would each do a section. After she finished, Katina and her husband Sam visited me on their way home to Wisconsin.

The Companion is written from the perspective of someone often going the "wrong" direction, upstream. The NFCT maps and official NFCT guidebook, *The Northern Forest Canoe Trail*, logically assume that most sane paddlers will go downstream.

Since its publication, Katina's book has truly been a companion for just about every thru-paddler. Given the 160-plus miles of upstream travel required to traverse the trail from west to east, its detailed maps and descriptions of portages and alternate routes are invaluable. In addition, readers will find advice on gear, skills, trail challenges, and thru-paddling philosophy, as well as a comprehensive guide to services along the trail. This guide, which is updated regularly, is useful for those planning shorter paddling trips, too.

On the map, I read: *"High to the northwest, Bald Mt. Fire Tower, used from 1912 to 1990 and now a hiking destination, stands on a large escarpment. It was the workplace of New York's first female Fire Tower Ranger, Mrs. Charles Mykel, who commuted in daily from Old Forge."*

I was cheered by Mrs. Mykel's example, as well as by the realization that we were almost halfway to our planned lunch stop in the town of Inlet. There was great satisfaction in seeing the map match the landscape and having the familiar words come to life.

From time to time, I scooped up a handful of clear, cool water to wash my red and gooey eyes. I fought the urge to panic, although by now I'd realized that one item that had ended up in the truck, rather than my boat, was the medicine that I'd brought in case of a relapse.

Oh well, I comforted myself, *every paddle stroke puts me closer to the truck.*

The town of Inlet lies between Fourth Lake and the tiny dot that is Fifth Lake, where the trail's first official portage begins. In the Adirondacks, portages are always called "carries," but no matter the name, they would be a big part of life in the weeks ahead.

Portages connect watersheds; bypass rapids, dams and bridges; and follow rivers, sometimes for long distances, when water levels are too high or too low. In addition, upstream paddlers must portage in other spots, where paddling would be delightful if only they could go the other way. Officially, the NFCT includes 63 portages, totaling 53 miles, but every thru-paddler will walk far more. Although I couldn't know it then, ahead of me lay 67 separate portages, totaling more than 125 miles.

Feelings swirled within me as we climbed the short hill to the Screamen Eagle for lunch. Along the way, Dad stopped several times to rest. Silently, I wondered how he was going to endure the long, rugged, and remote portages ahead. Ones where we would be forced to carry our boats and gear. Today was by far the easiest of our six planned days together.

Although the Screamen Eagle offered a tempting selection of beer, Dad drank a girly-pink bottled Saranac Shirley Temple with lunch, then popped into the store across the street for a minute. He emerged with a tacky plastic plate with a campfire and marshmallows on it, having forgotten his at home. I smiled to see him having fun, like a kid on vacation who has just spent his souvenir money.

Back at the landing, we put our boats on the "wheels" we would use whenever possible for portaging. Most thru-paddlers carry these small carts, which can be used to haul boats and gear in a single trip on wheelable portages, which often follow roads. We were both using Tuff Tires kayak carts manufactured by Wheeleez, with solid foam-filled tires and sturdy aluminum frames that weighed about nine pounds each. I had owned mine since 2011, when it had served me well during Paddle for Hope. Unlike many fellow paddlers, I had not experienced any cart tragedies, and Dad was happy to buy the same model.

With our boats carefully centered and strapped down, Dad caught his breath on a bench, then off we went, forgetting to sign the very first register along the trail.

The portage climbed a sidewalk, crossed the main road, and wound down to Sixth Lake. There, two older women with a friendly dog named Tyson paused in their gardening to help steady Dad's boat as he climbed in. They shared a moment on the joys of growing older, before we paddled on.

My eyes seemed no better, no worse. My mind churned through the what-if's. *Can I find a pharmacy or get a ride to the truck and back to retrieve my medicine? How bad will it get if this is really a relapse? Can I keep on going if it gets as bad as it was before?*

Meanwhile, Dad was still going strong, as Sixth Lake merged into Seventh. The camps and boats began to thin out, giving way to heavily wooded shores and the occasional loon. Our destination for the night, carefully entered on my planning spreadsheet, was the campground before Eighth Lake, which would be the last of the Fulton chain. We were still hoping to make it there, allowing us to pack up in the morning and wheel to the far end of the next portage, which ran right through the campground. Stopping sooner would leave us, on our first day, already a bit short of our goal. The trail, though, had not read my spreadsheet.

"It's so calm," Dad said suddenly, as our paddles dipped in quiet rhythm, "as calm as a millpond."

I simply looked at him in astonishment, not quite believing what I had just heard. He had uttered the "M" word, something we do not take lightly. It is a fact, proven more than once in other years, that the wind gods take the word "millpond" as a personal challenge.

Within minutes, the wind, which had cooperated for most of the day, suddenly picked up. It thrust us swiftly toward a small cove on the wilder north shore of Seventh Lake, two or three miles short of the campground. Here the first lean-to appeared, high on a bluff. I climbed up to discover it was delightfully, miraculously empty. It was time to listen to our bodies, the weather, my intuition. Quickly, I decided—we would camp here.

As he climbed out, I noticed Dad was shaking and knew I had made a wise decision.

It was Saturday on a popular Adirondack lake. An open lean-to was a gift. Later, I swam in the surprisingly warm water, admiring our site. A wide, gradual needle-strewn slope led up from the sandy beach to a bold bluff. There, an expansive granite ledge commanded a spectacular view of mountains draped with sun and cloud.

We love the homemaking of camp and always have. Here, Dad discovered that he could tuck his tent into the lean-to with no need to use the rain fly. I set up mine by the granite bluff. We had left our saw behind to save weight, but found one hanging on the wall beside a sturdy grill. Fresh food from our small cooler would soon be just a fond memory, but tonight Dad cooked steak and peppers over the campfire for our first dinner. Afterward, rinsing dishes down by the shore, I slipped, skinning my knuckles and drenching a pair of clean socks. We religiously guard our dry socks, and these had only lasted one hour. Before long, sleep called.

A few hours later, I was wide awake. Stretching every complaining muscle, I listened in disbelief. It was long after midnight, in this haven of peace, but loud voices had undoubtedly roused me. It had rained heavily. Who could be out there? There was yelling, singing, swearing, howling. Obviously close, were these crazy neighbors trying to camp here?

I worried especially about our boats. Almost $5,000 worth of high quality canoes, the foundation of the expedition, lay vulnerably along the shore. Finally, curiosity and concern pushed me out into the inky blackness. Blindly, I groped my way in the general direction of our boats, not wanting to use a flashlight. The noise was truly unbelievable, louder than any I had ever heard even in the middle of a crowded campground.

Suddenly, a strobe light flashed just off shore, on what morning would reveal to be a tiny island just below my cliff. I listened, determining that only one voice was clearly audible, a man's. Rain had drenched his hat and he was not happy, although he forgot his woes just long enough to sing a ballad before reverting to more swearing.

"So, you're going to stay here for some romance!" he finally bellowed to his inaudible companions. (Quote edited for family audiences). "Do you want the kayaks or the canoe? We're going to leave now. Don't forget, there are three canoe paddles. We brought an extra. Are you sure you know which way to go? Don't forget the third paddle. We're leaving now. Don't forget the paddles!" Then finally, it was quiet.

I carefully felt my way back to the tent and wiggled my damp feet back into the sleeping bag. From the romantic pair, there was only silence. Slowly, I drifted back to sleep, and in the morning, they were gone with no sign of a forgotten paddle.

A light rain still fell the next morning, as I followed Dad in his bright yellow jacket up the wild north shore of Seventh Lake. My eyes were the same, no better, no worse. The cold water still soothed them, so I tried to put it out of my mind.

In the stillness, there was time to daydream and my thoughts turned to Nessmuk. To fully appreciate the intertwining of early Adirondack history with my journey, you must meet the writer Nessmuk. A voice from the 1880s who lives on in those of us who still venture into wild places alone and simply, in small canoes with double-bladed paddles.

Nessmuk was his pen name, adopted in honor of the Nipmuck Indian who had befriended him as a surprisingly young boy growing up in Massachusetts. Imagine spending days in the forest learning wilderness skills, hunting and fishing instead of going to kindergarten. That woodcraft and a love of the northern forest would define his life and become his legacy, shared in the pages of the popular *Forest and Stream* weekly magazine.

His real name was George Washington Sears. Just one letter removed from my own great-grandfather, George Washington Searls.

Our Nessmuk was a tiny man, frail in health for much of his life, but bold in his love of adventure and in simplifying to the extreme. Tiny meant five-foot-three and around 112 pounds, smaller than me for sure. He needed small boats. Luckily, he had talented Adirondack boatbuilder J. Henry Rushton to craft them of native northern white cedar, each one smaller than the one before.

In his later years, after a life that interspersed his family trade of shoemaking with whaling, professional hunting, visits to the Amazon, and other improbable pursuits for a small and sickly man, Sears found his niche writing about canoeing, camping, and conservation. By then, the Adirondacks were becoming a destination, but one usually went with a guide, in an 80-pound Adirondack guideboat filled to the brim with what Sears called "impedimenta."

Sears had a different vision.

In his book *Woodcraft and Camping*, Sears wrote, "*The temptation to buy this or that bit of indispensable camp-kit has been too strong, and we have gone to the blessed woods, handicapped with a load fit for a pack-mule. This is not how to do it. Go light; the lighter the better, so that you have the simplest material for health, comfort and enjoyment,*" predicting, "*the light, single canoe with double-bladed paddle is bound to soon become a leading—if not the leading—feature in summer recreation.*"

Beginning in the summer of 1880, Nessmuk made three solo trips through the Adirondacks. He paddled some of the same waters that we were, experimenting with lighter and lighter boats, amid growing enthusiasm from his readers. The smallest Rushton canoe, christened the *Sairy Gamp* after a Dickens character, set out from Old Forge in 1883 for a trip of 266 miles. Her dimensions were a mere nine feet long and 26 inches wide. She weighed a feathery ten-and-a half pounds. Eventually, the *Sairy Gamp* became so famous that she was exhibited at the 1893 Colombian Exposition or World's Fair in Chicago.

Several years ago, my friend Russ Guibord, himself a fine Maine craftsman in cane and canvas, loaned me a book called *Adirondack Passage: The Cruise of the Canoe Sairy Gamp*. It was the story of a woman who had retraced Nessmuk's last and lightest Adirondack trip, which began with the first 70 miles of the Northern Forest Canoe Trail. The *Sairy Gamp* had passed this way, as had Christine Jerome over a hundred years later, in a tiny canoe she called the *Sairy Damp*. Her first night out, she and her husband had camped in last night's lean-to and mentioned the navigational light on "Arnolds Rock," the trysting place of our lovers.

It was the reading of Jerome's book that had sent me in search of a small canoe, rather than a kayak. One that I could paddle with a double-bladed paddle and reliably carry for a half mile or more. The goal for the rest of my gear was to condense it to just one additional load.

I was first attracted to a Wenonah model that weighed 25 pounds in Kevlar, called the Wee Lassie, after one of Rushton's larger designs. Like Sears, I would have sat on the floor of that boat. The NFCT, however, crosses a diverse variety of challenging waters that might require a little more canoe. Maine Sport Outfitters in Rockport, Maine, arranged for the loan of a 13-foot Wenonah Fusion instead, with a regular raised canoe seat. Paddling the Pemaquid River near home on a warm Christmas Day in 2014, I knew this was the boat I wanted.

Mine ultimately weighed in at 32 pounds. That included fore and aft skid plates and a comfortable clip-on canoe chair with padded back that came with the boat. Wenonah builds each of their canoes to order. Mine was constructed in April 2015—just for me.

Back on Seventh Lake, approaching the campground's boat landing, a tidy row of red and green channel markers beckoned us in. This seemed odd and foreign. The only freshwater navigational buoys I could remember from my Maine paddling were those marking the entrance to the Moose River from Moosehead Lake, an area of heavy boat traffic. Here in New York, buoys were everywhere.

The campground portage turned out to be simple, and no more difficult than strolling a mile for fun. I was sure we had made the right decision waiting until the morning. Already this journey was teaching me. Plans are good, but so are trust and the willingness to listen to your body and your intuition.

Wheeling easily along, we cheered on the sun as it made a valiant effort to emerge. At the far end's boat launch, a small boy in a striped shirt sat cross-legged on the dock. He watched solemnly as we went through the motions that were evolving into an efficient routine. Heavy stuff out, roll and launch the boat, fold the wheels, roll up the straps, everything back in.

"We have one of those," he finally shared, pointing at our canoes. I asked if he liked it and got a quiet nod.

After equally wild and scenic Eighth Lake lay the portage to Brown's Tract Inlet, a boggy fen that had intrigued me for months. Near the start of the carry, we stopped for lunch at a lean-to. I slumped wearily against a post, legs dangling off the edge, tired but happy. It was still sinking in that we were really doing this thing.

Dad and I had decided to bring our own breakfasts and lunches. I dug out a pouch of Mediterranean tuna, an apple, and a trail bar. These flavored tunas from the grocery store were great trail food. They came packed in sunflower oil, adding calories and eliminating the need to bring along mayonnaise and relish packets as I did with plain tuna.

We rested and chatted, relaxing. Then Dad tossed the last of his apple toward a snail exploring the fireplace, wondering aloud if snails even eat apples. Would it change direction? How long would it take to get there at its snail's pace? The snail surprised us. His tan body with cartoon antennae turned quickly, and soon he was climbing up the apple core. I couldn't help thinking we were a bit like snails, Dad and I, but hopefully we would surprise ourselves by getting farther quicker than we thought.

Brown's Tract Inlet was a highlight. To reach it, we wheeled well over a mile, getting a taste here and there of what lay ahead in abundance, namely mud and bugs, rocks and roots. Somewhere near the end, we reached the highest point on the trail at 1,825 feet and crossed from the Moose River to the Raquette River drainage.

Soon after, a sun-bleached boardwalk appeared. Refreshingly smooth, it curved away into the distance, our gateway into this fascinating ecosystem. Of course, we would have made better progress, rolling effortlessly along, if I hadn't needed to stop so often. There was just so much to see and I wanted to absorb it all, to savor every moment. Thus began the daily tug and pull between making miles and experiencing the quiet joys of observing, relaxing, listening.

This was a wet and wild garden alive with summer. Ferns mingled with plants unfamiliar to me, like one with large, shiny, cupped leaves and a light green fruit like a grenade. Never resting, a group of swallowtails danced among the wild blue flag iris, and everywhere, vibrant pink sheep laurel added more color. Even on the boardwalk underfoot, a group of mourning cloak butterflies clustered on a drab island of mud.

Soon, the map's promise of carnivorous plants "on almost every log" was fulfilled. We had reached the boardwalk's end and slid our boats smoothly into the water. Another portage in the books. Not long after, my eye was caught by a glimpse of dark purple. I maneuvered closer, to discover a pitcher plant. The shiny purples and greens of this voracious plant were hard to miss and I stopped to examine its exotic flower.

Later, I learned a bit more about its deadly efficient mechanism for trapping insects, condensed here from an article by John L. Turner in the *New York State Conservationist.*

The pitcher plant uses the pitfall trap strategy to catch prey. The drama begins when an insect enters the pitcher-shaped leaf, which has a layer of water at the bottom. *"Guided by downward pointing hairs, the insect works its way down the collar, which is populated by many nectar-secreting glands. Attracted to this area, the insect moves ever lower until it hits a surface like roof shingles that readily dislodge."* After the insect drowns, digestive enzymes in the water help the plant to absorb valuable nutrients and minerals from its unlucky victim.

The inlet moved in sinuous curves, and Dad reached for his new canoe paddle, a hand-crafted cherry work of art that put my battered spare to shame. Using a cross draw, he turned his canoe easily in the tight meanders. The lighting under ever-shifting clouds added to the feeling of a world apart from the bustle of our journey's start. It was Sunday and Father's Day. Thankfulness filled me at our chance to share this day and place.

That evening I journaled, *"Beavers ruled, their dominion marked by massive lodges and a series of dams, each higher than the last. Luckily, the water was high and we aimed and shot through where water moved most freely. Until the last—a chance for another Father's Day gift!"*

We had come to a dam higher than the rest. In a maneuver that would repeat itself with individual creativity a myriad of times this summer, I powered my canoe up on the dam as far as it would go, then gingerly climbed out. Balancing carefully, holding tight to the rope from my boat, I inched along to a strategic spot to pull Dad over.

Soon his boat, and then mine, were free and passing under a bridge into the expanse of Raquette Lake.

CHAPTER 3

CARRYING ON

We go to the wilds not so much to seek an adventure, a burst of excitement and thrills, but to live there. We like to go alone, to feel immersed in, surrounded by, and finally accepted into the embrace of wild and sublime places. We go out of a need to find that person in each of us who is obscured in the day-to-day of crowded, hectic living.

—**Alan S. Kesselheim,** *Going Inside*

The Raquette (RACK-et) River is the second longest river in the state of New York and probably one of the busiest. We would paddle on it and the lakes it runs out of and through for about 45 miles. In the small town of Raquette Lake, we signed the kiosk register and visited the general store for ice cream.

In the window sat a colorful beach ball that reminded me of a funny trail story. Chuckling, I sent a photo to my friend Peter, whose story it is, with the message, "Just in case you're ever in Raquette Lake and need one..."

Peter Macfarlane thru-paddled the Northern Forest Canoe Trail in 2013, without wheels, carrying everything in one load. He went in a canoe he built himself. That canoe, and Peter, will later play a part in my story. One day, Peter had been paddling, as he did for much of his 28-day trip, in rain. It was in driving rain, in the middle of Lake Champlain, that his canoe seat broke, a serious setback, less than six days into his trip.

Kneeling up, Peter pushed on, his mind churning through possible solutions. In the end, it was the improbable discovery of an orphan beach ball adorned with fairies that helped him. Using it as a temporary seat, Peter comfortably reached town, where he made the necessary repairs to his canoe.

By late afternoon, the moment when we had paddled away from our campsite on Seventh Lake seemed so long ago. We had portaged, watched our snail, wound through the bog, and navigated five miles of this large and busy lake. Dodging power boats and handling the confusing and conflicting waves from wind and wakes had drained the last of our energy. We were ready to camp, to reenergize. The rest could wait for tomorrow.

Tioga Point State Campground was comfortingly close. There, the ranger, Autumn, found us a well-situated lean-to with a small beach and wide view of the lake. The camping handouts included lots of detailed information on bear etiquette. Marveling, I faithfully signed an affidavit vowing to abide by the many rules. They took this very seriously. Last season a delinquent teenage bear had wreaked havoc in the campground.

We collapsed in weariness for a while, then roused to evening chores. For Dad, dry clothes felt good after an unplanned swim by Autumn's dock.

As we were building the fire, our thoughts on supper, a movement by the water made my heart race. Fearlessly, a sleek black, weasel-like creature ran gracefully along the pebbled shore, right through camp, just feet away. A mink, we both agreed. The mink falls in size between the much smaller short and long-tailed weasels and the larger fisher. To suit its life in and around water, it has partially webbed feet and can dive to a depth of 15 feet in search of fish and crayfish. This was the closest I had ever been to one.

The day ended with a new friend. I didn't know it at the time, but I would meet only a handful of other thru-paddlers in the weeks to come. As we were fixing supper, a spry, fit man in paddling clothes came briskly over from the adjacent site. He was about my size and probably older, and looked like he knew what he was doing.

"Are you Laurie Chandler?" he asked with a smile. Now that was a surprise. It turned out that the ranger had told him all about us.

John Mautner, we discovered, was 68 and just finishing his first day on the trail. He had paddled his 26-pound, 15-foot Placid Boatworks RapidFire canoe all the way from Old Forge. His boat, a carbon/Kevlar model, was two feet longer, but six pounds lighter than mine.

Later, John brought his supper over and we shared our wine and sat talking about the adventure ahead. Before he left, John mentioned how fun it would be to have someone else to share the journey. I wondered aloud, though, if I would ever catch him. He had done in one day what had taken us two. We all lingered a little later than we should have, then headed for bed.

In the morning, John left camp before us and was soon lost to sight. As we got going a bit later, the wind was a challenge at first. Soon, though, we rounded broad Bluff Point and turned northeast. The wind was pushing us now, funneling us up the ever-narrowing Raquette Lake to the first of the day's carries, an easy half mile to Forked Lake. These were the lakes that fed the Raquette River, which we had yet to reach.

"Keep Off Fence." The sign that sternly greeted us was not what we were used to in Maine. Here in the Adirondacks, though, many docks and shorelines had "No Trespassing" signs. In an act of defiant kindness, someone else had placed a row of benches in front of the fence. Gratefully we sat, to pull on the thin nylon liners and thicker wool socks we would wear under our river shoes. I had learned this lesson the hard way. Portaging without socks on my first solo adventure in 2010, I had ended up with serious, crippling blisters on both heels.

At the far end of the portage, we worked on our launching technique. After removing the straps, we tried wheeling right to the edge before lifting the boat off the cart and into the water. If done successfully, the wheels remained behind on dry ground. This improved efficiency was good, as there were would be three more carries that day, each one progressively more challenging than the last.

Forked Lake was pristine and quiet. There was not much talking, just the rhythm of paddles, the wind still behind us, our aching lower backs just hanging in there.

At the Forked Lake State Campground boat launch, where the next portage started, we met Katherine and Nat, who'd motored in from their island campsite to do some errands in town. They were an outdoorsy, outgoing couple, dressed in worn old camping clothes and sandals. With his John Lennon sunglasses and long ponytail, Nat looked at home here. Katherine, immediately friendly, was the type of person who asks you a question and then focuses intently on the answer.

I asked if they knew where the trash disposal was for the campground.

"Oh, we'll be happy to take your trash," Katherine volunteered earnestly. "We try to do a good deed every day!"

We had discovered our first trail angels. Trail angels are a beloved trail tradition, adopted from the thru-hiker world. They bestow trail magic, which is simply any kindness, usually unplanned and often involving food or drink. For today, we happily lightened our load by passing over the bag. This chore of trash disposal would be a constant litany in the weeks ahead. The "carry in, carry out" and "leave no trace" philosophies prevail all along the trail. Katherine and Nat were intrigued by our journey. Like many people I would meet, they had never heard of the NFCT. Soon, the map was out, draped across a seat, and Dad was telling them all about our canoes, the wheels, and the challenges that awaited down the trail.

When they asked us to show them where the trail ends, pointing to Map 1, I just smiled. Map 1 covers only the first 43 miles. Map would follow map until I had crossed all thirteen. On those maps lie the 58 lakes and ponds and 22 rivers and streams that compose the Northern Forest Canoe Trail. The scale of the trail had obviously not yet sunk in for them. In fact, I wondered if it had truly sunk in for me.

Two days ago, on the drive to Old Forge, Dad had voiced just what I was thinking.

"You know, we've been driving a really long time. You're going to paddle back all this way, not to mention going on almost to Canada!"

This was another easy portage. Although I had been helping Dad a bit on the uphills, the downhills were almost as effortless as just walking along. So, he went at his pace and I went at mine. When portaging with wheels, pushing often works better than pulling. Pushing allows the force of the body's forward momentum to propel the boat, providing a break for weary arm and shoulder muscles. This strategy hadn't been mentioned much in books or paddler blogs, but I did it a lot. On long portages, it was helpful to alternate between pushing and pulling.

Almost 11 miles into our day, we finally launched into the Raquette River and found our first fast water. Over the next five miles, the river would drop 116 feet. Here there were rocks to avoid and I was thrilled to recognize a feeling akin to wild Maine rivers lined with fir and hemlock. Sadly, after not much more than a mile, the fun came to an abrupt halt at Buttermilk Falls. Portaging was about to take on a very different character. For the first time, we would not be able to use our wheels.

In a way, this was a moment of truth. Of course, I had practiced carrying my canoe, going in proud circles on the lawn around my house. But this was a true Adirondack carry, albeit a short one, winding around

Most portages were wheelable, but we had our share of true Adirondack carries, too. Pushing was often easier than pulling, just a stroll in the park.

and over rocks and boulders, with a significant up, then down, and a good look at the turmoil of frothy Class IV whitewater that we were avoiding.

For the first of many times to come, I unbuckled my canoe chair and rebuckled it upside down, under the canoe seat and out of the way. Next the yoke slipped neatly into its place. Dad had designed and built the wooden yoke, which I sanded and varnished before attaching a pre-fabricated foam pad. Four small bungee cords secured the yoke and both paddles in place and I wore my PFD, completing what would become the first load of every well-organized carry. The rest of my stuff comprised a second load, so that on non-wheelable portages, the distance walked was tripled.

Taking a deep breath, I reached for the gunwales and rolled the canoe up, with a little bounce. Another wiggle or two got it perfectly balanced and I was off. This choreography would get smoother as the weeks went by, but even this first time, it worked.

There was something about my firm grasp on the thwart and the yoke settling solid on my shoulders that carried me back in time. As it has throughout the centuries, the trail ahead disappeared beneath the bow, shyly emerging a bit more with each careful step. The balance, the rhythm of the carry—look up to find the way, look down for sure footing—was repeated again and again, in a dance that connected me to all those who had ever gone this way before.

Back on the buoyant, flowing river, we didn't get to rest for long. Approaching the day's fourth and final portage, Deerland Carry, Dad was out of sight ahead. I stayed alert, searching the right bank for signs of the takeout. Paddlers call this "river right," the designation always based on travel in the downstream direction. In other words, if you are traveling upstream, anything on your left is on "river right." Try figuring that out in a panic!

However, this takeout was easily visible. Dad was standing on shore, waiting for me. Optimistically, we were hoping to be able to use our wheels, although *The Companion* described this portage as "not easily wheeled." But hope springs eternal, particularly when you are exhausted. Stashing both boats out of the way near the start, we stumbled wearily along the twisting path with less gear than we could have carried. It was over a half mile of rocks and roots, a muddy, slippery mess from all the recent rain, and certainly not wheelable.

By now, I was at that point where the connection from brain to feet was slowing. Carefully, I stumbled along with the exaggerated care of a drunk. Dad, who had already walked over three miles, including carrying his boat at Buttermilk Falls, continued to amaze me.

Near trail's end, we were grateful to discover an empty lean-to. In the gloom of late afternoon, it looked a little dreary, but wonderful to us.

Dad started work on a fire to confuse the bugs. Meanwhile, I found some more energy somewhere and made two more round trips with gear, leaving the boats for tomorrow. When the mud sucked one of my shoes right off my foot, I was heartily glad that I didn't have a canoe on my shoulders. Trudging out to get the second load, I met an older couple, with two friendly dogs, a boxer and a Lab, walking back toward Dad. They stopped to chat with him, a conversation that would change our evening.

"Do you like beer?" Tom astonished Dad by asking. Or maybe it was, "How would you like some beer?"

Well, there's only one answer to that! Before I finished transporting gear, Tom had walked to his lakeside house and back with an assortment of beer and enough wood for a campfire, something he and Judy often do for weary paddlers. More trail magic that quickly brightened our spirits and our camp.

The kindness of people was a sharp contrast to all those no trespassing signs.

The rabbit comes out, runs around the tree, and goes back down his hole. After all these years, I still silently repeated the words that my father had used to teach me how to tie a bowline knot. I wrapped the end of the rope around itself, poked it down through the loop, and pulled the knot tight. It needed to be secure.

It was the next afternoon and waves surged the flooded shore of Long Lake, uncomfortably close to where I had flipped my canoe over, putting it to bed for the night. The wind that bent the trees above had been growing steadily stronger as the afternoon progressed. This early camp had not been in the plan. Yet I knew, in my heart, that it was a gift. My blog entry started like this: *"Only 7.5 miles, you say? Well, let me tell you our story!"*

During the night, violent thunderstorms and torrential rain had rocked our world. Thankfully, Dad had helped me squeeze my tent into the lean-to, the difficulty being in securing it. Dad's tent was free-standing. Mine was not and would collapse if not staked to the ground or somehow tethered to random nails and crevices in the lean-to. Later, we learned that it was not considered good etiquette to put tents inside a lean-to.

The sky was still muttering when I left Dad sleeping and set out to retrieve my boat in the early light. The trail had been transformed. The leafy, damp path was now just mud, deep puddles, and, astoundingly, a rushing stream, nowhere near either of the two boardwalks. I crossed, carefully and securely placing each foot in the tumbling water, wondering how I would manage to carry a canoe back across this treacherous way.

Once the canoe was up, though, I covered the entire distance in one carry, including the stream. Dad would be surprised when he woke up, I thought, as I thankfully slid the canoe down at the river's edge. Later, after breakfast, I carried Dad's boat while he brought the rest of his gear. Even Dad's longer canoe balanced easily and I could adjust its angle to see ahead down the path. Finally, at about ten in the morning, we were ready for the river.

Trail angels Tom and Judy reported more weather on the way when we stopped at their dock to say goodbye. Then we flew north with the wind at our backs. Of this morning, one moment stands out. A pair of loons zoomed straight at me, at eye level, then split around me like a well-planned maneuver of fighter jets. They passed so close that the clarity of each brilliant feather will forever linger in my memory. That was certainly a fireplace bird moment!

The town of Long Lake, near the start of the lake of the same name, marked the end of Map 1. Grinning, I posed for a photo with float planes as a backdrop. We needed some more fuel, which I found in the well-stocked general store just up the street. The charmingly authentic Adirondack Hotel, where we'd hoped to stay the previous night, served up a scrumptious lunch instead. For me, a turkey and Swiss bagel with red cabbage and special mayo.

For the next 25 miles, the trail would run far from any roads or towns. There would be no retreating. Luckily, my eyes were clearing up, although I would certainly grab that medicine when we reached the truck. In my mind, though, I realized that I had been wondering if Dad would decide to call it quits, to give his body a rest and meet me later. I needn't have worried. There was no way he was going to stop.

After our leisurely lunch, the wind had picked up more and on we sailed, at speeds approaching five miles per hour, torn between hugging the shore for safety or flying free down the middle. Then came that delicate point where fun goes from exhilarating to a bit scary. Then probably scary. Then definitely scary.

Was it the result of prayer that there was a lean-to right there, on the lake's east shore? The waves carried us in with minimal help from two tired paddlers and guided us firmly to shore, where the crashing surf made just getting out a bit tricky. The flooded shore had been stirred into a vegetation slurry that, from a distance, looked like solid ground. We would make an early camp. As I tied that bowline knot, I thought how blessed I was with family.

Dad had mastered the bowline in Boy Scouts, but later he'd learned many more knots from Grampy, my mother's grandfather. For years, Grampy spent summer weeks camping on the untamed dunes of the Jersey shore, recording their wild beauty with an antique folding camera. I'd known Grampy well, and his daughter, my Grandma Jan, had shared her love of birds and books and wildflowers with me for over four decades.

We had two other families we camped with growing up. Together we ranged from West Virginia to New York, with a tangle of kids in the back of a woodie station wagon. We made our own fun, the times when we were truly living found in the serendipity of the unexpected.

A favorite photo from our many years of family camping (Joan Apgar photo)

In my memory, this all too often involved a dripping tarp or poison ivy or triaging one of the boys. It was a way of life that so many children today are missing.

In the early 1980s, Harvard's Dr. Edward O. White used the term biophilia to describe the intrinsic love for the natural world that he believed was present in everyone. As more scientists began to study the role that the outdoors plays in our lives, they learned that we have not just a love, but a need, for nature. Immersion in the natural world encourages creativity, makes our bodies healthier, reduces stress, and improves cognitive functioning.

Growing up, we just knew it was fun. All those hours spent searching for salamanders, whittling sticks, and crossing rushing streams on slippery logs had fed our souls. For me, they'd given me a passion for wild places that had led me here, to the blustery shores of Long Lake.

That afternoon was a deep breath in our journey. We spent the windy hours doing chores and talking. "*Just remember to put a large rock on anything you set down or it will blow away!*" my blog explained. "*And when you are done washing yourself and the laundry, you will need to pick little leaf bits out of all the crevices.*"

Appalachian Trail thru-hikers swear by Vitamin I, ibuprofen, to keep them going day after day. For Dad and me, it was Aleve. Aleve, and all that extra rest, had us out on the lake, paddling strongly, surprisingly early the next morning. That was good. The wind had changed direction since the mayhem of yesterday and there was a major hurdle ahead.

The Raquette Falls portage, more than a mile around two 15-foot cascades, had long been on our radar. Like yesterday's Deerland Carry, *The Companion* described it as "not easily wheeled," with a particularly steep initial climb. Mack Truax, a fellow member of the NFCT Thru-Paddler Class of 2015, had called it a "monumental portage."

And Mack was tough. The community of thru-paddlers is a close group, even those of us who have never met in person. Back in April, I had discovered Mack's trail journal and been inspired by his rigorous training regimen. Mack, from Michigan, had finished the trail before I even started, paddling a 17-foot sea kayak that weighed 66 pounds. Like me, he had used a SPOT. From May 20 to June 13, we had watched him rocketing along, on pace to match or even break the solo paddling achievement of 25 days, at least until he got seriously lost one day on remote Maine logging roads. Raquette Falls had been one of the few places where he went slower than planned. I knew that today would challenge our endurance.

Pushing deeper into the heart of the Adirondacks, we seemed to have left the crowds behind. Long Lake stretched ahead, doing justice to its name. Seven more miles to cover before returning to the river. Dad ranged far in the distance as I poked around, taking photos and trying to capture the spirit of the place. Our early start had given the day a feeling of promise and possibility that suited the beauty surrounding me.

A parade of "Adirondack Great Camps" gave character to the rugged shoreline. Their greens and browns, their architectural individuality, just felt right. The builders had utilized the palette and materials around them. Native stone, twisted saplings, bark-covered logs echoed the character of the forest they blended into. I, too, felt at home. Spruce and cedar clung precariously to mossy rocks, their roots somehow penetrating deep within the cracks. Where the forest met the shore, sheep laurel struggled to keep their heads above the flood.

Loons were here in abundance. Their dramatic, glistening colors and serenading calls reminded us fondly of home. I had just caught up to Dad again when a loon with a chick appeared. The small one rode on its mother's (or perhaps father's) back, as they do for up to three weeks after hatching, for protection from predators and chill water. Her bravery surprised me, as parents with chicks are usually wary and we avoid them as much as possible. Unconcerned, she never wavered, swimming a course that would take her right in front of my now stationary boat. I snapped picture after picture. Picture after picture that I later deleted when I realized that my "chick" was an odd tuft of ruffled feathers. The joke was on me and now I would have to dig in again to catch Dad.

Reunited, we paddled on toward the layered mountains, alone on the lake. In three hours, we had come farther than in all of yesterday's abbreviated paddle. We were thankful for the GPS, which led us straight to the outlet. Far above, the morning's solid cloud cover had become dots of puffy white in a deep blue sky. It was a sunscreen day.

The swollen Raquette River flowed out of Long Lake into a mysterious world of silver maples, the current alone a vigorous two to four miles per hour. A mile farther and we rounded a bend to find a group of people clustered on river right. A single canoe was visible among the shore's greenery. From a safe distance, we back-paddled, shouting questions and straining to decipher the answers. A second canoe had been pulled into a strainer and lay hopelessly submerged, swept into the powerful tangle of limbs and current.

Dad couldn't wait to help. He has always been a Good Samaritan, rescuing farm animals wandering rural Pennsylvania roads or prying fishing hooks out of the kids of strangers. He was in his element, strategizing and shouting advice.

"Don't go close," I yelled, knowing my urgent warning probably wasn't necessary. We both respected the river's power, having had our share of catastrophes in the past. We struggled back upstream to the protected lee side of a huge fallen log, not far from the drama.

"What you need is a rope," Dad advised them. "If you can get tied on to the canoe, you can use leverage to get it out."

It was a sound idea. Near the submerged canoe, a large and sturdy maple leaned solidly out over the surging river. Its horizontal branches would provide a safe platform for the difficult rescue. More shouting revealed that, unfortunately, the group didn't have a rope.

It was my turn to help. Carefully, I climbed out onto the log and worked my way to my bow, undoing the bowline and then the one on the stern, too. Tied together, the two ropes might be long enough. The log bobbled and rolled a bit and I held my breath until it stabilized. As I pieced together the rescue rope, the canoe that was still floating paddled over and joined us. Dad's canoe, then mine, then the new boat, packed like sardines in a can.

Paddling stern was a hefty, sunburned raft guide type with lots of curly blondish hair. Big baggy shorts and tiny professional-looking PFD. But his confidence seemed to exceed his knowledge, and I was glad to see that he seriously hugged the shore while carefully wading and swimming down with the rope. He was a camp counselor, part of the staff hired to guide a group of Brooklyn high school students and their two teachers for the week.

That left Vincent to hang with us. He was a veteran of one previous wilderness canoe trip. Several hours of companionship in the bright sun, swarming bugs, and careful immobility of our canoes and log jumpstarted our friendship and we talked of many things, even working around to what life was like for a black teenager in the city. We touched on racism and gangs, a world as foreign to me as the Adirondacks probably seemed to him.

Vincent did not like bugs, and the brush of a branch as his canoe shifted would cause him to lean alarmingly in panic. More than once. And much to the consternation of his teacher, who soon joined the crowd, with two more boys in his canoe.

So, we got to know J.W. and Jamal, who was as quiet as J.W. was talkative. The boys were good company and thanked me repeatedly for sharing my sunscreen, bug spray, and, sadly, the last of my Snickers bars.

"If you believe in the Big Man, you should thank him we're safe," their teacher threw out after a while. This was the group's second scare. Yesterday's wind had capsized one of their canoes out on the expanse of Long Lake.

"Yeah," Jamal surprised me by saying, "lots of blessings, nice day."

Dad wanted to be out there helping. He paddled closer, where he could watch the rescue in progress. Although our early start had long since evaporated, we would not leave before there was a happy ending. After a while, the girls from the school arrived, too, with their teacher and another batch of counselors. The crowd gave a cheer when the green canoe was finally pried from the grasp of the current and hauled up toward the sprawling maple. After more than two hours balancing on that precarious log, my cheer was as heartfelt as any.

The spirit of victory was still with us as we arrived first at Raquette Falls. There were many boats behind us, the boys and the girls, and we wasted no time humping our canoes up the steep start of the portage.

Dad carried his own, and it was obvious that his conditioning had taken a leap in the days behind us. At the top of the hill lay the first campsite. We tucked our gear out of the way and sat down, ravenous for lunch.

Soon we were joined by the crowd of young girls. Two topics and two only were being discussed—the quantity and quality of the food and disbelief and astonishment that they were going to have to carry their canoes. Sort of like the two topics on our minds.

Dad and I each tackled the portage differently. I carried my boat the whole way, in three shifts, resting by moving my other gear along. Dad optimistically strapped on his wheels and rolled part of the way. Most often, though, one of the camp counselors or I would grab the other end of his canoe to lift it over the many rough spots. In places, remnants of an ancient corduroy road could still be seen. Keeping us company and entertaining us were the campers, cajoled along by the adults. Some suffered in sullen silence, others joked all the way.

At the far end, the girls had already claimed the lean-to. More than a century ago, travelers would have stayed in this small clearing, too, in Mother Johnson's boarding house, home of "the best flapjacks in the wilderness." The flooding had turned the end of the portage trail into a stream, which we waded down to sign the trail register and rejoin the river, navigating a few small rips at the start.

We discovered the first lean-to on river right empty. Dad left his canoe in the river, tied securely to a tree. I wrestled mine up the steep, slippery, washed-out path and flipped it over. When I scrambled up the bank and into camp, he was relaxing in an Adirondack chair, a huge grin on his face. Some kind soul had even left a supply of dry split pine for the campfire.

My blog enthused: *"From my tent window I could see hemlocks reaching out over the water, sun shimmering through, with the sparkle of water behind. Our cooking has gone from steak with potatoes and fruit to beans and franks to just franks rolled in tortillas. It still tastes good! Heard a group of coyotes right across the river at dusk, powerful and eerie."*

Grit, not the kind in your shoes, was needed the next morning to pry us out of our tents and on down the river. Packing up was a comfortable routine, by now, though, and soon we were on our way. Within a mile, we passed the boys of yesterday, with a shout of farewell to J.W. and Vincent. The weather was clearing after rain in the night, and the current gave us a helpful push as we drifted lazily along.

In my journal, I tried to capture the contrast between the tranquil morning and the exertions of the day before. *"Would one mean as much without the other? You trudge along with aching shoulders, shrugging the yoke to try to find comfort, mud sucking and trying to wrestle away your shoes, with bugs and grit...the hopes ahead and the memories behind are a powerful fuel. Then, you paddle and drift through a flooded mysterious world of silver maple, to the melody of unseen songbirds, rounding bend after bend with Impressionist reflections doubling the beauty. Water stretches as far as the eye can penetrate, into the depths of the forest, between yellow aster and white cedar and you know it's a gift that is bestowed only on those who persevere."*

After five miles, the entrance to Stoney Creek was clearly marked with a sign in the middle of the stream. Onward we went, through a maze where the channel flirted with us, sometimes obvious, but often puzzling even our GPS. Dad was enjoying finding obscure paths that worked. Eventually we emerged from a fun, but likely inefficient, "shortcut" into the first of the Stoney Creek Ponds, where a few cabins hinted at a return to civilization.

Between the two ponds was a small bridge, sitting right on the flooded waters. We had no choice but to unload and carry our boats across the private road and put back in on the other side. I made a note to add this extra portage to the NFCT paperwork that I was filling out.

On their website, the NFCT maintains an official list, recognizing paddlers in several categories. There are section-paddlers, who have completed the entire trail, taking more than one year. Then there are thru-paddlers, who paddle the trail as one expedition, during a single season. Since 2012, they have been recognized at three levels:

Self-Propelled Paddlers are those who complete the entire 740 miles in one direction using their own power to paddle, pole, and portage. Leaving the trail via other means of travel for lodging, shopping, or other reasons will not count against the self-propelled paddler as long as they return to the same spot to continue the journey on the trail. Consideration for deviations to this definition will be given to safety, inclement weather, and extreme low water. Self-Propelled Paddlers are designated with a double asterisk (**) on the Thru-Paddlers List.

Integrated Paddlers are those who paddle the trail as one expedition during a single season in one direction and use a shuttle for one or more of the carries, not to exceed 10% of the total trail distance (74 miles). Integrated Paddlers are designated with a single asterisk (*).

Integrated "Downstream" Paddlers are those who paddle the trail as one expedition, during a single season, reversing direction on one or more rivers to increase downstream miles. There will be no mark to designate this category.

Those two little asterisks meant so much to me.

To join *The NFCT List*, one must submit a lengthy form, including a detailed description of each portage and campsite. So, this bridge just before Indian Carry became the first of many tweaks I would make to the carefully folded paperwork I was carrying with me and filling out as I went. It's a good thing I did, because I would never have remembered all the details.

As I climbed the first half of Indian Carry, the canoe seemed lighter on my shoulders, my feet surer on the wooded path. My strength was growing. At the height of land, we crossed from the Raquette River watershed to that of the Saranac, a bold river that would drop 1,400 feet over the next 63 miles, in its journey to the shores of Lake Champlain.

CHAPTER 4

JUST ENOUGH COURAGE

You will never do anything in this world without courage. It is the greatest quality of the mind next to honor.

—Aristotle

I can just go at my pace," Dad said, allowing me to pull ahead on the wheelable second half of Indian Carry. Delicate woodland flowers, club moss, and princess pine dotted the forest floor, beneath tall hemlocks. I hurried along, hoping there would be time for a swim. At the put-in on Upper Saranac Lake, I tied up my loaded canoe, then waded in. The sun felt strong on my skin, the water balmy. In the Adirondacks, I had been swimming every day, enjoying the change from the brisk Maine lakes back home.

Dad was determined to get as far as we could, to give us more "town time" tomorrow. Like the slow but steady tortoise, he caught up, loaded up, and was soon dwindling in the distance, while I was still drying off. I left the sheltered cove and paddled after him. Out on the lake, a strong wind greeted me, gusting vigorously from the northwest. Unfortunately, our route lay along the unprotected eastern shore. Two miles north, then we would turn east into Huckleberry Bay, to find Bartlett Carry to Middle Saranac Lake.

We both wore whistles clipped to our PFD's. They were a standard item on safety equipment checklists, used to communicate across the water. Whistles are a low-tech tool—no batteries, no instructional manual, and everybody knows how to blow a whistle, right? Well, the trail was about to teach us yet another lesson.

Indian Point gave me a short break and then a gauntlet of large, confused waves as I went around it. I spotted the yellow dash of Dad's canoe, far out on the lake. Way too far out. For some mysterious reason, Dad was heading straight for the large green outline of Birch Island, well beyond our proper turn.

Finally, I get to use this whistle, I thought, justifying its presence on all those gear lists.

As you may have deduced, we had never actually tested our whistles on the water. The GPS, yes of course. The SPOT, too, with our friends getting mysterious messages from land and water months before, proudly proclaiming our location on some random lake, or our backyard. But a whistle's a whistle, right? However, it turned out that Dad can't hear it!

At first, I thought he had, as he paused along the island shore. I blew some more and used my paddle to signal the proper course. Patiently I waited, then blew and blew some more, putting my whole self into it. Nothing. Then Dad made a move. He was backtracking, the wind now hurtling him along at a good pace. Where was he going?

Reluctantly, I left the hard-won prize of the calmer bay and took off after him, still futilely blowing that darn whistle. My shoulders and back spasmed as I dug in, determined to catch his attention before too much ground was lost. Finally, he saw me.

"I was watching for you to paddle into the lake and you never came. I thought for sure you had a problem and was going back to help," he explained.

Against the shoreline, he hadn't seen my boat. He needed some convincing with the map in one hand and the GPS in the other to believe he'd been on the wrong course. With that sorted out, we had another go at the wind, made short work of wheelable Bartlett Carry and found ourselves on Middle Saranac Lake.

The shore was lined with attractive campsites. After a shaky cell phone call, we secured one, which we could pay for tomorrow on our way out. The high water had turned the small point into an island, where we waded to the outhouse. The site did have an ideal tree for hanging our food. This evening ritual is part of proper bear etiquette and requires finding a sturdy tree limb, within rope-throwing reach, on which to suspend your bags of food and cooking gear. It's often surprisingly difficult to find a branch that works.

It was my turn to cook. I started with tortillas, my trail bread of choice. They're versatile, durable, and already flat. I loaded them with chicken from a pouch, cheese, refried beans, chopped peppers, olives, and hot sauce. For dessert, we had hot chocolate. I'd be eating this meal often, as I'd purchased a giant bag of dehydrated refried beans, tiny plastic cups of black olives, and packets of hot sauce. The website minimus.biz is an excellent source for small packages of everything from duct tape and anti-fungal ointment to apricot preserves.

Then we headed for bed, where the cries of loons wove their way into my dreams.

I take a lot of pictures of my feet—immersed in mud or propped on the canoe's gunwales, with a wild river in the background. In the morning, my feet were warm in their wool socks and Tevas, resting with a mug of coffee on a granite bluff. I snapped a photo. Dad was still asleep. Only a family of cruising black ducks, gilded by the early sun, disturbed the mirror of the lake.

In my heart, I was already saying goodbye to Dad. This camp had been our last together. Tonight, we would have a real bedroom in the Saranac Lake home of two NFCT supporters, Dave and Patti, who were offering thru-paddlers what they called "trail angel housing" for a small cost. We would have hot showers, cold beverages, breakfast and, it turned out, lots of warm hospitality.

Our travels today would take us through two locks, smaller versions of those found on the Erie or Panama Canals. Constructed around the turn of the century to allow motor launches to travel farther upriver, the locks eliminated carries above and below Lower Saranac Lake. We would paddle down through three lakes to the town of Saranac Lake, without a single carry.

My only concern was the operation of the lock mechanisms. I was glad to have my mechanically minded father with me. In the busy summer months, there were usually lock tenders on duty. If not, though, boaters must operate the locks themselves.

A mile of quiet river, dotted with white water lilies, brought us to the first lock. We slowed down when we spotted a brown cabin on river right. Cautiously, we approached the Upper Locks and were glad to find lock tender Margaret on duty.

Area tradition has pluralized what is really a single lock. It was already full of water, and we simply paddled in and waited. Margaret shut the gate behind us, lowered us down a couple of feet, and deftly pushed the downstream gate open with her foot, swinging with the ease of practice to the other side. Quick, efficient, and she made my day by saying I had the lightest thru-paddler load she'd seen this season.

After Lower Saranac Lake, we stopped as promised at the campground headquarters to pay for our campsite and have lunch. From there, it was a couple of miles to the Lower Locks, again just one, built to bypass a rocky 5-foot drop.

Before the lock was built, there was a hand-operated windlass at the falls that used a cable to raise and lower boats. A 1985 article in the *Adirondack Daily Enterprise* gave a thorough history of the Saranac River locks. The author shared a story from the 1940s or 1950s when Ed Lany was the tender at the Lower Locks. A woman traveling through had accidentally dropped her diamond ring overboard. Distraught, she pleaded with Ed to find it for her.

"Ed feared that if he opened the wickets to drain the lock, the ring might be washed downstream and lost forever, but by keeping both gates and wickets closed the ring would surely remain in the confines of the lock. In another boat waiting to enter the locks were a couple of young men whom Ed knew. He enlisted their services to dive for the ring. After repeated dives the boys brought up a book, three watches, a set of false teeth and finally the missing diamond ring. Ed later claimed that he lived all winter on the generous reward received from the grateful lady."

The rest of the afternoon was anticlimactic. It was simply work, dodging power boats and fighting the wind to make it to the town of Saranac Lake and the end of Map 2. We were ready to be done, to rest our aching backs and shoulders, to regroup. The first 90 miles of the trail had taken us seven days, rather than the six we'd planned, but we were content. Together, we'd met the challenges of what Dad called my "shake-down cruise."

Having completed Maps 1, 2, 11, 12, and parts of 10 and 13, Dad was now well on his way to section-paddling the NFCT. We would be together again on Maine's St. John River, the final miles for him of Map 13. Until then, he and Mom would become my support team.

Our host Dave met us at the river. I'd wheeled my boat to where I'd start alone tomorrow, then put it up on Dad's truck for the night. We followed Dave home, then agreed to all go out to dinner after we'd had showers and some time to rest.

Outers, Nessmuk's term for sportsmen and women, were not the only folks who came to the Adirondacks a century or more ago. Patients with tuberculosis came, too, in search of a cure, in the days before antibiotics.

After dinner at the Downhill Grill, Dave kindly drove me to the store, pointing out the ancient paths of "Tray Boys" along the way. These crooked, overgrown steps traced their way from street to street, connecting the town's many cure cottages. The cure cottages, recognizable by their many-windowed porches, had once housed hundreds of hopeful patients. Windows were kept open year-round to let in healthful air. Patients followed a strict regimen of exposure to the elements and large amounts of milk and healthy food. Meals were cooked in special kitchens and delivered by the Tray Boys, some of whom were actually girls.

We had so much fun visiting that I didn't get much done. I woke insanely early to sort photos, write, and pack. Before long, Dave had coffee ready, with a delicious breakfast casserole and fresh fruit salad. We said goodbye, then drove through town, quiet and thoughtful.

Our first stop was St. Regis Canoe Outfitters, right on the Saranac River. Owner Dave Cilley and his manager Sarah were enthusiastic about my journey and loved my new boat. They promised to stand on the riverbank in a few minutes to watch me go by. We learned that John Mautner was two days ahead, and I stocked up on water, supplies, and some excellent advice. Dave scribbled notes on a copy of his custom river map and filled me in on the flooded river conditions. Eventually, however, it was time to go, to face what lay ahead.

Surprisingly, bears don't scare me. I have fond memories of a trip with Mom to Shenandoah National Park in the summer of 2004 when, in one week, I saw eight. Posing cooperatively along the Skyline Drive, passing in a blur of black through an abandoned apple orchard, strolling trailside in the early dawn, and even a cub playing hide and seek among some tall grasses. Truthfully, that cute bear cub did make me nervous. I never spotted its mother and froze until another hiker came along to keep me company as I continued down the trail.

Neither am I bothered by being alone or by the dark or by snakes. There was something, though, that did scare me. At first, I'd been nervous and worried, now I was terrified. Something far more evil than bears or snakes might be lurking downriver. A desperate escaped convict was on the loose and could be anywhere.

Dannemora, home to New York's maximum-security Clinton Correctional Facility, hovers at the edge of Map 3. For weeks now, my eyes had been traveling the short distance, representing about four miles, between the gray dot that marked the town of Dannemora and the winding blue line of the Saranac River. Late at night, safe in my bed at home, my mind had churned, replaying bits and pieces of a story straight from Hollywood.

In the early morning hours of June 6, two weeks before I was scheduled to depart, Richard Matt and David Sweat had pulled off a daring prison escape. It was the stuff of legends, or the plot of *The Shawshank Redemption*. First cutting through their cell walls weeks before, they spent many midnight hours penetrating the bowels of the prison, making a plan. Later, news articles would characterize the pair as vicious, cunning, and MacGyver-like. They were predictable, too, fashioning dummies from sweatshirts to leave sleeping in their beds.

One was a brutal cop killer who had shot his victim 22 times. The other a psychotic who had kidnapped, tortured, and dismembered his first victim, his boss. He escaped to Mexico, where he murdered again.

To make matters worse, on June 11, CBS News reported that dogs had picked up the men's scent in Cadyville. They had apparently bedded down in some vegetation, leaving behind food wrappers and a footprint. The Saranac River runs right through Cadyville, where I would face a complicated two-mile portage.

Rumors flew. They were headed to Vermont, or Mexico, or they hadn't even gone a mile. Your mind can do a lot of late-night churning with that material.

I remember, though, just three days after the prison break, listening to a radio devotional on the Christian station. The Old Testament scripture spoke reassuringly right to me.

The words I heard from Deuteronomy 31:6 were: *"Be strong and courageous. Do not be afraid or terrified because of them, for the Lord your God goes with you; he will never leave you nor forsake you."* What could be clearer? I continued my preparations for the trip.

As my departure drew closer, I wavered, but my faith gave me the courage I needed. Plus, I would have my father with me to keep me safe. But now came the moment of truth.

One of the killers was still out there, and, unbelievably, Dad was truly going to leave me as planned and go home. Yesterday, as we'd been taking photos at the kiosk, a parade of serious black SUV's had roared by, punctuated by the occasional police car. Sirens screamed and lights flashed. At Dave and Patti's, the TV talked of nothing else.

Richard Matt was dead, shot by a border patrol officer after getting drunk on whiskey stolen from an empty cabin. David Sweat remained at large. Patti thought his partner had done him in early in the escapade, but who could know?

All along, I had been able to rationalize plowing forward, my plans unchanged. I had been convinced that if I just had faith, the problem would be resolved before I had to venture down the river alone. The convicts would be caught or proven to be in Mexico. Then we were paddling closer and closer, but I still had Dad with me.

Now, though, there was just me and a decision to be made. I halfway expected a call from Mom, begging me to come home. Or that Dad might issue an ultimatum or offer to hang around, to keep me safe. But none of those things happened.

Leaving Dad was a wrench. We traded kayak paddles, as his was lighter and longer. He stayed in the truck, while I made several trips up and down from the parking lot to the river. Finally, I just had to go, before I lost my courage.

"That moment of leaving Dad gave me butterflies," I wrote that night. *"I know how precious this past week was and hate to see it over. And yet I yearn to test myself, to have less of people for a while…to write."*

Once committed, the river did not let me linger. Dave and Sarah

Be-on-lookout-for convict poster on footbridge across Saranac River, a terrifying reminder of the danger that I faced

passed in a flash, and a bunch of fun little rapids took my mind off my sadness. Although the river had dropped overnight, it was still high and flowing briskly. There were bridges ahead, some with possible low clearance issues. It was time to focus, to stay alert.

Red-winged blackbirds were abundant in the grassy marshes. The first few bridges were fine. At the bridge marking a hiking trail to Moose Pond, I stopped for a quick bathroom break. Five miles had already gone by and I was still alive, not murdered yet. I climbed up for a look at the bridge and there they were. "Be on Lookout For" signs with the two faces that had been burned in my memory for weeks. The glance over my shoulder was automatic, then I scuttled down to the boat and back to the river, paddling the exact center.

The Saranac River flows for 11 miles to Permanent Rapids, and today it never slowed, due to the high water. The danger, the bugs, the forecast rain, all shouted, "Hurry!" And the river cooperated, as I averaged over four miles per hour along this section.

At the McCasland Bridge, which was literally sitting on the river, I went around through a gravel parking area. Below, the flooding had created dangerous strainers. I weaved my way between downed trees, as the river began a series of sinuous curves.

Blind to the scenery, my eyes darted from bank to bank, wishing I could penetrate the tangled alder. It did register that the manicured lawns, the colorful powerboats with massive engines, in fact human presence in any form, had faded away. Instead there was the papery rustle of grass, its whisper loud in the gloomy silence. Darkening clouds shrouded the sky.

I am going nowhere, I thought, as the river continued to double back on itself. Just when I wanted to hurry, to get these miles done. It felt like I was paddling in slow motion, although the GPS said otherwise. I began to wonder, *If I were a convict, where would I hide?*

There were plenty of places to choose from. Any of these faded cabins would welcome a desperate man. To sleep in safety away from prying eyes, scrounging food left from summers past. Invisible eyes seemed to watch me from dark windows framed by sagging shutters. I shrugged off those disturbing thoughts and tried to remember God's comforting presence. *What was that Bible verse I heard on the radio? I wish I could remember it!*

A couple of miles before the Permanent Rapids portage, a barn appeared on river left. It was a testament to what must once have been a grand farm. Painted red and gray, its elegant peaks and gables now contrasted wickedly with broken and boarded windows. *A truly fitting hideout for an escaped convict.* I surged forward with renewed vigor.

Suddenly, a mighty crash in the bushes, probably just a deer, sent me airborne. My heart jumped, racing in terror. I thought how crazy this was and wondered if I should even go on.

Eventually, my heart rate slowed and my courage returned. I did go on and reached the portage safely. Now I was wheeling along within easy lunging distance of the woods. Cars passed from time to time, and I couldn't walk the center of the road. I had a plan though—bug spray in the eyes. A can of Off hung from a carabiner in easy reach.

What a relief it was to finally put in on secluded Franklin Falls Pond, to paddle far from shore. In this weary hour, the quiet pond backed by mountains felt longer than it looked on the map. Near the end, a fisherman had caught a 32-inch northern pike and a bunch of walleye.

"If you can't catch fish here, you can't catch 'em anywhere," summed up his day. He was still talking fishing as I paddled on into the wind. It was not a spot to stop and chat.

Union Falls Pond was equally wild. I headed for the red circle that Dave had drawn around Bear Point. There I found a secluded campsite, drew my boat up well out of sight, and built a cheerful fire. For dinner, I steamed Patti's cut-up vegetables and added them to instant cheddar and bacon potatoes. I was still spooked, though, and crouched down to hide behind my tent when a man motored up and then away in a small boat.

I woke to rain drumming hard against the tent. My system of having most of my gear inside with me had paid off this morning. I wiggled around, packing for a day of drenching travel. For breakfast, I brewed coffee under the tent's small vestibule and ate handfuls of homemade granola. Soon, I was as ready as I was going to be. After a deep breath and a prayer for strength and safety, I unzipped and emerged.

Out on the water, a stiff northeast wind whistled down the length of the lake. I fought into it, hugging the shoreline. In a small cove, a group of three mergansers materialized from the gloom, as surprised to see me as I was them. In less than three miles of paddling, the canoe took on almost three gallons of water, and I stopped along the way to bail.

Thus began a day of endurance of body and soul, in which I walked over 14 miles in cold rain. After the pond, my brain must have been water-logged. I stopped to photograph the dam, standing on Casey Road, my intended portage route. By walking, I would avoid a long stretch of difficult, dangerous rapids. In past years, the ledges below Tefft

Pond Falls had destroyed boats and even ended some thru-paddles. Casey Road obviously paralleled the river.

Inexplicably, I started up an intersecting paved road instead, at a 90-degree angle away from the river. By the time I realized my mistake, I had walked an extra mile-and-a-half.

Back on Casey Road, it was quiet, far too quiet. Five miles of lonely walking on a sandy, uneven, barely paved road, like a movie set for a thriller's final scene. I had thought yesterday was remote and the bushes close? Only three cars passed in more than two hours. I was relieved to turn onto much-busier Silver Lake Road, where a red antique sleigh was one of the few charming sights of a blurry, gray day of nonstop rain.

I followed the plan I'd made yesterday with Dave, turning next onto busy Route 3. I was a machine. Stopping meant getting colder and already my hands were fumbling and my lips felt blue. Separator Rapids, far below, looked as though they would quickly separate you from your boat. At my intended put-in, I double-checked the directions.

My fumbling, tired body is supposed to go down there? I may have even muttered it aloud. High grass, with just a hint of a faint path, covered the slope that dropped sharply to a mire of flooded cattails well below. The energetic river promised to make launching tricky.

I wavered, then returned to the busy highway. Not far ahead there was supposed to be a convenience store. Soon, an oasis of colorful neon emerged from the gray mist.

It was Maplefield's, the home of the perfect survival food, the Michigan.

"You don't know what a Michigan is?"

I had amazed the young man behind the counter with my ignorance. Soon, though, I had wolfed down two of these hot dogs with meat sauce and mustard, followed by a banana and two cups of hot cocoa. A while after that, I finally stopped shivering.

The cashier knew of a far easier place to get back on the river. A short way up Route 3, I crossed the Pup Hill Road bridge and wheeled right to the water. Great blue herons kept me company as I flew through miles of easy Class II water, at speeds up to seven miles per hour.

The High Falls Carry was a must for every paddler, as it bypassed a dam and Class V-VI rapids through High Falls Gorge. *The Companion's* accurate directions guided me carefully between two rows of warning buoys to a point, then along a potentially confusing network of roads that could have used better signage. By now, I felt as if I were nearing

Tolkien's Rivendell and the last homely house of safety. Baker's Acres Campground and a hot shower were just several easy miles ahead.

Ron, the campground owner, kindly dried my soaked tent in his dryer.

Later, from the depths of my dry and toasty sleeping bag, I reconnected with family and friends. This was the first time in days that I'd had cell phone service. My first call was to Dan Brown, who had shuttled us to Old Forge. We were working out the final details to paddle together with Peter Macfarlane on the big waters of Lake Champlain.

It was Sunday and many friends had been praying for me. Those prayers were answered when Dan gave me the news. David Sweat had been captured alive that day. He'd almost made it to Canada. Dressed in camouflage and running for the cover of a tree line, Sweat had been shot twice by a New York state trooper. With my mind truly at rest for the first time in days, I drifted off while the sky was still light.

CHAPTER 5

ONCE YOU'RE WET, YOU'RE WET

Sunshine is delicious, rain is refreshing, wind braces us up, snow is exhilarating; there is really no such thing as bad weather, only different kinds of good weather.

—John Ruskin

People are often surprised to discover that rivers run north. On a U.S. map, many large rivers—the Mississippi, the Colorado, the Rio Grande, the Hudson—flow south, or down the page. In coastal regions, rivers typically head for the ocean. Always, though, the flow of water must follow the terrain, traveling from higher to lower elevations at the whim of gravity. Logically, then, rivers can run in any direction. For the past week, since Brown's Tract Inlet, I had been following the rivers of the NFCT northeast. In its final miles, though, the Saranac River would turn southeast, toward mighty Lake Champlain.

The Saranac was a strong river, temperamental and moody. For centuries, its strength had been harnessed to serve the needs of man. Sawmills, iron forges, woolen and grist mills, and a glass factory—all had been run by water power captured and controlled by a host of dams. Most dams were later repurposed for the generation of electricity. A sense of history lingered here and was reflected in the names of the dams and portages that lay ahead—Cadyville, Kent Falls, Treadwell Mills, Indian Rapids, and Imperial Mills.

The day began gently. In the gray light, a family of Canada geese cruised silently away from shore, the only ones awake to see me go. A chilly hour passed before the sun climbed higher and fell across my shoulders, bringing life and warmth and comfort. A chorus of ecstatic bird song said that they, too, were happy for the sun. From the sky above, a tiny feather drifted down, hung balanced for a moment on the gunwale, then dropped into the river.

My thoughts wandered, gathering energy and purpose for the challenges ahead. Plattsburgh, on Lake Champlain, was more than 20 miles from Baker's Acres. If I made it in a day, I would be back on schedule. For six quiet miles, the river rested. Perhaps it, too, was gathering energy for the run to Plattsburgh.

The day's first portage wound through the village of Cadyville. I bumped along the crooked sidewalk, watching shiny cars leave dark garages for another day of work. What a contrast to my summer, I thought, to this adventure of a lifetime that I was living.

Every day is a gift, was the message I'd been sharing as I signed in along the trail. I always tried to squeeze the words in, next to my departure date and destination and the description of my canoe. I thought of Chris and what he would have given for a summer full of days like this, however strenuous.

The portage returned me to the river once again. There, my heart fell, and I stared in astonishment at the transformation. Sullen, murky water churned and boiled its way downriver and crept among the shoreline trees. Any calm eddies had been devoured by the flooding. I scouted a good distance along the riverside path. There was simply nowhere to safely put in.

What am I going to do? I gazed blankly at the raging river, trying to think.

Then I remembered something. I'd written down the number for St. Regis Canoe Outfitters, just in case. Thankfully, my phone had service and Dave answered. He was quick to comprehend the challenge.

"I'd say err on the side of caution. I've never paddled that part of the river when it was that high." It was confirmation that I wasn't crazy to be cautious. The two miles just ahead were the most difficult, he said, and I could walk by road to Morrisonville, then put in.

Along the way, I stopped to study the inscription on a roadside monument, made from a triangle of worn millstones from local nineteenth-century pulpmills. Not far past the monument, I finally reached a spot where a grassy bank met calmer water. I launched and for an hour, raced downriver, hurtled along as fast as I would go anywhere on the trail. The thrilling ride ended at Treadwell Mills Dam, where I resumed walking. One by one, I put the last of the dams behind me, until I stood again undecided beside the river.

I was now on the edge of Plattsburgh, at a spot where I had a big decision to make. Somewhere ahead, within the city boundaries, the contaminated residues of a coal plant were being dredged, randomly closing parts of the river. Past paddlers had even encountered cables strung across the full width of the water. To make it more complicated, there was a large surfing wave, Class III in high water, under a bridge and lots of trash. In 2011, Katina and Sam had seen a mattress and a refrigerator door in the water, then torn a hole in their Kevlar hull, probably on a piece of old rebar.

Sunlight filtered down through arching shoreline trees and the river ran along, cleanly and swiftly. I deliberated, weighing unseen dangers against the exhilaration of flying past city streets in a victorious finale to my ten days in New York. On my right was the river. On my left, an ordinary street led up into a residential neighborhood. My thoughts went back to my talk with Dave and then to that afternoon on the Dead River, remembering the grip of churning whitewater, relentless and uncaring.

In the distance, far up the street, a woman in a colorful sweater walked a small dog. She paused, calmly letting the dog sniff. The scene was so suburban, so comforting in its simplicity and calm after the turmoil of the river. It looked amazingly good, in fact. At that moment, I made up my mind. I would not try the wild ride into Plattsburgh with all its question marks.

The street led up past sprawling apartment complexes, then segued into a neighborhood of single family homes. On the right, well-kept athletic fields surrounded the local high school.

On the sidewalk by the school, I pulled out my map and balanced it atop the load of gear. I was on course to intersect Rugar Street, a major east-west artery that might lead to a hotel. Plattsburgh was a large city, with lots of lodging, but I didn't know where any of it was.

Then I looked up and there were people. From a tidy split-level across the street, a man and woman were walking purposefully straight toward me. They had spotted me from their front window. Friendly and comforting, was my first thought, and a grin spread across my face.

"Hi. You look like someone who could help me find a hotel."

"Hi. Are you paddling the Northern Forest Canoe Trail?" the man asked, almost at the same time. Tom and Nancy had recently finished section hiking Vermont's Long Trail. When they brought me inside, piles of unpacked gear awaited sorting and I felt right at home. They offered help, starting with a backyard space to park my boat until tomorrow.

For days, I'd been brave and decisive. Now, I wavered on this simple decision. In the busy urban environment of Plattsburgh, I knew, there would be no casual storage near the kiosk, no locking my precious canoe to the nearest sturdy tree. Instead, I tried to find an outfitter near the river to store my boat overnight. Tom hurried between computer and kitchen island, cheerfully bringing little pink sticky notes with phone numbers for me to try.

Meanwhile, Nancy cut up watermelon, piled grapes and cheese on a plate, and made hot tea. I found a hotel, but nowhere to store my boat. Perhaps the boat could ride with me to my hotel, I threw out next.

"We can take your boat in our truck," Tom quickly agreed, jumping into action to hunt up some straps. Before he could find them, though, the tea and calories hit my tired brain and I realized their first offer of backyard boat storage would work just fine.

In the fenced backyard, my boat looked secure and content, locked for added peace of mind to the wooden steps. Most of my boat gear hid underneath.

Gratefully, I sank into the comfort of the truck's backseat, tucking one last sticky note into my pocket. It had Tom and Nancy's address, to give the taxi driver in the morning. Within minutes, we were pulling up at the Comfort Inn. At the end of the building was a restaurant, its glorious sign reading "Plattsburgh Brewing Company." It doesn't get any better than that.

When the taxi dropped me at the pink-sticky-note address the following morning, Nancy volunteered to walk with me along the Saranac River Trail. This paved path followed the winding river through the SUNY Plattsburgh campus and a bit of downtown Plattsburgh to the NFCT kiosk. The striking Macdonough Monument, a 135-foot obelisk crowned with an eagle, towered high above the city. It commemorated the victory of Commodore Thomas Macdonough in the final naval battle of the War of 1812, fought on Lake Champlain.

After taking my end-of-Map-3 photo, Nancy hugged me warmly, then tactfully went off to do her errands while I got organized.

For months now, Lake Champlain had sat like a huge blue blob in the middle of my route. A mental blob, too, in which giant canoe-eating ferries, mysterious spiny softshell turtles, and legendary pastries swirled.

I had known from the beginning that I would love some company in crossing Champlain, the sixth largest lake in the United States.

Some thru-paddlers had been windbound here for days. Others had resorted to taking the Grand Isle Ferry to eliminate one of the hazardous open crossings. Wind and adverse weather were the norm and could build to epic proportions on this long lake.

Once again, trust and faith were rewarded by details falling into place. Earlier, in May, the NFCT had hosted their first spring Freshet Fest, a paddlers' gathering in Burlington, Vermont, featuring a panel of successful thru-paddlers sharing their stories. Of course, I had gone. I camped with Katina and Sam, the first time I'd seen them in years.

At the Freshet Fest, I'd met Dan Brown and his wife Michele and solved the Old Forge shuttle piece of the planning puzzle. Peter Macfarlane had been there, too. Peter, with his intent blue eyes and quick smile, looked rather different in person, clean-cut and saner than in the increasingly scruffy photos of his drenching thru-paddle.

Peter generously offered, "If you'd like some company on Lake Champlain, just let me know." This was a huge gift. He would rearrange his busy summer schedule of fiddle lessons and Celtic music to be available for the time window when I might reach the lake. Later, Dan volunteered to come along, too—the more the merrier. That would make twice that he'd left his Vermont inn to help me, with Michele kindly filling the gaps, I'm sure.

First thing this morning, though, I was by myself. Given the logistics of shuttling cars, Peter and Dan were meeting me near the ferry terminal. To reach them, I would cross Cumberland Bay alone, paddling two miles east. Another mile southeast around Cumberland Head would bring me to the rendezvous. On the map, which showed only half of the enormous lake, the bay looked rather small and protected, a breeze to paddle.

Well, it was a breeze all right. More like a gale. A short distance from the kiosk, the full extent of the bay came into view. Before she left, Nancy had pointed out a bright patch of green in the far distance. That was my first goal. From there, I would follow the shore to the tip of the peninsula and around to my friends.

On my right, at a large marina, boats danced and bucked on the waves. A police boat idled reassuringly, just out from the marina. A source of rescue perhaps. Or a witness to a disaster. A southeasterly wind was driving up into the bay, and it was already nine o'clock.

Conditions would likely get worse. Out on the bay, there were no other boats in sight.

This was by far the biggest water I had paddled yet in my new canoe, or maybe ever. I quickly discovered the swells had a pattern, coming in sets of two or three big ones, with a break in between.

Just focus on what's coming next, I coached myself. *The waves about to reach you are the only critical ones right now.*

After what seemed a very long time, a quick glance showed the marina was now as distant as the bright patch of green. Halfway across. A few tongues of white flickered among the rollers. The waves lifted my boat impressively, then dropped it, giving me time to adjust and go on. There was, of course, no choice but to go on. Soon, it would be a far different story. Peter, Dan, and I would be together, sailing north with the wind at our backs. Up along the shores of South and North Hero islands toward the Missisquoi (miss-SIS-kwoi) River, with options for which shore to paddle. Here there were no options. Somewhere across the sea of waves lay the promised land.

Near the end, I was fading and I knew it. The words of the 23rd Psalm came to me and I repeated them again and again, remembering God's presence and promises. *"The Lord is my shepherd...he makes me lie down in green pastures, he leads me beside still waters, he restores my soul."*

I fought for that crossing, digging in and using what felt like all the strength I had. Finally, a surging wave deposited me at the bottom of a set of steps that led up to Route 314, right in the middle of that bright green I had been aiming for. The road looked so wonderful, so safe, and my map showed that it led right to the ferry landing that was our meeting place. With my wheels, I could safely walk to where the guys must by now be waiting. I couldn't reach Peter on my phone when I tried, but he quickly called back.

"Oh, I'm so happy to hear your voice," I blurted. "I made it." And breathlessly, "I'm right by a road. I could wheel to the ferry. You don't think it's safe to keep paddling, do you?"

That wonderful cheery voice with its British accent was immediately calming. "It's perfectly safe, you don't need the road. There's nothing out there that can touch your canoe. Shall we paddle round to meet you?" If I hadn't had Peter, I know I would have walked to the ferry.

After a dicey launching into pounding surf, I labored on. I'd eaten an enormous breakfast. The eggs and bacon, yogurt and English muffin, coffee and orange juice, were powering me toward Cumberland Head.

Seeing the specks of Dan and Peter's boats gave me another burst of energy. When we met, they turned, to battle back into the wind the way they'd just come. Peter gently suggested that I release my death grip on the paddle and stay further from the shore with its confused waves.

It seems safer near shore, but really isn't, he explained.

Cumberland Head's romantic ivy-covered lighthouse was a sign of victory, soon after we rounded the point. We crossed the path of the ferries with no problems, and, with the wind at our backs, had energy to visit. Dan was in training for an Alaskan wilderness trip and paddled a sea kayak. Peter was in the boat that he'd built for his 2013 thru-paddle— a 14-foot Sylva Tripper cedar-strip canoe by Otter Creek Smallcraft, his boatbuilding business.

Peter had once raced kayaks. Like 2011 thru-paddler Skip Ciccarelli, who had paddled with and coached me at the Freshet Fest, Peter understands the physics of paddling.

"What did Skip teach you?" Peter asked to start.

"Plant your feet. Your canoe should have a foot bar. And use your whole body; paddle from your feet and your torso. Plant the paddle, then pull the boat by."

Peter added more, much of it about my grip. I needed to get rid of that death grip and stop rotating my wrists.

"Do you ever have wrist pain?" he asked.

I described the stabbing pain and numbness that had grown worse during Paddle for Hope, finally making the handwriting in my journal almost illegible near the end. And I had been living on pain relievers. The trick, Peter said, was to open your hands every few strokes and concentrate on not rotating your wrists.

Dan chimed in, "Every time I see Peter look over at me, I think about my form."

I, too, would reassess my stroke countless times in the weeks ahead.

My friends made another common-sense improvement that would be with me for the trip. My SPOT had been transmitting sporadically at times. The reason was its location. I had been clipping it in random spots in the canoe, where it swung back and forth all day. At our first snack break, Dan and Peter devised a way to secure the SPOT with small bungee cords in the frame of the seat, always facing up. It lived in that same place for the rest of the journey.

Peter observed and made suggestions, but always he would say, "This is your trip."

I would choose the route and how far the "flotilla," as we called ourselves, would go. Tonight we would camp on Knight Island, where Peter had reserved a site with two lean-tos. We planned to stop first on North Hero Island, at Hero's Welcome, a store whose pastries had been calling to me like sirens since Katina and Sam had brought some for our breakfast in Vermont. Pastries from Hero's Welcome were a true trail tradition.

In honor of Peter's British heritage, we were headed there for tea that afternoon. With the lovely tailwind, we flew up the lake, through the much calmer waters of "The Gut" between the Hero Islands, and northward again, surfing the waves. At least Peter was surfing and I was attempting to perfect the technique. As a wave passed and a big one could be spotted over my shoulder, I waited for the bow to drop into the trough and then paddled like crazy. Peter just flew, surging ahead on the crest of wave after wave, which gave him time to take some nice one-handed action shots of me with his waterproof camera.

"There is nothing here that could capsize a canoe," Peter reiterated.

As we drew closer to the spot where we would detour west for tea, though, I knew that Dan and I were exhausted. The wind was picking up as storm clouds gathered. Rain was coming and the pastries would have to wait for tomorrow. A couple of times, Peter asked if I felt comfortable in the rougher conditions and seemed pleased when I answered yes, and that I would have even if I had been alone.

The best part of camp that evening was the stories. I tried to absorb all the details I could about the trail ahead. I had my own lean-to and the guys had theirs. Instead of having to pack up a wet tent, I decided to just use my sleeping bag, but it was buggy and warm inside the head net that was practically a necessity. When morning arrived, those pastries and a cup of strong coffee couldn't come fast enough. Dan was not feeling well, and would be leaving us on North Hero Island.

The display of baked goods at Hero's Welcome was a work of art and fully justified trail legend. After much thought, I chose a chocolate-filled flaky concoction, a peach scone, and an enormous ham and cheese pastry for lunch. Hero's Welcome had lived up to my expectations.

Dan, meanwhile, had found a ride back to his vehicle with some cycling friends, and we wished him a speedy recovery. Fueled by sugar and a southerly wind, Peter and I made good progress up the east shore of North Hero Island, finding plenty to talk about as we paddled.

There were endless notes to compare on gear and philosophy.

Peter had been following the track of my SPOT since the beginning and was surprised at how quickly I started portages.

"The SPOT pings, it pings again, and you're off," he said, referring to the blips the SPOT sent every 10 minutes showing my location. "Do you leave the straps on your wheels set up?"

"No. In fact, if the boat slips, I'll take it all apart and redo it mid-portage if necessary." Speaking of those straps, they were now living handily in the net pocket on the back of my canoe chair. As the days on the trail added up, I continued to fine-tune my gear organization.

We were both fascinated by that time long ago when glaciers shaped the landscape. Not only did they sculpt mountains and valleys and leave behind intriguing geological features like moraines and eskers, but their enormous weight pushed the land's surface down. The last glacier, the Laurentide Ice Sheet, was up to two miles thick and depressed the earth 600 feet.

The map described the retreat of the most recent glacier:

About 12,500 years ago, the ice sheet began to melt. Water from the retreating glacier filled the great valley between the Adirondacks and the Green Mountains, forming the massive, freshwater Lake Vermont. At its highest volume, Lake Vermont was 500 feet above Lake Champlain's current level. Can you imagine the surrounding hills as islands in the ancient lake?

As the melting glaciers receded farther north, salt water flowed from the Atlantic Ocean through the Saint Lawrence Valley and into the Champlain Valley. Lake Vermont became the Champlain Sea, a brackish arm of the Atlantic. Whales and seals inhabited its waters until the earth rebounded, closing the connection to the ocean. Today, a few seashore plants still live on this freshwater lake.

Peter and I were wind-powered, wind-driven, on an exhilarating ride that was conquering this intimidating lake at a great pace. And it was about to get even more memorable. The rain began, gently at first. Serious clouds overtook us from behind, and gone were all thoughts of stopping at North Hero State Park where Dan had camped or searching for the threatened spiny softshell turtle. The crossing from Stephenson Point to Clark Point was one and a half miles of open water. It grew darker and then we were simply inside the rain. If you have ever been there, you know what I mean.

Then, something about the weather must have changed for Peter, and he shouted above the wind, "This would be the time to head straight for the closest shore. Say that white house over there." Luckily,

Drenching crossing of Lake Champlain (Peter Macfarlane photo)

we saw no lightning, but we did find out we could go faster.

On shore, we stopped to bail and Peter suggested just flipping my boat. Why hadn't I thought of that? After agreeing that we both were crazy, we continued, on through the wall of rain. The ferocity of the storm ebbed and flowed, at points allowing us to see the island we had left behind. Then it would disappear in a gray monochromatic world where we seemed like the only living creatures. Crazy perhaps, but also very fast.

We passed under the Route 78 bridge, near where Peter had parked. He was feeling "a bit nippy," so we stopped at his car. While I inhaled my ham and cheese pastry, he rid himself of excess gear and put a dry layer under all the wet. Yet another trick that does work, as I found out when I did the same. The dry thermal shirt that I put on under my saturated raincoat felt warm for hours.

In the end, I was on Lake Champlain for only twenty-eight hours.

Best of all, Peter decided to go with me a short distance up the Missisquoi River, the first of my many upstream miles. As we entered the river, still peering through rain, we were in the Missisquoi National Wildlife Refuge, teeming with birds. We saw herons, eagles, osprey, and a multitude of ducks.

Peter started his upstream paddling lesson with a simple question.

"Where is the strongest current in the river?"

My answer? In the middle of the stream and on the inside of curves.

"Half right," he smiled. Also half wrong.

Actually, anyone who doesn't know the answer to that should probably not be paddling. Or perhaps they should be sentenced to a couple of hundred miles of upstream paddling to learn. (By the way, I would face at least 150 miles of upstream travel.)

The correct answer, of course, is in the middle and on the outside of curves, which I certainly should have known. That leaves the inside of curves as the place to be, to discover tiny eddies that make a giant difference. Peter demonstrated. We were going to hug the banks on the inside of curves, crossing from left to right and back as the river curved.

When Peter said, "Hug the shore," he meant it. We wove in and out of trees draped over the river. We stayed so close to tall banks of marsh grass that there was barely room for the paddle. When crossing at a bend, we searched for the elusive point of least resistance to cross, something that is only learned by practice.

"See," Peter encouraged me after a while, "you're doing over three miles per hour upstream."

I was still amusing myself looking for turtles.

"It's not exactly basking weather," Peter said, although the sun was struggling to appear.

Four miles upriver, at Louie's Landing, Peter would leave me to retrieve his car. There we found a new boat-washing station, one of several that NFCT had installed at strategic spots along the trail. Their purpose was to prevent the spread of aquatic invasive hitchhikers, plant and animal, from one water body to another. The Clean-Drain-Dry campaign was common sense, and the new wash stations made the process much more efficient. There were good instructions. You scrubbed your boat with a brush, inside and out, on a conveniently provided rack, then rinsed and even dried it, although we found no towels there that day.

When leaving Lake Champlain, thorough cleaning was critically important. In 2014, lake monitors there had discovered their fiftieth nonnative invasive species, the spiny water flea. This tiny crustacean, a relative of shrimp and crabs, is less than half an inch long, including the stout barbed spine that makes up most of its length. It caught my attention because of what I didn't do. I forgot to wash my paddle. Later, I read that spiny water fleas attach themselves to paddles and fishing tackle by their barbed spines.

I'm always amazed at how much there is to learn in this world. Out on the trail, there are bits of knowledge or intriguing questions that pop up, on topics you would never have foreseen. The spiny water flea turned out to be sadly and grotesquely fascinating.

In 1984, this invasive species was discovered in Lake Huron, probably brought there in the ballast water of a ship from Europe. A robust reproducer and clever traveler, it can quickly spread. In the warmth of summer, adults produce offspring every two weeks. In the cold of winter, their eggs survive, buried in lake sediment. Preventing their introduction to other waters is challenging. Adults can live in a thimbleful of water. Their eggs can survive a trip through the digestive tract of a fish.

This tiny crustacean illustrates the complex impacts that a nonnative invader can have on an ecosystem. As a predator, it competes with juvenile fish for the same food, microscopic zooplankton, leaving less for native fish to eat. The spiny water flea also eats crustaceans that help to keep algae populations in check, significantly reducing water clarity. This could prove disastrous in Lake Champlain, which already has algae problems caused by high levels of phosphorous.

As if all this wasn't enough, as the population explodes, spiny water fleas can attach to fishing lines in such numbers that they look and feel like wet cotton. Rod guides clog and the line can't be reeled back in. Sadly, the spiny water flea is just one of many nonnative aquatic invasives that are spreading in New England's waters.

Peter left and I went on alone. Hugging the shore was a great way to see and hear wildlife. A mighty crash and scramble in the shoreline bushes must have been a startled deer and then, finally, I found a turtle. The rain had stopped, the sun came out, and basking could commence. The turtle, larger than a painted turtle but similar in appearance, was straddling a midstream log. It stayed there, posing cooperatively for the camera. Later, I identified it as a common map turtle, named for the yellow lines, like contours on a map or chart, that covered its head, legs, and shell. It was a new species for me.

In the planning months, when you picture trials, they tend to be dramatic. You're on the water—caught by lightning, capsized, lost.

My day ended with trials of a different sort. I pulled into the takeout after 28 miles, still damp and disorganized, and couldn't find my credit card anywhere. My tired brain remembered having it in Plattsburgh, at the ATM that staunchly refused to give me any cash. I dumped my boat and systematically searched each bag, with no luck.

Admitting defeat, I trudged to the NFCT kiosk, somewhat cheered by its familiar colors and bright logo. I signed in and remembered to send a SPOT message, as tomorrow I would return to the kiosk to start. Up the hill I went, into town, undoubtedly the only person pulling a canoe across the crosswalks and among the sidewalk wares of a busy thrift store, to the haven of the large library. It was there I missed my GPS. With disbelief, I pictured myself flipping the boat, the GPS falling unseen into the grass. Twice as fast, I set out to retrace my steps. Crosswalk, town park, crosswalk, thrift store, down the hill, to the takeout. A family was there, the two young children exploring along the water's edge.

"Hello. I think I lost my GPS here. Have you seen it?" I sheepishly asked the mother. She looked friendly and said something to the small boy. Miraculously, he reached into his pocket and handed over my GPS. Thank you, God, and thank you small boy and honest mother.

From there, it was about a half mile back through town to the Swanton Motel. Erin at the desk was kind and helpful, understanding my plight and allowing me to call Dad and use his credit card number. Next to my room at the end of the building, I locked my boat tightly to a solid metal railing. Bit by bit, I brought everything else inside. Then I collapsed, literally collapsed on the bed, after shutting and locking the door like a barricade.

Outside was the world of lost credit cards, towering waves, bugs, chilly rain, and uncertainty. Although there were restaurants in town, I would not leave my room until checkout time tomorrow. I had a microwave, fridge, well-stocked Keurig, warm shower, and bed, all the luxuries of the finest palace.

CHAPTER 6

MUDDY, MONOTONOUS, MARVELOUS

Be able to be alone. Lose not the advantage of solitude, and the society of thyself.

—Thomas Browne

At home, I'd been simplifying my life, and life on the river is by nature simple. What we carry is pared down to the essentials. Our cares shift from pleasing people and satisfying a thirsty schedule, to navigating the intricacies of the ever-changing trail. Our thoughts focus closer, deeper, truer. We are content with less, and often find more.

Having only a little money and no credit card was something I could live with. Instead of a Quebec resupply, Mom and Dad had agreed to meet me in a few days, in Vermont. Until then, I had about twelve dollars.

My schedule also felt suddenly unencumbered. There was no one to meet, not much official camping available, and I was now a day ahead of my original plan.

The Missisquoi River makes a loop around the town of Swanton. About three miles of paddling can be saved by walking in the other direction from the hotel. A purist, though, would surely go back to the kiosk and launch from there, which I did.

For the native Abenaki, this river had been an important travel artery. At this bend had once stood a large, strategically placed settlement. It must have been something to see, sitting high on a bluff, surrounded by a palisade of vertical logs. There, the people, perhaps as many as 5,000 during the summer, were well protected against their ancient enemies, the Iroquois.

The Iroquois nation was a confederacy of tribes stretching across the state of New York. Their representative government was highly successful in working together to wage war, make peace, and promote trade. In the Adirondacks, I had paddled through the territory of the Mohawk tribe, the "Keepers of the Eastern Door" for the confederacy.

Lake Champlain formed an important natural boundary between the Iroquois and another confederacy, allied for similar purposes. The Wabanaki, meaning "people of the dawn," lived throughout New England and parts of Canada. The Abenaki were one of five Wabanaki tribes, and it was through their historic lands that I would paddle until I was well into Maine.

I returned to hugging the shore, looking for the sweet spot to switch sides, and embracing the shoreline shade, as the miles gradually fell behind me. I focused on relaxing my hands, not twisting my wrists, not hurrying. The Victorian pink of one of my favorite wildflowers, Joe Pye weed, and the company of an Eastern kingbird kept life interesting, at the start of a day that would be filled with wildlife.

At the takeout for the Highgate Falls Dam portage, I met a young woman and three young men, college friends, who had been gradually section paddling the NFCT. We compared notes on campsites, and they lamented the wind. Going in the opposite direction, they were fighting the wind, which had been helping me work my way upstream.

"This portage is a bitch!" said one of the guys. "It's all washed out."

I should have paid more attention, although I guess it wouldn't have changed anything. A short distance up the hill, I discovered an NFCT campsite, shady and clean. John Mautner had signed the trail register two days earlier, noting that he'd had a bear swim across in front of his canoe. I was jealous. One of my hopes was to someday spot a black bear on the water.

The portage was awful, much worse than what I'd expected. Before I finished, I had the boat on and off the wheels three times. First the canoe was bounced off-center by ruts, then had to be fully unloaded to lift over a locked gate amid an impassable row of boulders, then a third time to cross a huge washed out gully. By then the put-in was close. I just gave up and carried everything from there down to the water.

Lots of people were around on this Thursday before the Fourth of July. I was glad to move on, through the murky green Missisquoi water.

A washed-out portage trail can really mess up your day

Months ago, I had been surprised to learn that water from some rivers along the trail isn't safe to drink, even when it's filtered. The Missisquoi was contaminated by agricultural runoff from its many dairy farms. The water even had a funny smell. For drinking, I carried gallons of bottled water with me in the boat.

Every day had its joys. Here there would be no swimming in the dubious water, but a spotted sandpiper flitted ahead and young families of ducks scuttled to safety along the banks. A rustling in the shoreline grasses became a parade of young beavers. One by one, they popped out, then slid into the river. *Plop, plop, plop.* Meanwhile, two adults swam back and forth in agitation, tail slapping, diving, then coming back to keep an eye on me.

Nearly twenty miles of the Missisquoi now lay behind me. So far, the quiet upstream river had been doable by being patient and hugging the shore. Along my second portage, where I dodged combines on a curvy road, newly paved, I glimpsed a changing river. The half-mile walk around Class II ledges and rapids brought me to a lively put-in. I half-carried, half-pulled my boat to find enough water to get in, then fought through to the inside curve. It was a foreshadowing of things to come. By then, the afternoon was growing late and I was hoping to make it to an informal camping spot called Dickies, where other thru-paddlers had stayed.

It was not to be. I rounded a bend to see some significant rapids. They looked as though they'd require shoreline bushwhacking to get around, but not today. There were no buildings in sight, and it was time for my first stealth camp.

I love stealth camping, discovering a safe and quiet nook where perhaps no soul has slept before. Embracing this option provides greater flexibility on water with few established campsites. It's a fun challenge to truly leave no trace of your presence when you quietly pack up and leave the next morning. For me, a good spot is high and dry, fairly open, and not accessible by road. I like to be completely out of sight, even my boat. Finding all that requires patience.

I tramped around and found a bit of higher ground, only a little damp and sheltered beneath the branches of a small tree. I flipped the canoe, tucked my boat gear underneath, and set my tent up among some ferns. The rest of my gear went in with me, to spend eleven hours in a bubble of dry, bug-free space. Stealth camps never have a campfire, and tonight I didn't even use my stove to cook. Supper was a cheese and pepperoni wrap and some dried apples. From my tent windows, I looked up to the edge of a mown field and down to the river, where the moving water churned and gurgled.

That evening, I found my credit card. It had been sandwiched in between the cardboard of two packs of batteries, stored back to back in a sandwich bag. I was carrying both AA for my GPS, which needed new ones weekly, and AAA for the SPOT, which so far was going strong on its first set. Unfortunately, the cancelled card was now useless.

In the morning, I wrote, "*I'm glad I didn't stay awake all night worrying about those rapids! Instead, I rested well and woke to bird song, as good as an alarm clock at four fifteen. The sun rose higher, stronger, warmer, conquering the early morning chill. Somewhere a woodpecker hammered and I wrote up a storm. Victory—my journal is caught up. And I conquered the rapids in a half hour, carrying my gear first, then lining the boat.*"

Lining, or guiding a canoe by two ropes, fore and aft, was a skill that I occasionally used in shallow rapids, going upstream or downstream. Moving up the river through rapids was working, I thought, elated that I was finally here, just doing it. After all the daydreaming, research, and doubts, here I was. Unbelievably, I'd already come 220 miles. Of course, ahead lay more daunting challenges, stronger upstream rivers without the shallow, mostly peaceful nature of the Missisquoi, which soon slowed again around a large oxbow.

For two miles, I gratefully rounded bend after bend to the same boring sight. Then more rapids and another phrase of Peter's came back to me. *Time is on your side.* More carrying the heavy gear, then lining with the light stuff still in the boat. Slowly, steadily, I was making progress, staying safe. Soon I was approaching another landmark.

Surprisingly, the Sheldon Springs power facility was as attractive as it was welcoming. There were two ways to portage through the property. Reaching the takeout for the easier, wheelable route would be tricky. I would need to power across between the turbulent discharge from the power plant and some frothy rapids. More confident now, I decided to go for it.

Safely across, a young man working at the plant walked down to offer me a ride. Instead, I asked him to take my picture, and we chatted about the paddlers that he meets. The owner, Enel Green Power, generously shares their space, allowing camping anywhere except beneath their extensive field of solar panels. The portage followed a well-manicured and landscaped road that reminded me of the long green entrance to a state park.

I ate my lunch in the shade of an informational kiosk, while a nice breeze kept the bugs at bay. Reading while eating, I learned that the run-of-river hydroelectric plant here was built in the 1910s and enlarged in 1988. The solar panels, which produce enough energy annually to avoid 1,800 tons of carbon dioxide production, were added in 2013.

Back on the river, I was surprised to meet a large group of kingfishers, seven by my count. Usually they are found in pairs or, more often, alone. Although they act disgruntled and grumpy, belted kingfishers are one of my favorite birds. They are easily identified by their appearance, behavior, and call. Blue-gray and white in color, they have a large crest and a long thick bill designed for catching fish. With a staccato rattle, they continually move ahead along the shore to yet another dead branch overhanging the water. Females have two chest bands, one blue, one rust-colored, on a white breast. Males have only one blue one.

The kingfishers were still with me when it was time to walk once more. For months, the interlude ahead had shone as a bright spot of surety and respite in my planning. To avoid the rigors of Class II–III Abbey Rapids and environs, thru-paddlers typically hopped onto the

Missisquoi Valley Rail Trail (MVRT), walking anywhere from three to 17 miles on this smooth dirt and gravel trail. I planned to use it for eight miles, to the town of Enosburg Falls.

Despite embracing the simple life, it hurt, really hurt, to have to skip the ice cream stand whose grassy backyard was the takeout for the MVRT. I needed to save my cash for another surprise, further down the trail. For not only would I walk for miles on a smooth path away from busy traffic, but not far ahead a real restaurant sat right on the rail trail. The Abbey was a much-anticipated stop for paddlers, and probably for cyclists, too.

The rail trail baked in the noontime sun and I thought wistfully of ice cream. Lots of cyclists passed with friendly hellos, though, and the wheeling was going well. Suddenly, my phone found service and I quickly called the credit card company. And begged. They were understanding and helpfully reactivated my card for three days, for face-to-face transactions in Vermont only. It would be enough.

The Abbey was far larger than what I'd been envisioning. I locked my canoe to a long bike rack and disappeared into the dim, cool interior, soothing after the hot trail. For a while, I was the only customer. The food was awesome—a crisp salad loaded with vegetables, a juicy mushroom Swiss burger, hot salty fries, and coleslaw. I wrote and wrote, sitting at a clean table, on a clean seat, far away from any bugs. Best of all, I found a place to camp for the night.

As the days passed, my natural shyness was being overcome by basic need and the cumulative power of good karma. Each person who helped or encouraged me, each detail that miraculously fell into place, was changing me. Outside, I'd noticed a wide, grassy path that curved away down toward the river. I hardly hesitated before asking if paddlers were ever allowed to camp down there. A quick call to the owner and I had a spot for the night.

I locked my canoe to a tree, hidden from above. My tent went up on a firm gravelly spot on the side of the path. Soon the sun was drying the last of the morning's dampness from my sleeping bag and pad and for an hour, I relaxed. From the rail trail, no one would ever know I was down here. Best of all, just up the hill was an evening of food and drink and company.

I slept to the lullaby of rapids and was up early. It was the Fourth of July. By 6:30, I was walking the rail trail. A local old-timer had been in the pub last night, visiting with the bartender. Punctuated by deep laughter, he'd told me river stories and convinced me that the miles to

Enosburg Falls could be paddled, not walked. Reading *The Companion* with breakfast had solidified my resolve to put in not far ahead, at the North Sheldon Bridge.

At a gravel parking area, downstream of the bridge on river right, a precipitous bank led down to the water. I was thankful for the early hour. There was no one around to see me hesitating, unsure of how to safely enter the river. These are the situations that demand careful thought, visualizing the worst-case scenario, not rushing.

Just navigating the slope with a single bag was tough. I scrambled up and down, carefully, strategically dropping and tossing my gear bags. They could easily have landed in the river. Getting the canoe down without catastrophe seemed improbable. At a few other steep ups or downs, there had always been something to anchor a rope to, a fence or a tree. Here, there was nothing, the path like a toboggan chute.

I pondered. *Time is on my side.* Suddenly the solution came. Rather than try to carry or slide the boat down the path, I would ease it down through the brushy vegetation on the side of the path. Maneuvering 13 feet of canoe through the stiff, resistant brush provided enough friction to slow its descent. Soon I was balancing on the river's edge, loading my bags.

"Muddy, monotonous, and marvelous," my blog philosophized about that day, *"those sections of the river where you can just stay in the boat and paddle. Most of today was like that. Muggy, too, later in the day. Great blue herons led me upstream and I amused myself noting all the animal tracks in the muddy banks. Pink morning glories and Canada lilies were bright spots of color amid the blah, blah, blah of mud. My phone was on and working for a bit and Megan called. 'So, are there more people on the trail there than in Maine?' she asked. That made me realize that the only people I had seen in boats on this river in days were the group at the Highgate Falls carry!"*

The town of Enosburg Falls marked the end of Map 4. There, I detoured from the portage route to sign in. I found the NFCT kiosk where the Bridge of Flowers and Light arched across the bubbling river. This 1915 bridge, once essential for dairy farmers transporting their milk to local creameries, was saved from decay by a group of local citizens. From the kiosk, a path led between perennial borders onto the old bricks of the bridge that horses once trod. Now visitors could linger on granite benches, dreaming of days gone by.

For days, the smell of the river and adjoining fields had confirmed the continued importance of the area's dairy industry. Enosburg Falls,

A quiet section along the Missisquoi River

said the *Guide to the Missisquoi Valley Rail Trail,* had become known as the "Dairy Capital of the World." During the first weekend in June, I could have attended the Vermont Dairy Festival here and watched pig races, a kids' milking contest, and the cow plop contest, whatever that was. Too bad it was now July.

Around lunchtime, back on the water, an authentic Vermont country store came into sight just past where a bridge crossed the river. *"Pulling over to the easiest access from the bridge, I secured my boat and started walking up a tiny muddy stream. With every step, I sank deeper, until I was literally in mud to my knees, worried that if I lost a shoe I could never retrieve it. Humbly, I struggled back, clinging to the meager vegetation, and paddled away, eating trail mix."*

My tan pants were filthy. I rinsed away giant mud clumps to find my feet, still clad in their river shoes. Those shoes had been a splurge…Chaco Outcross Evo 1 water sandals that I researched online and purchased at REI, after trying on everything that might have worked. For once, money was no object, and my Chacos turned out to be worth every penny.

At one pound, two ounces, they were lightweight, durable and secure, with good traction and a minimum of drainage openings to admit pebbles and sand. The neoprene lining also helped. Still, humps of sand and mud would work their way in, packing around my toes and building up into a small mountain that painfully prodded the arch of my foot. With time, I learned that stopping in surrender to rinse and regroup was time well spent. I would even turn my socks inside out and rinse them too.

From Enosburg Falls, it was 16 miles on the Missisquoi to the town of Richford, where I was meeting Mom and Dad. *"Only the Samsonville Dam ruins and Magoon Ledge break up an otherwise flat section of river,"* said *The Companion* about this stretch. *"There are no established portage trails around either of these minor obstacles."*

The tranquil river had been winding through the pastoral country-side toward rugged Jay Mountain. Gradually it segued into a shallow, rocky obstacle course. Approaching the Samsonville Dam ruins, I discovered that I needn't have worried about my muddy pants. For a full half mile before the ruins, I was constantly in and out of the river, washing my pants quite thoroughly in the process.

In a way, I welcomed the challenge. I had expected it and there was much satisfaction in tackling the puzzle, as I called it in my journal. By trial and error, I was learning where the footing was safest. In a spot washed clean by the current, the sandy bottom would be a brighter color

Later, the river became a shallow, rocky challenge

and less slippery. Clumps of cushiony water plants also made a soft, secure landing place, especially for my left foot, which had developed an annoying ache. The surface of the river told its own story, giving clues to where the water might be deep enough to hop in and paddle.

At one point, where a small stream entered the river, I paused to rest. Suddenly I saw an intriguing sight, a clump of bright green vegetation floating in the current. *But wait,* I thought, *that clump is going across the current.* Only then did I see the small brown tugboat pushing the barge. A beaver, or more probably a muskrat, given its size.

A small block building with empty windows and a rusting metal roof stood watch over the remains of the breached dam. This was part of the original powerhouse at the site of the old Samsonville Butterchurn Factory. I portaged along the shore on river left, an improvised route. I carried my gear first, then pulled the canoe through tall weeds. The long day was ending. It was time to think of camp and leave the unknowns of Magoon Ledge for tomorrow.

The map's description of the NFCT Doe campsite looked intriguing. In the clay of the tall bluff were something called varves, *"annual sediment layers creating visible stripes, like tree rings...formed when the last ice age receded and this area was underwater. From your camp watch for long- and short-tailed weasels swimming and diving for crayfish."*

Sadly, I couldn't find the site because the riverside sign was missing. I thought I was looking at the right cliff, but it would have been a long, fruitless climb up if I was wrong. I continued wearily on for another mile as clouds darkened the sky above.

At the rumble of thunder, desperation provided inspiration, and I quickly got off the river by a small creek. I scrambled up the bank to a small, weedy flat area big enough for my tent. Lightning flashed briefly and there were trees around, but I'd have to chance it. With that, the race was on. I beat the rain, barely, diving into the tent and onto a pile of jumbled gear just as it started in earnest. The storm passed and still I lay there, too tired to write. Through the tent windows came the sound of a breeze stirring the maple leaves and the soft lullaby of the river.

I startled awake to the sound of much louder rapids. Glancing out, I saw that my "rapids" were a doe, splashing across the river, right toward me. Almost to my side, she saw or smelled me, whirled and ran back across the shallow water. Then she paused and looked back a moment, as if thinking, "Did I really just see a tent?" Then she snorted danger and disappeared.

Later, after dark, distant fireworks reminded me that it was still July 4th. Across the creek, a motorbike tore around the fields, and I was glad to be safely on the other side.

The morning's fresh, storm-cleared air brought with it a short and simple day. Magoon Ledge truly was just a minor obstacle. I started out up the middle, slid right to walk briefly on a sandbar, then edged over to the left slowly and carefully, in current which was deeper and stronger than any I'd yet experienced going upstream.

In paddler's jargon, this wading with the canoe is called "tracking." The design of the Fusion was an asset here. The canoe could float in very shallow water. It was stable in deeper current and provided a sturdy support. As the days wore on, I developed a fluid dismount and reentry. I would tuck the paddle on the far side, held by gear, hop out and walk with both hands on the near gunwale. Preparing to hop in, I'd put the paddle across the gunwales, ready for action. As soon as the water seemed deep and slow enough to be able to achieve forward momentum, I'd jump in, trying to paddle even as I landed in the seat.

After just five miles, I arrived at Richford's Davis Park. Across the street was one of the trail's most unique lodging places, an 1890s Queen Anne Victorian masterpiece.

Tim and Deb Green's Grey Gables Mansion B&B was not to be missed. Painted gray, it had a quirky assortment of gables above windows highlighted here and there with stained glass. Below, a wide porch with a row of wooden rocking chairs hugged the front and sides. Everywhere there was color. The red and white of gingerbread-house trim and a profusion of flowering plants and green ferns, in earthen pots and vibrant hanging baskets.

I felt shy, a bit overwhelmed by the abrupt transition from muddy riverbanks to this elegance. Tentatively, I knocked on the door. Tim took a while to answer. He had probably been enjoying a well-deserved midday break. Sure, I could roll my canoe around back and spread my stuff to dry. I did, then walked to town for a pizza loaded with vegetables and bacon. I filled the time until Mom and Dad arrived by catching up on my blog.

Just seeing my parents was a comfort, like a home-cooked meal. Before long, our spacious room was covered with mysterious piles of gear and supplies that I continued to arrange and rearrange, as I talked nonstop. From the flow of stories, one thought emerged, as if I had needed to share these miles with family before I could understand what they meant to me.

After two weeks on the water, I was as strong, as confident, as I had ever been. For the first time, I believed that I would finish the trail. If I didn't wreck my boat or my body, each day would give me its gifts and its challenges, and I would accept them, deal with them, survive them. Going into a 12-day stretch alone, it was a good place to be.

CHAPTER 7

BONJOUR, QUEBEC

Far away there in the sunshine are my highest aspirations. I may not reach
them, but I can look up and see their beauty, believe in them, and try to follow
where they lead.

— Louisa May Alcott

Years ago, Grey Gables had been the home of a schoolteacher, Hazel
Weatherby, who every year brought her first and second graders here
for a visit, to play hide and seek in the mansion's twenty-one rambling
rooms. In the morning, we were joined at breakfast by Hazel's grandson
John, in town for a family reunion. Along with a grand breakfast befit-
ting this elegant old dowager of a home, came news that the U.S. women
had won the soccer World Cup.

Fresh fruit with yogurt and granola, white chocolate cranberry
muffins, banana walnut pancakes with bacon, orange juice and coffee.
Chef Tim had years of practice in fueling thru-paddlers and was a loyal
NFCT supporter. If all the Grey Gables rooms were full, paddlers could
camp for free across the street in Davis Park and still have breakfast at
Grey Gables if they ordered it the evening before.

Tim and Deb had achieved a balance between grandeur and
hominess. The interior was a gem and a delight to wander. Ornate carved
woodwork framed boldly patterned, richly colored walls, their original
character undisturbed. Antiques graced every room, but Oriental rugs
and period oil paintings kept company with a dining table set with plain
white dishes on a practical burgundy oilcloth. A paddler needing to

recharge would be comfortable here, even arriving with the aroma of mud and days on the river.

Today I would paddle into another country. The border crossing into Canada was just seven miles ahead. The Missisquoi River between Richford and the Quebec border was shallow, very shallow, and I had been reserving a decision on strategy until talking with Tim. At breakfast, he encouraged me to go for it, to try paddling rather than walking.

Afterwards, we stood chatting in the yard, postponing the inevitable goodbyes.

"Look, there go two paddlers now," Tim exclaimed, nodding toward two women walking a large green canoe down the sunny street. They wheeled in to say hello. Sydney Aveson was athletic and boyish with super short hair and a contagious smile. Her mother Marji, with a twin smile, had just come from California to fill the shoes of Sydney's injured boyfriend and thru-paddling partner. Sydney's journey was more than just fun. It was part of her thesis for a master's degree in Expeditionary Studies from, of all places, SUNY Plattsburgh. Can you imagine the fun of majoring in taking journeys like this one?

After finally hugging Mom and Dad goodbye, I headed toward town and the put-in. It would be almost two weeks and 170 miles before I saw them again, near the Maine border. Sydney and Marji had left before me, but I soon caught up, wheeling my much lighter boat.

"Are you going to try the river or walk?" they wondered. "We need to get some groceries and go to the post office first."

I had found the grocery store yesterday, memorably housed in a renovated old mill that had once manufactured hard maple furniture. I pointed them in the right direction and shared Tim's thoughts about the river. Like me, Sydney and Marji were hoping to camp tonight at Canoe & Co., a Quebec outfitter located right on the Missisquoi. I had won a night of camping there in a recent NFCT silent auction. The Canadian border crossing closed at four o'clock, giving us a firm deadline. We had six hours to travel seven miles upstream.

The conversation with Sydney had started me thinking again. I went on, pulling out my map and notes to refresh my memory. The road, *The Companion* warned, was not easily accessible once you committed to the river. The guidebook listed the challenges ahead.

"An almost two-mile section of braided islands…creates continuous Class 1 rips at high water or exposed gravel fields at low water. After passing by the old mill (site), there is one last set of the largest rapids to ascend within this

area. An exposed cobbled shoreline provides a route to carry around it. You'll need to cross clear-running Stanhope and Mountain Brooks before putting back in above the head of the rapids. You can now return to paddling—mostly fast-running flatwater—up to the border. Lucas Brook joins the river just before the U.S. Border Patrol take-out, creating a final set of up to Class II rapids."

Could I possibly navigate all that by four o'clock or leave the river if I needed to? I didn't know, but my confidence was growing and I trusted I would find the answer. Much later, after I was safely home, Dan wrote to ask, "Did you really not have at least one of those spots that you were so tired, so wet and so cold that you wondered why you were doing it?"

The answer was no. Any day that I could keep going and both my canoe and I were uninjured, was a good day. And any day could be broken down into bits—every bit that was done without giving up, when both my canoe and I were uninjured, was a good bit.

Dan went on to say, "I just love those times—I really hate them but they show me who I really can be and do. Because sitting down and doing nothing just does not work."

A closer study of the map reassured me. A mile from the put-in, the river would return to the road for another mile before veering off, giving me a chance to retreat if necessary.

At first, there were open fields along the gently curving river and progress was good. The first mile took 35 minutes and my hat. It was inevitable, I suppose, that sooner or later a low-hanging branch would grab it as I ducked underneath. I snatched the dripping hat from the river and put it back on, gasping with shock as cold water cascaded down my neck. I had discovered something, though. In the hot sun, a wet hat was wonderfully refreshing and I would dip my hat on purpose countless times in the weeks to come.

Things went downhill from there. Before long, I was out of the boat more than in it. The discouraging ruffled surface of shallow riffles became more and more frequent. The river still had its bright spots and plant clumps to aim for when walking and it wasn't dangerous. It was just impossible to make much progress. Meanwhile, the current was noticeably increasing, and I wondered how Sydney and Marji were faring.

As the river prepared to depart from the road, I abandoned it without guilt. I had given it my best try. At the edge of a field, I found a good take-out. A firm bank and gentle climb up, hidden from the road above. I edged around the row ends, being careful of the farmer's corn. I would have liked to load up on the wheels in a hidden corner, sheltered from view, but the ground was much too soft. When I reached the road, already feeling a bit guilty, there was a very large and visible "No Trespassing" sign. Well, I was committed now, but could just imagine a sheriff's deputy arriving at any moment.

Across the road stood a simple white house. Bright flowers in a well-tended garden gave it an encouraging appearance, and I debated asking for belated permission. I decided I should and nervously walked over. Still breathing heavily from hustling everything up, I knocked, then stood waiting. Honestly, I was glad when no one answered and quickly went on my way.

Although I was nearly flattened by a speeding motorcycle, the walk to the border was delightful. Flowers, intriguing old homes, and a surprising number of downhill sections along an upstream river added to the charm. Before two o'clock, I made the final turn onto Glen Sutton Road. After a couple of miles, the U.S. border crossing station appeared on the left.

Under the baking sun, I pulled my canoe off to the side and walked slowly toward the building. No matter how many descriptions you read in advance, preparing to cross an international border in a new way is intimidating.

The border patrol officer on duty, a man, said hello in a friendly enough way, but not much else. I explained my mission, in case he had not been able to figure it out from the canoe. With his approval, I plopped down in the shade to have some water and revive.

Soon, a woman emerged from the customs building to join us. As I ate a snack, they warmed up, and soon we were chatting away.

"If you're comfortable," they offered, "you can leave your boat here, take your passport and walk up to Canadian customs. If they're happy with you, then you can just come back here and launch."

That sounded good to me. An old metal bridge spanned the river, with a sign delineating the international border. Up and around a curve, I found Canadian customs. In answer to the usual questions, I admitted that I was carrying two folding knives and a small bottle of red wine, was meeting no one, and would be gone in three days. When the friendly officer didn't ask to see my boat, I thought how simple the process had been after all.

A short path near the U.S. Customs building led to an easy put-in. Back in my canoe at last, I could finally rest. As if the river knew that it had crossed a notable boundary, it deepened, and I paddled quietly toward layers of hazy mountains. A bright yellow warbler flitted among the shoreline shrubs and then a far more surprising sight appeared.

Tubes, kayaks, families sprawled in striped beach chairs, people swimming in the suddenly cleaner looking water. I had discovered summer. The river was alive with folks having fun, with *bonjours* tossed back and forth. I don't know how much further I paddled in the sweltering heat before it hit me. I, too, could swim, in the new black L.L. Bean bathing suit that Mom had brought to replace my old torn and faded one.

I lay back in the refreshing water as the current flowed past, washing away my weariness, restoring my energy. It was equally invigorating to paddle the last couple of miles just for fun. I pulled my boat into the sandy shallows a couple more times to swim, smiling and waving to the friendly rivergoers. These Canadians knew how to enjoy their river.

At Canoe & Co., a clump of boats and a young couple just loading up their kayaks confirmed I was at the right place. From the upstairs of a gray house on stilts, two kids peeked down, waving. Later, they emerged and nodded yes, I could camp on the edge of their lawn, above the river. I am not sure it was an official campsite, but I was all set up and had even eaten a burrito loaded with fresh vegetables from town before their parents returned.

Francois and Rachelle Turcotte reflected the Quebec ethic of cheerful hard work and were good friends of the NFCT. Rachelle showed me around and visited for a while. There was a trail register, which the four section-paddlers from the Highgate Falls carry had signed, and a lovely, clean restroom with real plumbing but no hot water. Later, Rachelle's small daughter came down with a shy smile to bring me an apple and two bananas.

Every so often, I would gaze downriver in hopes of spotting Sydney and Marji, but finally had to conclude they had missed the border deadline. More new friends, thru-paddlers like John Mautner, who I would probably never see again.

Dawn found me packing up. Breakfast was a quick cup of coffee and the next to last of Tim's delectable muffins, with a banana. A pileated woodpecker drummed loudly in the quiet as I gently paddled away, the first soul on the river.

This would be my final day on the Missisquoi. From the riverbank, cows watched curiously as I went past, and I snapped one of my favorite photos of the trip. The tranquil pastoral scene was like a seventeenth century Dutch painting come to life. The nearby village of Glen Sutton had its own well-known landscape painter, Aaron Allan Edson, whose art captured the beauty through which I was paddling.

The lazy river presented few obstacles until I turned left into the North Branch of the Missisquoi. Here the river narrowed, the current quickened, and there were fallen trees to get around. After more than nine miles, I started to look for the takeout for the Mansonville portage. My GPS, I had discovered, had no maps for Canada, a detail that had escaped me in my planning. They would have helped today. As I went on, the river quickened, until I had to admit I was in small rapids. This did not look right. It was time for some scouting.

Backtracking, and two sweaty trips traipsing up to the road, got me oriented. Earlier, I'd paddled carefully by a young fisherman and his girlfriend, trying not to disturb the fish. Sure enough, I paddled back to find two yellow portage signs, partially covered by sumac branches. By now, a lovely audience of tourists had gathered. They seemed surprised when I declined their help, as I struggled up past the fisherman and his tackle box, which blocked the steps.

In Mansonville's tidy town square was a gazebo with the most unique piano I'd ever seen. Painted to look like a yellow farmhouse, it had a sloping black roof, curtains in the four-pane windows, and a bright red door. The porch with plants and a small cat gave it a lived-in look. In front sat a three-legged stool, just waiting for someone to play a tune.

I locked my canoe to a nearby bench and went to find lunch.

Just across the street was the Boulangerie Owls Head, a bakery and eatery with a display of desserts reminiscent of Hero's Welcome on Lake Champlain. *What a contrast there was between trail food and town food*, I thought. One day, peanut butter and jelly on a tortilla with water. The next, a braised pork sandwich on soft, homemade milk bread with caramelized apples and onions, a garden salad, and fruit custard for dessert.

As I ate, I debated what to do next. Not far ahead was the Grand Portage, an almost-six-mile climb up and over the divide between the Missisquoi and St. Francis watersheds. At its far end was Lake Memphremagog (mem-fruh-MAY-gog), straddling the border between Quebec and Vermont. Tomorrow, I would paddle south down the lake to return to the United States.

There were three possibilities for tonight, all unofficial places that generously allowed thru-paddler camping—Mansonville's town square or a park not far beyond or all the way at the end of the Grand Portage, at Perkins Landing, a small park and boat launch on the lake. Already it was early afternoon and the sky looked iffy, timing and weather that made it hard to decide. The bakery manager kindly checked the forecast and said I would be good to go on.

Intriguingly, the town of Mansonville had been founded in 1803 by Joseph Chandler and John Lewis, who together built a mill here. In 1811, the property was sold by Chandler to Robert Manson, who ran both a sawmill and grist mill there. Manson was a Loyalist, one of many area settlers who had come here from New England after the American Revolution. If history had been just a little different, I reflected, I could have been walking through Chandlerville, Quebec.

In town, I passed a large and well-preserved round barn, constructed in 1911. Although the building was not open, a photo showed the elaborate pattern of wooden beams on its ceiling, reminiscent of an old cathedral. The barn's history and architectural design were documented on an attractive display, written in both French and English.

"Circular barns owe their design to the Shakers, a religious sect from New England, who saw the circle as a perfect design. It was a most efficient way to feed the cows while preventing the Devil from hiding in the corners!

Round barn in Mansonville, Quebec

It has three levels, used as follows: on the ground floor, the cows were held in stalls laid in a circle all around the barn; above, is the hayloft, from where the hay was thrown down through openings in the floor; finally, the upper floor, reached by a ramp, similar to a covered bridge, was used by the hay wagons to unload for the hayloft below."

Walking on, I made up my mind. By three o'clock, I should reach the start of the Grand Portage. I felt strong, full of energy. I would go on to the Grand Portage today.

As I had no GPS map, I carefully compared the river's curves with the NFCT map, tracking my progress toward the bridge where the Grand Portage began. From the NFCT website, I knew that many paddlers had been taking out across a farmer's field on river left, without a landowner agreement. The approved Diorio Access on river right turned out to be a steep uphill, firm and rocky, a strenuous warm-up for the walk ahead.

Carpenters say to measure twice, cut once. Paddlers should check twice, walk once. While I rested, looking over my map, a woman pedaled up on an expensive road bike. She lived up the way I was headed and shared the news that the road I would climb, called Chemin Peabody, was being resurfaced. Right now, it was all torn up, loose gravel.

She was determined that I should paddle back to Mansonville and walk a different, smoother way. Well, there was no chance of that. Like Mud Pond Carry in Maine, the Grand Portage, which NFCT calls its "most significant portage," is a rite of passage for the thru-paddler. With her pretty accent, the woman eventually accepted that I would go on and described the route in some detail, for it would be a stiff and possibly discouraging climb.

"Psychologically, it is good to know when you are at the top—many large stones like so," she explained with her hands, referring to the large boulders with petroglyphs on the summit.

After sweetly asking to take my picture, she rode away and I loaded up, mentally ready to be tough and endure, gravel or no gravel. The beginning rose gradually. Then the road got serious, climbing up and up, passing picture book homes, all neat as a pin. Tidy custom-built trash enclosures, matching house numbers, and immaculately tended lawns and gardens. Only the barns were worn and weathered, adding to the charm of the scenic climb.

Every hundred feet was a victory, celebrated by some trail mix and water. I climbed a total of 670 feet by the GPS altimeter to cross

Near the top of the Grand Portage, Quebec

into the new watershed, about three-and-a-half miles along. Two kind souls offered me rides and were surprised when I didn't accept.

Reaching the height of land was a summit of spirit as well as altitude. A brisk, refreshing wind swept the world clean, and my whole soul felt victorious. At the crest was a gently undulating field of green, bordered by the march of the ancient boulders. Perhaps their petroglyphs, indecipherable scratches to my eye, told of the victory of reaching this point. Behind the field nestled a red farm with a herd of cows, backed by a sun-dappled mountain peak. For me, this moment will always define the "grand" of this portage.

Then, it was simply taking my boat for a stroll, down, down, down through the calendar scenery, to the lake, which I'd glimpsed once from way above.

Perkins Landing had a sprawling, shaded picnic area and plenty of room for camping. The most delightful surprise, though, was the sight of Sydney and Marji's green tent, already set up. They'd taken a shuttle with Francois, from Canoe & Co., across the Grand Portage. They welcomed me with cheese and crackers. Tomorrow we would go on together down the lake.

Morning arrived in a cold and steady rain. It couldn't dampen my

First evening camping with Sydney and Marji Aveson, at Perkins Landing

spirits, though, thanks to the kindness of a stranger. The man in charge of the boat landing walked over from his house, coming on duty at five o'clock, ready to inspect boats and issue the mandatory certificate for cleanliness that was required for travel on the lake.

"I like it when I see someone do a long trip," he said, when he heard I was a thru-paddler. "I give you permit for free." Usually the cost of the permit would have been $30.

"What will the weather be today?" I asked.

He leaned back in his chair, looking ready to share the wisdom of his years living on the lake. He looked at me intently through his glasses.

"This," was his simple answer, with a sweeping gesture that embraced the gray and misty world beyond his little building.

"And the wind…?"

"Will be fine." And, indeed, it turned out to be a help, rather than a hindrance, on this long and open lake that often delivers large and uncooperative waves.

"You see all these boats?" he went on. "You can stop anywhere, any boathouse, you go inside, no one say anything." I felt that I had made a friend. He also showed me an island on my map, about three miles to the south, where we could take shelter if needed.

By 6:30, I was ready and headed out first, enjoying the wooded hills that came steeply down to touch the shore. Here and there among the green, a house clung bravely to the slope. Seagulls wheeled and bobbed, unaffected by the damp and dreary weather. Though I often see gulls, they seem to my mind creatures of the sea, and I usually ignore them. Today, though, they suited the wild, untamed feel of the lake, and I wrote about them in my journal.

Before long, Sydney and Marji caught up. Sydney was an experienced paddler, with kayaking trips in Newfoundland, Scotland, and Wales on her résumé. Paddling stern, her handling of the canoe was natural and effortless. The island quickly fell behind, as we talked about Sydney's intriguing major and the goals for my book. On the water, our pace was well matched and time flew by. The wind pushed us along and soon we could see the buoys marking the international boundary between Canada and the United States.

I had certainly enjoyed Canada's French-speaking province and had rediscovered the fun of summer there. But in my blog, I wrote, *"I felt more vulnerable to logistics traveling by canoe than I ever would have with the security and mobility of a car. Quebec was clean, delicious, welcoming, and swift, but I was comforted to return to the good old United States."*

CHAPTER 8

WEAVING NEW FRIENDSHIPS

There is nothing…half so much worth doing as simply messing about in boats…whether you get away, or whether you don't; whether you arrive at your destination or whether you reach somewhere else, or whether you never get anywhere at all.

— **Kenneth Grahame,** *The Wind in the Willows*

Lake Memphremagog had gifted us with just enough wind at our backs. By ten in the morning, we were approaching the marina on Newport, Vermont's bustling waterfront. Here, we would check back in with U.S. customs. In April, my parents and I had scouted the area on Maps 6 and 7, and I'd marked some waypoints on my GPS. Now I aimed confidently for our destination, as Sydney followed me in. We cruised past rows of magnificent sailboats, straight to a gray building with a cupola and two peaked gables like eyebrows.

Customs, reached via a video phone on the dock, surprisingly had just one question for me. Was I bringing anything from Canada back into the country with me? A simple and honest no and I was officially back in America and ready for an early lunch.

Newport Natural Market & Café served up homemade chipotle black bean soup and a "Vermonter" panini stuffed with smoked turkey, cheddar cheese, apple, and honey mustard, all washed down with hot tea. After a stop at the library, we signed in at the kiosk, where Sydney took my belated end-of-map photo. Map 5 had ended yesterday afternoon at Perkins Landing.

Sydney and Marji had been having problems with their wheels and would be portaging at a slower pace. They encouraged me to go on ahead and they would catch up. I thought of the similar interweaving of journeys on the Appalachian Trail, where partnerships are fluid as each hiker hikes his or her own hike. Mine was a solo journey at heart, but it was fun to have the companionship of two kindred spirits for a time, a blessing and a surprise on the much-less-travelled Northern Forest Canoe Trail.

When the route for the trail was being decided, back in the late 1990s, much research had gone into incorporating traditional native travel routes. The three old friends who dreamed up the idea were uniquely qualified for the challenge. Professionally, Mike Krepner was a Maine guide and pack manufacturer, Randy Mardres a computer systems designer, and Ron Canter a cartographer. Their passion, though, was unraveling the complex history of historical canoe routes, in the jungles of Belize as well as New England. To accomplish this, they formed a nonprofit organization called Native Trails and willingly tackled the dirty work.

"Since college days," explained a 1997 article in *AMC Outdoors, "the three have been cheerfully obsessive canoeists. They will pole upstream for hours in four inches of water trickling through four feet of mossy rocks, hacking at alders with machetes, and call the struggle a fine outing."*

Displays at the kiosk and along the corridors of the nearby state building told more of the story. In the Adirondacks, the Raquette and Saranac Rivers had been major river highways for the Iroquois. Here in Vermont, Lake Memphremagog was the hub at the heart of the Western Abenaki homeland. From the center, spokes extended in every direction. To Lake Champlain in the west, along the Missisquoi River that I now knew so well. To the St. Lawrence River in the north. And east to the mighty Connecticut River, reached just as I would reach it, traveling up the narrow, winding Clyde River and down the narrow, winding Nulhegan River.

The Northern Forest Canoe Trail truly was a journey back through time.

Before the Wabanaki and Iroquois, 9,000 to 3,000 years ago, the Archaic people lived along the trail. This long span was filled with innovations, including the first canoes, dugouts. Carved and burned out of huge logs, using stone tools like the gouge and adz, these simple boats changed life dramatically. For thousands of years, there were no other canoes.

By the time of the Wabanaki, the birchbark canoe had appeared. It was far lighter and much quicker to construct than the dugout. Surprisingly, though, dugouts continued to be used on large rivers and lakes, where they were stored underwater when not in use.

Canoes were also less commonly constructed of spruce, oak, or elm bark or moose hide. Native peoples used the materials and routes that were the most available, appropriate, and straightforward. It was simply a matter of what worked. Many centuries later, my philosophy mirrored theirs. Traveling solo, relying on my own strength and wisdom, my decisions would need to balance safety and practicality to navigate the trail as efficiently as possible.

The Companion described the challenges ahead, "*While the first section of the Clyde River from Newport to Salem Lake constitutes only a few miles of the NFCT, it is arguably one of the toughest sections of the trail for thru-paddlers. The swift-flowing narrow river is flanked by steep banks and…full of fallen trees, continuous boulder fields and other debris.*"

I would embrace the philosophy of common sense, of doing what worked to travel in the simplest manner possible. I like to think that if a smooth meadow path had existed parallel to a river, native peoples would have walked, too, instead of risking upstream travel through Class II–III+ rapids, like those I'd circumvent today and early tomorrow.

The first mile of the Clyde could be paddled, though, and I went slowly. "*A deer stood sculpted among the grasses,*" I later wrote, "*as we looked eye to eye, my mind slowly grasping her shape.*" At the Western Avenue bridge, I took out and began walking along a small street, soon passing a hydro plant that was harnessing the energy of the turbulent little river. The steepness of the climb rivaled that of the Grand Portage, rising over 300 feet on my GPS altimeter. Gratefully, I stopped for a chat with a man in a straw hat, who was busy filling his bird feeders.

"Are you headed to Maine?" he wanted to know. He knew all about the trail, had family in Maine, and looked forward to greeting paddlers as they trudged past.

Following this route, I missed paddling Clyde Pond, which I deeply regret. I could have put in, paddled a short distance, and had all 58 lakes and ponds, rather than 57.

Tonight, I knew for sure where I would sleep, had known for months, in fact. The wood-fired pizza at the Vermont Pie & Pasta Company in Derby had been delicious when we ate there in April. Pizza to die for, near a motel and a supermarket, on a little strip of civilization by Interstate 91. Sydney and Marji and I had made reservations from the library. After walking three miles and ending up on busy Route 5, I arrived at the Derby Four Seasons Inn. I locked my boat around back and began the familiar drying routine. At dinner, we ate a lot of pizza!

I took full advantage of the motel's breakfast the next morning, too. *"From the minute breakfast started until it closed,"* I blogged, *"I was consuming protein and calories to replenish my hardworking body, the body that has lately been amazing me. They had hard-boiled eggs and yogurt and peanut butter and bagels and real Cabot butter. Overall, a real surprise to me is that I am craving 'real' food more than sweets, except for the fabulous bakeries I've visited."*

Between sleeping, writing, and reorganizing, it was 11:00, checkout time, before we settled the last dry bags in our boats and were gone. Sydney had done considerable advance research and planned to try a shortcut to Salem Pond that was not discussed in any of the books or maps. I was confused and hoped to find some guidance along the way. We said goodbye, hoping to camp together that night on Pensioner Pond, where *The Companion* mentioned an unofficial campsite on corporate property, complete with picnic tables and an outhouse.

My journal that night began, *"Today was a grueling challenge, one that I met, one more in line with what I expected in the way of uncertainty and, yes, even danger."*

The day built to its climax. The first order of business was getting back on the water. It was disconcerting pushing my boat at its snail's pace on the (luckily) wide shoulder, alongside cars racing to get up speed for Interstate 91. After crossing the interstate, though, I could relax. Walking along quiet West Street, a man in a late model truck stopped beside me.

"What are you *doing?*" he asked incredulously.

I explained, which frankly didn't change his expression much. He did recommend a helpful garage ahead, where they sent me by the longer route to the beach on Salem Pond. Walking there, I met a man named Ray, who stopped his van in the street and hopped out. Ray was a caller for square dancing and looked the part in his plaid flannel shirt and blue suspenders. He had just bought a 17-foot, 91-pound canoe and wanted to learn all there was to know about my wheels. It felt good to be giving out information for a change.

Salem Pond was a gloomy struggle of clouds and wind, with nothing to recommend it. After a tiny river section, though, Little Salem

Pond seemed brighter. In no hurry, I searched among white water lilies and swaying grasses for the passage back to the Clyde. Navigating that was a small warm-up for what I would face in two days, in a notoriously confusing bog that is simply called The Fen. From there, my journal description of the ascent of the Clyde continued:

The mud of the Missisquoi had been replaced with clear water and a sandy, rippled bottom that later changed to pretty gravel and rock. Curve followed curve and I thought how a Google Earth image would make a great maze. There were even dead ends and several fabulous spots where a giant tree had fallen all the way across, creating a magnificent arch or a choice of small tunnels through its branches. Damselflies, mostly black and a brilliant green, flitted among the grasses.

The first mile and a half was peaceful, with strong current you could work against, make progress against. Rounding one curve, though, I had a little déjà vu with the South Branch of the Dead River in 2011. Quick, get your PFD, your shoes, your gear in order. I paddled a bit more, then I was walking. Luckily, I had three slices of pizza left to eat and plenty of water. For the most part, the river was still shallow, so on I trudged, grateful to be still making miles (or feet) on the river. With each step, the current got stronger, less manageable, more dangerous. And why are you more resistant to resting as you grow more tired, less steady, less rational?

Eventually, I was finding internal strength when my muscles were less responsive. I remember edging my way around a strainer on river left— wanting to hold the tree for stability, while also wishing to be far away from it! Then river left became impossible and I was forced to cross, aware that my strength and reflexes had been sapped. Each step was a mental exercise— wedge your foot/test/commit.

For a time, grudgingly, the other shore let me pass. The river and I continued to battle, my stubbornness against the power of its swollen waters. And where would I have retreated, even if I wanted to? On the GPS map, my destination, the Fontaine Road Bridge, was tantalizingly close, but not yet visible ahead. Along the banks, thick vegetation guarded the shore. The strong current would have made an early take-out even more dangerous than what I was now doing. What I needed was a small beach or other opening, but I saw none.

In the underwater current, masses of light pink undulated and danced at the edge of the river. *Algae*, was my first thought. A second look revealed thick clumps of tiny pink tree roots, waving brightly in the current. They beckoned me upriver, distracting me from my weariness.

And then, just like that, the bridge appeared. Its utilitarian concrete and metal were beautiful, as was the grassy yard that stretched down to the water, on my shore. In the distance, I could hear the comforting sound of a lawnmower. I secured my boat and walked up toward the sound, waiting for the man on the riding mower to make another pass back toward me.

"Would it be possible for me to take my boat out from the river across your yard?" I asked, in my most friendly and polite voice. I wondered if I also sounded a little desperate.

"Sure, that's fine."

"And do you mind me wheeling my cart on the grass?"

"No, that's fine and, no, don't worry about interrupting me. I was finished mowing."

My body needed rest and something less challenging. Not far ahead was tiny Charleston Pond, which many paddlers walk around. To me, it sounded heavenly and I headed toward it.

Perhaps fatigue and stress were factors, but the small crossroads of West Charleston just didn't feel friendly. As I crossed the bridge, a boy of about eleven came running up, clean-cut and helpful, and asked if I needed a place to put in my canoe. Then, incredibly, he pointed me to a spot in the middle of the mayhem above the bridge, described in the NFCT guidebook as "a run of Class II+ ledges." This was one of the few times that my inner self said to move along. Thankfully, after a short half mile of portaging, I arrived at the put-in.

A loon followed me across Charleston Pond to the NFCT Great Falls campsite. It was on the same small scale as the pond, but secluded from sight if I pitched my tent just so. It was enough for today. Although short of our goal of reaching Pensioner Pond, I knew that if Sydney and Marji made it this far they would surely see me, as the campsite was right on the portage route. I hung my food for the first time in days and slept deeply for nine hours.

I woke to find myself still alone, but had news of my friends as I continued up the Clyde. Chris, the owner of Clyde River Recreation, on the river just past the portage, told me he had seen them wheel by. He kindly let me charge my phone while we visited. When I asked about current water levels, he told me that dam releases kept this section fairly constant. This proved true, as the river returned to peaceful, flowery curves into and out of Pensioner Pond.

There is an unsolved mystery here, in this quiet river valley.

"According to some historical accounts," read the map, *"the Clyde River valley was once covered by Long Lake, formed by a natural rock dam at West Charleston Falls. During the 1700s, Abenaki lived along this ten-mile-long lake. A 1775 earthquake felt throughout New England may have broken the dam, draining the lake. Silt and vegetation filled the area, so that the first European settlers found an impassable morass that they called the Great Swamp."*

I was intrigued and continued my research after the trip.

When we think of earthquakes, we don't usually think of New England. On an evening in October 2012, though, in Bristol Mills, Maine, I was busy taking minutes at a parks and recreation meeting. Without warning, the windows of the town hall shook as if a train had just roared past. Except there were no train tracks, and no train. I had just experienced a Maine earthquake, magnitude 4.0, centered west of Portland.

It is doubtful, though, that an earthquake was responsible for destroying the lake. The three strongest New England earthquakes in the historical record occurred in 1638, 1727, and 1755, estimated at magnitude 6.5, 5.9, and 6.2, respectively. There was no significant earthquake in 1775. One primary document that provides strong evidence for the lake's existence clearly states that it was still there in 1763, after all the major earthquakes. Written by Alpha Allyn, the 1877 article tells the story of his conversation with a group of older Abenaki in the year 1824.

The members of their tribe had been divided in their loyalties during the French and Indian War. Those who sided with the English left their home in Canada and came to the Clyde River valley, where they lived for nine years near a 10-mile-long pond. When peace came in 1763, they returned to their Canadian home.

Allyn wrote, *"They showed where they camped, where they put their furs and potatoes, and also showed old marks on maple trees where they had been tapped 9 years in succession. This sugar lot, which was one of their camping-grounds, was situated on both sides of the town line between Charleston and Brighton. They related each circumstance so clearly from time to time, and gave the several proofs with so much correctness, that no one doubted the truthfulness of their assertions. And as years have passed from that interview* [to] *the present, the changes observed in the meadow lands, corroborate their testimony. The bog meadows that a man could not cross in safety in 1803, had so much increased in density, that in 1824, hay was cut and carried out by hand. Now both people and teams pass over them secure from danger."*

West Charleston Falls was close to where I had camped last night. Although I hadn't done the research yet, the thought of the vanishing lake fascinated me. Along the trail, man had constructed many dams and, therefore, created many lakes. This was one, though, that the workings of nature had somehow removed. How surprising it must have been when the first Abenaki returned to the valley, to find that their beloved lake was there no more.

Halfway through the day I caught up to my friends. Two different pairs of kayakers had told me Sydney and Marji were just ahead. Then, sure enough, there were the familiar light blue and light green shirts that I was coming to know so well. They'd persevered, making it to Pensioner Pond last night after all, but missing me as they'd walked around Charleston Pond.

We were heading to a unique place. Pat Moyer and Bill Manning, passionate trail supporters, had made an ordinary boat landing into a destination. On this quiet stretch of the Clyde, their Northern Forest Canoe Trail Farm Stand sold seasonal fresh produce and, most importantly, ice cream. Bill and Pat also allowed thru-paddler camping. Dreaming of ice cream, we hurried over the last beaver dams and fallen trees to the landing at Ten Mile Square Road.

The doors of the small wooden farm stand building stood open wide in welcome, behind a hand painted sign with an ice cream cone on it. This time of year, there were bags of crisp salad greens in the fridge and Vermont maple syrup for sale. All on the honor system, for we found no one around. Inside a chest freezer were homemade ice cream sandwiches, hard maple ice cream between Pat's homemade chocolate chip cookies. We sat in the cool shade of the farm stand eating and taking pictures of each other in this epic moment.

Later, I walked up and found Pat working in her greenhouse. She willingly agreed to our request to camp in the farm stand yard, by the picnic table and sink. The tents went up with practiced efficiency, and soon our clothes and gear were drying in the bright sun.

In their first week together, Sydney and Marji had become a team. Marji seemed to have no regrets about dropping everything, lightning shopping for gear and clothes, and flying across the country from California to allow Syd to continue her journey. As they problem solved or planned strategy or just decided what to eat for dinner, Marji's respect for her daughter as trip leader shone through. Luckily for Sydney, she had a mother with an adventurous spirit and the patience and endurance to tackle the trail's many challenges.

Sydney possessed an inner confidence and the bravery and determination to undertake this journey in a canoe far heavier than mine. The pair did everything by the book. Their food traveled in a bear-proof plastic barrel. In the mornings, they cooked healthy concoctions for breakfast and a riverside lunch. Hats and long-sleeved shirts guarded them from the sun, and they never ever took off their PFD's. Ropes were spliced, gear tied in—I would give Syd an A in Expeditionary Studies. And the best part was seeing how much fun they had together. Hearing them laugh, you knew they were friends as well as mother and daughter.

Later that summer I also discovered that Sydney was humble. I knew she was a college ice hockey player, but she never talked about it much. Not in all those days did she mention that she was the 2014 Division III National Player of the Year. Since then, she has played goalie for professional teams in Canada and Austria.

At dinner, we shared a fresh salad made with Pat's greens and reread the hints on navigating tomorrow's maze. Many paddlers had gotten lost in the Fen. In fact, something told me that getting through might have as much to do with luck as anything else.

The beauty of the fen in the gentle light of morning was doubled, reflected back in the perfect stillness of the water. An abundance of glossy black red-winged blackbirds moved among the tall grasses, their perches ever-changing. Above was pure blue sky. Near shore, shadows stretched long across the subtle reds and greens of a vast field of lily pads. I looked over to Sydney, paddling stern as always, and Marji, just touching her paddle to the water and there they were again, mirrored in the river. We were delighted with the fen so far.

As the sun intensified, though, the ephemeral beauty of early morning began to slip away. We passed large stands of dead trees, home to nesting ospreys. At first, we had little difficulty following the channel among the delicate pink swamp roses and yellow water lilies. Watching the undulating underwater plants flowing backwards, pulled by the current, confirmed that we were truly following the main channel upstream.

Several miles passed before the river, now much narrower, began to split and branch. High water further confused things, in this bog that was constantly reinventing itself. Our maps, my GPS, and *The Companion*'s advice to stay to the left all helped, but soon we found ourselves confused again and again.

Under the sun's ruthless glare, we paddled vigorously up a likely channel, only to round a bend and discover a dead end, choked with vegetation. Meanwhile, tantalizingly close, were glimpses of bright blue water on the far side of a tangle of green.

Reflecting back, though, I think I would have been disappointed if we hadn't gotten at least a little lost. And always, after some hot and scratchy bushwhacking or backtracking, we would go forward again. We were never seriously lost. It was just a lot of work. At last a cabin appeared—we were almost to Five Mile Square Road, a good place to stop for lunch.

Four miles of the Clyde were left, until we reached its source at Island Pond. We began this stretch by entering "The Tubes," a pair of giant culvert pipes that luckily had enough headspace, barely, to allow us to duck down and pull ourselves through.

From there, the navigation promised to be simpler. Only it wasn't. I paddled confidently along, following the little blue river on my GPS. Sydney and Marji paddled confidently along, following me. The channel was wide and obvious, until suddenly it just petered out to nothing. There was positively no outlet where the GPS showed the river. Refusing to face reality, I pulled and grunted and scooted myself a little farther along, then had to back out, scratched, sweaty and defeated. Here was one spot where I would have much preferred to be alone in my misery and uncertainty, where the wrong choice would only inconvenience me.

Back we went and up the smaller left channel, where we were soon confronted by a huge fallen tree. Maneuvering my light canoe over it would work, I thought, but Sydney and Marji had had enough. They would paddle back to Five Mile Square Road and walk to the town of Island Pond, hoping to find the post office still open and their new wheels delivered.

That last remote section of the Clyde was beautiful. Not far in, the river briefly curved close to the road and I looked up at just the right moment to see a few cyclists' heads fly past. Otherwise, it was a time of solitude and peace and journaling, that afternoon. Alone, I could stop to write, as the current gently drifted me backward. After I passed the fallen tree and a massive beaver dam, the shores were higher and home to cedar, fir, and spruce.

The river flowed with crystal clarity over the shallow rippled sand. Line after line after line of ripples curved in perfect unity. That simple pattern spoke to me of purpose, of God's hand in the natural world surrounding me, when I paused to look. Long tendrils of green waved in the current, and a brilliant trout appeared, then as quickly flashed away.

An easy portage path led me around the ruins of an old dam, to a tougher challenge—two or three tenths of a mile of rapids to walk up. After that, the river narrowed and returned to its usual shrubby alder shores, with scurrying duck families and the familiar black and shiny green damselflies. Then, around a bend, a white church with a steeple appeared above the grass and roses, and I knew I must be getting close to Island Pond.

Surprisingly, the Clyde River begins its journey from Island Pond by passing underneath an old hotel. Before long, I was paddling up under the hotel into the pond and the Clyde was finished. I treated myself to a haddock sandwich with fries and a Blue Moon, then spotted Sydney waving to me. Instead of camping with me at the state park, she and Marji were going to stay in town and wait for their new replacement wheels to arrive on Monday. We might not see each other again, I thought, as two days at my faster pace would probably carry me far ahead. Our time together, I wrote, had been a bright spot in my solitary adventure.

The Clyde River exits from Island Pond beneath an old hotel

CHAPTER 9

AN ABUNDANCE OF ANGELS

Friends…they cherish one another's hopes. They are kind to one another's dreams.

—**Henry David Thoreau**

A canoe with wheels. A canoe with wheels. Look, Daddy, a canoe with wheels."

The adorable little boy tugged vigorously on his father's arm and pointed toward my boat, which was parked on the road above my campsite. Brighton State Park was charming, full of quiet nature lovers and friendly families. Last night, it had also been full. I'd trudged wearily the half mile up to the office from the park beach and discovered the bad news.

"Don't worry, though," the young ranger reassured me. "We keep an overflow site for nights like this." He kindly pulled out a campground map and pointed out the way to go.

My tent was thoroughly dry, and its lingering mustiness banished, by the time I crawled out into the bright sun of morning. It was Sunday, I realized, and I said a prayer of thanksgiving for being there, safe and secure, on such a glorious day.

Hoping to avoid the walk back to the beach, I went a short distance up the road to where the lakeside sites began on the left. At the first one, a large and friendly-looking group of teens and adults were gathered around a picnic table, just finishing breakfast.

"Good morning." I began. "I'm paddling the Northern Forest Canoe Trail, thru-paddling actually. I don't know if you've heard of it?"

As their faces lit up, I knew they were familiar with the trail and would let me put in through their site. I went back to get my boat and gear, then they made a place for me around the checked tablecloth. One question followed another. I answered around bites of the huge chunk of apple pie that they'd set in front of me, along with a large glass of orange juice.

I felt the now-familiar feeling that our meeting was meant to be. We certainly had a lot in common. Paul, a casual looking guy with a reddish beard, had come to ministry later in life, after teaching kids with behavioral needs. He'd also been a wilderness canoe instructor. No wonder he got so excited over the NFCT. His wife Katy and the others, Paul's brother Rick, Rick's wife Laura, and their friend Colleen, were all outdoors people, too.

"I've gone 320 miles so far and I'm almost finished with Vermont. It's just 18 miles to the Connecticut River, which I'm really looking forward to, because it's downstream. I'll paddle that along the border with New Hampshire, then turn up the Upper Ammonoosuc."

"What do you do about food?" someone chimed in.

"Well, before I left, I packed up five resupply boxes with food and stuff like toilet paper, batteries, and cans of fuel. My parents have been meeting me to bring me those. But until I get to northern Maine, there are also plenty of stores along the way. In Island Pond, I just bought oatmeal, tortillas, an avocado, soup, and mandarin oranges. That's pretty typical."

Seeing a good chance to share more of the NFCT story, I explained that this portage route through small, sparkling Spectacle Pond was new since my map had been printed.

"That's why NFCT's website is great. There's a section called 'Trail Updates.' It shows what's new since the various editions of the maps were published. And my friend Katina Daanen has written a guide for thru-paddlers, too, which she revises often."

"Does the NFCT organization own land along the trail? Or are there easements?"

"Not really, that's what makes it very different from the AT. NFCT partners with landowners, businesses, and communities to add campsites and improve portages and water access. This new portage is shorter by a mile and a half than the old one."

"So, are you headed down the Nulhegan River next?"

"Yes, into a new watershed that drains into the Connecticut. I'll go down the Nulhegan for the next day or two, although I'll be walking along Route 105 for the last half of it."

Last winter, I had read and reread the description of the Nulhegan in *The Companion*, hoping there would be sufficient water to paddle the first half.

"The Nulhegan River is a unique ecosystem full of wildlife, native trout, great birding and wonderful wildflowers, but due to the location, degree of difficulty and/or seasonal low water levels, many through-paddlers miss covering part or all of this river. While the first half originating out of Nulhegan Pond typically has deep enough water—thanks to the numerous beaver dams—there are no services at Wenlock Crossing to assist paddlers around the Class II–IV Upper Gorge and Old Stone Dam sections that follow or when navigable water is absent before reaching the confluence of the Connecticut River. From the put-in near Nulhegan Pond, it will take four to five hours to paddle the 7.25-mile winding upper portion of the Nulhegan River to Wenlock Crossing."

I also wondered if it would truly take four or five hours. After all, it was not much more than seven miles, going downstream. It was time to find out.

After heartfelt thanks to everyone, I paddled away across Spectacle Pond. What I really wanted to do was give them all a hug. *The world is full of friends we are just about to meet*, I reflected, *and the trail is turning out to be a great way to find them.* The portage led me on a pleasant path through open, sunlit woods, then down Route 105 to Nulhegan Pond, the river's source.

At first, the distant roar of motorcycles drifted from the highway. Still, there was a sense of tranquility and retreat from all that was urgent, modern, or manmade. At the start, the aldery stream was so curvy and narrow in places that I maneuvered carefully for each stroke, holding the paddle upright as I squeezed through tight spots. Sometimes there was only room for a single paddle stroke, until I drifted on. Dad, I knew, would have urged me to use my single-bladed canoe paddle, but stubbornly I didn't.

Back on Brown's Tract Inlet, weeks before, I had written about beaver ruling. Here, though, their dominion was absolute. Crossing an impressive number of dams was the price to be paid for venturing down this small river. Some dams could be run in the canoe or scrambled over with a certain wiggle and scoot, but many required getting out to maneuver over.

One of dozens of beaver dams to be navigated on the Nulhegan River

Not far along, a tiny, delicate nest of woven grass rested near the water's edge. The wet, sandy shores were also home to an eye-catching flower, new to me. Its spiky heads were made of many small yellow five-petaled stars, each with a red circle in the center. My friend Chris Gill later identified the species as swamp candle, from a photo on my blog. Chris, a very active voice in the NFCT community, was a trail maintainer who would complete his section-paddle of the trail in 2015, after starting in 2008. He was often the one to identify the mystery flora and fauna that I encountered on my journeys.

Soon, the river began to widen and the beaver lodges retreated to the banks. The scenery, the treasures, the challenges, I thought, could be little different from those the Abenaki knew so long ago. The whisper of wind in the grass soothed my senses and I knew a single spoken word would have made this a different place.

To those who have never paddled solo, the experience may be hard to comprehend. You can travel for hours and hear only the sounds that are always part of the wild. Gradually, your mind quiets and all that is other fades away. You become truly present in the time and place where you find yourself. Suddenly, your alert senses notice things you other-wise might miss. Colors, textures, or the exquisite detail of a single flower petal. And if you're lucky, you reach that moment when you understand that you, too, belong. You touch the water, the paddle slices in and out, a tiny whirlpool drifts behind and you simply are a part of the flowing river.

One inner conversation that I often have when I reach this place and depth of thinking concerns the ownership of land. Native peoples had a very different understanding of this concept. How could one own what belonged to the Creator? What one could use for but a tiny moment in the history of the world?

Many are the hours I have spent in wild places where I have known I was at home and I hope for many more. These, of course, are places that I will never own. Subtle woodland trails that I may cross thirty times in one winter, snowshoeing, and no other human ever does. Or new places, where some moment of connection simply happens, leaving a memory that will linger forever in your soul. If, in that moment, you are there and fully present, how could anyone own that place more than you?

Such deep thoughts and the beauty of the peaceful river stilled me and carried me along for a time, but then the endless curving began to get monotonous and slow, even though I was going downstream. A pattern emerged. A sharp curve with a backwater, then a gentler curve with a sandbar, then a beaver dam, or sometimes two together. This work of water and beaver seemed to follow some grand scheme, creating oxbows, clear evidence that the river was in a constant state of change, as the longer way around became silted in. This was a river in flux, evolving, adapting, living.

Rounding yet another bend, I came upon a fledgling bird, its presence betrayed by the quivering of branches where it hopped and flapped. As I eased toward it for a photo, it flew awkwardly to the other bank, landing in an alder. Its species was soon determined by the frantic actions of four or five adult red-winged blackbirds wheeling and squawking above.

"I will go quickly and not harm your little one," I whispered gently.

Another couple weary hours and I finally pulled out at Wenlock Crossing, more than ready to switch from paddling to walking. The river had by now entered the Sylvio O. Conte National Wildlife Refuge. I had high hopes of seeing a moose on my long walk. There must be some, I reasoned, after discovering an elaborate moose observation platform along the road. The square wooden building, raised high above the woods and bugs, was a comfortable spot for a snack, but I never did spot a moose. I passed the visitor's center, but it was closed for the day.

No camping is allowed anywhere in the wildlife refuge and I wanted to respect that, so I continued walking to a Vermont River Conservancy campsite on the East Branch of the Nulhegan. It was as intensely buggy as anything I'd experienced on the trail so far. Black flies breed in running water, and this was a low, damp, ferny kind of place right by a stream.

In the safety of my tent, I squirmed into my bathing suit, hat, and head net, then hurried down to the water. There were a few deeper spots in the shallow stream. Near shore, I found a place where I could lie down with my back against a rounded rock and let the cool, rushing water flow over me. Most of my body was covered and for once the bugs were stumped.

They couldn't get me! my journal gloated.

A head net, at the cost of just a few dollars, literally preserves your sanity during the swarming spring and early summer. After my swim, I retreated to my tent, refreshed.

I woke the next morning to the pleasant sound of the gurgling stream and none of the predicted rain. The sun was even trying to break through. Day after day, the beautiful weather had held, with storms at night or not at all. Mornings always inspired me to write. I caught up in my journal, while water for breakfast was boiling out in the tent's vestibule. It was a puzzle sometimes to juggle everything to cook from inside the tent, but very rewarding to have a peaceful hour away from the bugs or tucked in a warm sleeping bag on a cool morning.

Perhaps it was inevitable, but today my juggling went awry. During the winter, reading thru-hiker tips, I'd learned that instant oatmeal can be eaten right from its paper pouch. Just add hot water, stir, eat, and throw away, with no dishes to wash. This time, though, I fumbled the packet and tipped boiling water onto my stomach. What a bizarre accident, and it hurt! I thought of running down to jump in the stream, but settled for a soothing towel soaked in cold water instead. The pain soon abated and I thought no more about the burn.

My thoughts instead were on the sad fact that paddling the East Branch of the Nulhegan was impossible; it simply didn't have enough water. I had missed Clyde Pond and now this. Of the trail's 22 rivers and streams, I would paddle 21 at most. At least it was a pleasant walk to Bloomfield, in the peaceful cool of morning, past weathered barns and a cemetery where I found many French names and one worn stone written all in French.

At the kiosk, still in Vermont, I took my end-of-Map-6 photo. Across the Connecticut River bridge was the town of North Stratford, New Hampshire, where Claudette and Dean's Place had great food and wifi. A cheeseburger, salad, strawberry shortcake, and endless iced tea made the walk worthwhile, and I sat writing until they closed at two o'clock.

The Connecticut River is a reprieve for thru-paddlers, twenty miles of downstream bliss. For me, it was a race from the start, as the first distant rumbles of thunder began before I even got on the water. There was weather building. You could feel it in the air and see it in the towering clouds and it was already three o'clock. The closest campsite was a couple of hours away, and I wasn't going to end my day having gone less than three miles.

After a scratchy start, shallow and rocky, it was an awesome paddle. How quickly you again get used to flying onward, as the memories of the upstream struggles quickly fade. The first few miles interspersed some simple rapids with islands and just a few rocks to make it interesting. The current helped to boost my speeds to a whopping four or five miles per hour, faster than I'd gone for many days.

Not far along, a strong smell hit me, drifting from the shore where water trickled down a heap of rocks stained orange-brown. The tiny stream flowed from nearby Brunswick Springs, whose sulfurous waters the Abenaki and early settlers had believed were healing. The resort hotels that had once grown up around the springs were long gone now, though.

Overhead, a bald eagle wheeled against the increasingly angry sky. A single bolt of lightning sent me scurrying to shore, but when no more came, I impatiently chanced the river once again. Giant clouds continued to build, but the storms stayed mainly to the northeast. Surprisingly soon, I was approaching the first possible campsite, seven miles from Bloomfield, by the granite foundation of an old railroad trestle.

The massive block structure was hard to miss, planted as it was firmly in the middle of the river. As I drew near it, I thought I heard voices. They drifted from the shore, where a green canoe was pulled up on the gloomy bank. I saw a light blue shirt and then a light green one, too. Suddenly, I realized who it was. Sydney and Marji were somehow ahead of me again. As it turned out, Sydney's boyfriend had never ordered their wheels, so they'd shuttled that morning from Island Pond to Bloomfield, bypassing the Nulhegan. They reported a dismal, buggy, muddy site, with no flat tent spots, so we went on, aiming for the next campsite, six miles farther. Gratefully, I realized that the day's mileage would be quite respectable after all.

The storms passed and the weather cleared, as kingfishers and an osprey enlivened this last stretch. We found NFCT's Samuel Benton Campsite high and dry above a sandy beach. The flat tent sites on the edge of a freshly mown hayfield were a vast improvement over the last option and there was even a new composting privy. The mosquitoes were fierce, though, and I escaped into the river for a swim, like the evening before.

Later, our campfire made no impression on the voracious swarms. Supper was in the tent again, a simple meal of avocado, tortillas, fruit, and tea. Sunset gilded the sky, as I thought gratefully of the generous landowner who allowed camping on his property. The buzz of mosquitoes, a few in the tent and others thick on the outside of the window netting kept me up for a while. Then, deep in the night, I woke to the roar of a train and looked out to see a ghostly lighted engine fly past over in New Hampshire, a state away on the other bank.

Our incredibly buggy campsite meant breakfast in the tent, too, very carefully this time you can be sure. I was shocked to see my stomach in the morning light. The burns were an angry red and two large brown blisters had formed in the center of the red streaks. Carefully, I covered them with clean gauze pads and gently settled my paddling pants in place. That day, though, the blisters broke. By evening, the wounds were raw and open. They would continue to bother me for many days to come.

The river was peaceful in the early morning light. A family of mergansers was reflected against a massive rock, the mother's vivid orange beak and stronger colors leading a row of five more muted youngsters. My thoughts, though, were not as tranquil as the scenery.

Soon I would be going upstream once again on the difficult Upper Ammonoosuc River, where, several miles away in Groveton, more trail angels waited. Our upcoming rendezvous was on my mind, and I wondered whether my new companions would still be with me then.

Back in May, Peter had introduced us through email. Ray and Hildy had been his "support crew extraordinaire" in the greater New Hampshire area, during his thru-paddle.

"If in that region you need help, fancy a comfortable night in a real bed, need a hot shower or a good meal, or whatever, feel free to get in touch," Peter had written.

Not long after, another message came from the trail angels themselves, "Ray and Hildy here just to second Peter's offer of help, a bed, a shower, a meal or two from us as you pass through New Hampshire. We've enjoyed the thru-paddlers we've met and are always happy to meet more and follow their adventures vicariously." They were headed to a family reunion soon and this was the last evening we could have connected.

After finishing the Connecticut, I made a left turn onto the Upper Ammo, inwardly sighing at going upstream once again. I'd gotten ahead of Sydney and Marji, but they arrived at Weston Dam in Groveton not long after I did. When Ray and Hildy drove up, they were not at all surprised to see the three of us, as they'd been following my blog.

"We're happy to have all three of you," Hildy quickly said, as we loaded up the canoes and piled into their vehicle. I felt that same instant kinship and connectedness that I'd felt with Katina and Peter and so many others, yet another gift of the river.

On my blog, I gave the following recipe for hospitality for NFCT thru-paddlers:

1. *Pick up paddlers and countless pieces of gear and equipment, filling vehicle to bursting.*
2. *Drive the long way home (who cares about gas), visiting covered bridges, ski jumps, logging boom relics, and towering mountains.*
3. *Also scout rivers ahead, sharing river conditions, portaging suggestions and other valuable wisdom.*
4. *Stop at grocery store.*
5. *Bring smelly, tired, famished paddlers and aforementioned gear, also smelly (and wet), into your home.*
6. *Provide tea, homegrown peas and hummus, showers, beds, laundry facilities, home-cooked supper, well water, grease (for wheels), band aids, coffee packets, more time poring over maps, and warm, caring hearts.*

Inside her spacious country kitchen, Hildy showed us the cups and the kettle and told us to make ourselves at home. Ray asked if anything needed fixing. He greased my wheels and gave me some more grease for the road, carefully double-bagged.

Our cassoulet supper drew heavily from the farm's bounty, with salad, greens, and cobbler made from some of the 14 quarts of cherries Ray and Hildy had picked that year. The shower was wonderful, particularly for thoroughly cleaning the blisters on my stomach. They were still a mess. All I could do was carefully cover them and hope they would heal soon.

The next morning, which happened to be Ray and Hildy's 48th anniversary, we all pitched in to make breakfast. The table groaned with farm-fresh eggs, bacon, English muffins, coffee, tea, and fruit salad. Our hearts were just as full, grateful to have shared Ray and Hildy's home and family life for an evening of rest.

The overnight rain was clearing, as Hildy dropped me at Weston Dam, alone. Sydney and Marji had town errands, and this time my farewell to them was more honest. I had thought carefully about my words and hoped I said them kindly.

"If I was going to have paddling partners, it would be you two, but this is a solo trip."

It was time for me to journey alone again, rediscovering all that I had come for. To go to the places deep inside where my thoughts and reflections were worth exploring. To pause for a tiny bit of red moss that adorned a stump or to gaze upward for an hour at the dance of sun-filtered leaves. And, for my faith journey, to commune with God in the place where it comes simplest—alone, outdoors, confronting creation in all its delicacy and power, variety and patterns, blahness and beauty, exertion and comfort.

I will try to camp where I won't hinder my friends' journey, I promised myself.

*With Dad, camping on the Maine coast at eight months and canoeing
Rollins Pond in the Adirondacks at age 8 (Joan Apgar photos)*

Paddling Brown's Tract Inlet on the second day of the trip (George Apgar photo)

The first of my thirteen end-of-map photos, in Long Lake, New York (George Apgar photo)

Morning reflections on Middle Saranac Lake in the Adirondacks

Following Dad into the Lower Locks along the Saranac River

Good shepherds Peter Macfarlane and Dan Brown pass through The Gut on Lake Champlain

Surfing the waves on Lake Champlain (Peter Macfarlane photo)

*Missisquoi River rapids at the site
of an old butterchurn factory*

*Tim Green's Grey Gables Mansion B&B
serves a legendary breakfast*

Pastoral beauty along Quebec's Missisquoi River

Sydney and Marji Aveson ready to check in with U.S. Customs by video phone (above gas pump)

Difficult stretch of the Clyde River where I struggled upstream to a grassy yard

With my husband Chris on Bigelow Mountain's Avery Peak above Flagstaff Lake in 2006

Almost to the haven of Middle Deadwater on Little Spencer Stream

*Sue raises her paddle in victory after
crossing Moosehead Lake in 2011*

*Historic Mud Pond Carry resembles
a stream for most of its two miles*

Mud Pond before the storm

Chamberlain Lake lit from within a glorious bank of cloud

Echoing loon on Eagle Lake in the Allagash

Taylor and Dad on the Allagash during Paddle for Hope in 2011

Uncanny noon stillness on Umsaskis Lake

Chris loved fly fishing

Picture-perfect Allagash Falls

Last lucky moose, just past the official end of the Allagash Wilderness Waterway

CHAPTER 10

GRIT IN THE GRANITE STATE

I write as the birds sing, because I must, and usually from the same source of inspiration.

—Gene Stratton Porter

As my canoe slid cheerfully down the soft grassy bank and into the water, a surge of confidence rippled through me. The paddling plan that Ray and I had marked in red on Map 7 was doable and would keep me on the river more. I was well rested after an evening of healthy food and good company. Most of all, I had shared my need to travel alone, probably the most difficult hurdle I would have to face today. I felt strong and ready for anything. Familiar, comfortable Maine now lay well within my grasp.

Four evenings from now my parents and I planned to meet in Errol, New Hampshire, where I would collect my next resupply box. The following day, I would cross the state border on Umbagog (um-BAY-gog) Lake, merging with the 2011 route of Paddle for Hope. The way there, across the top of New Hampshire, was all upstream, 19 more miles on the Upper Ammonoosuc and 19 miles on the Androscoggin. The two rivers were linked by a five-mile portage through the small town of West Milan. It was a distance I could wrap my mind around.

The day started well. I soon passed under a covered bridge, rather faded and ordinary compared to the one that waited nine miles ahead in the village of Stark. We had stopped in Stark yesterday, delighted by the calendar-worthy covered bridge in a quintessential New England town. A statue of Revolutionary War hero John Stark, whose words "Live Free or Die" are on the state's license plate, stood watch over the village green.

Stark was my next goal. Back in June, Ray and Hildy had paddled this part of the Upper Ammo with Peter and his wife Viveka, going downstream. Yesterday they'd confirmed what Peter had written to me back in June.

"It was good to put that to rest, after I walked too much of it in 2013. Had I known then what I know now, I would have put back in at the Emerson Road bridge and struggled another 600–800 yards against shallow rapids (well, somewhere between Class I and swift-water). It then gets much deeper with less current, barring the occasional shallower riffle, and so is much more paddlable than the lower section immediately above Red Dam. This could have saved me a carry about the length of the Grand Portage!"

After portaging around two more dams, I followed the highway and then a quiet, flowery country road to the easy put-in at the Emerson Road bridge.

The first half hour truly was a struggle just to get out of sight of the bridge. I fell once, hard, collecting an impressive bruise. Nash Stream, entering vigorously on river right, had created a shallow gravel bar that was treacherously slippery for walking. In general, spots where

Struggling up past Nash Stream on the Upper Ammonoosuc River

streams enter a river are challenging for upstream paddlers. This was a prime example.

Once past the stream, though, the river quieted and deepened as promised. Paddling the inside curves still left energy to watch for moose and I kept my camera at the ready. For two miles, I relaxed. Deep in the shaded forest, the thrushes trilled joyfully and I cheered on the bit of blue sky that peeked through the layered clouds. I felt thankful for the great river advice that had given me this brief respite in a section I hadn't originally planned to paddle.

The river didn't let me rest for long. Slowly it grew more troublesome and shallower, the current flowing faster over the sand and gravel. Hopping in and out of the boat was refreshing at first. The cool water felt great on my feet and it was a chance to stretch my stiff back. As the hours wore on, though, my tired legs were less reliable on the increasingly slippery rocks. I tried to focus. Mental stamina, determination, and an optimistic attitude needed to take up the slack. With each careful step, I thought of what could go wrong and tried to be more analytical.

At several points, that déjà vu sense from the Dead River returned. Then, as always when that happened, I carefully walked the sand of the shallow inside curve. Approaching Stark, my speed slowed to one mile per hour, even though there were a few deeper sections.

One place stands out in my memory. The river swept to the left around a tight curve. On my right rose a towering eroded bank of sand, where the river was relentlessly nibbling away at the cliff. High above perched an eerie row of gravestones, their slightly awkward angles hinting at advanced age. I wondered what would happen when more of the sand had gone and bones or caskets started to appear.

Eventually I reached Stark and pulled my boat from the rapids just below the covered bridge. The village was every bit as picturesque as I remembered. The buildings, all a tidy white, could have been borrowed from beneath a Christmas tree, beside a tiny train. The school, the library, the steeple on the church. It was all perfect. I would have liked to explore the village more, but it was buggy and all I really wanted was to find camp for the night.

Back on Highway 110, a mile's walk around a boulder field brought me back to a deeper and gentler river. The afternoon was growing late, and, by now, I had passed all the official camping and lodging options. I began to look for anywhere to camp along the muddy, brushy shores. The spot I found, several miles upstream, will forever be a special place to me.

Safely tucked away stealth camping on the Upper Ammonoosuc River

"A small place in the world can have a spirit all its own," I later journaled. *"From the river, my eye was caught by a flat, pine-needle-brown opening high above. The towering trees and steep access looked no worse than some Allagash sites. Landing conveniently on a tiny, pebble beach, I scrambled up. A miracle on the Ammonoosuc. A small clearing, bordered on the north by a teetering row of fence posts and rusted wire. What story had created this perfect, soft, open campsite? Whatever it was, my heart was grateful, my enthusiasm supplying the energy to get all my gear up. Just late afternoon, there was precious time to flip the boat in a hidden nook, hang the food bag rope, mop out the little water that had snuck in my bags, and set up camp."*

I cooked my potatoes and bacon outside, with only a few mosquitoes for company, my feet propped on soft dry needles, not deep wet grass. I slept deeply, interrupted only by the deafening arrival of two trains deep in the night. If I hadn't known with certainty that there were no railroad tracks beneath my sleeping pad, I would have been terrified. Actually, let's be honest, it was the most terrifying event of a long day.

Discovering that site was truly a gift. Yet it was just one of so many concerns and needs, small and large, that were being met along my way. That little white church back in Stark had reminded me of folks back home, at the Bremen Union Church, where my best friend Kathy Maclachlan is the pastor. I'd given them a list of concerns for different parts of my journey and they'd been praying for me. Many other friends were praying, too, giving me confidence as I faced the many unknowns of the trail.

I was also discovering that trust and faith complement and build on one other. As the days went by, I found I was worrying less and less about those unknowns—where I would camp or store my boat or navigate a tricky section. There was a synergy between trusting and succeeding that was making me more relaxed about the details of each day.

"The same is true in life," I reflected. *"As the years have come and gone, with their joyous peaks and tragic valleys, my trust in God's caring presence has kept on growing. This life of faith is working for me. I worry less and trust more, although the path ahead may still be uncertain."*

There was a Bible study we did a few years before my thru-paddle that had helped clarify my thinking on the whole topic of God's plan for our lives. It wasn't that long after Chris died when we read a book called *Why? Making Sense of God's Will* by Methodist pastor Adam Hamilton. He explored what it means when we say that God has a plan for our lives.

One possibility is that God has already planned every detail and takes responsibility and credit for it all. The blessings, the accidents, and the decisions, good and bad, that we make.

There could, however, be another interpretation. Perhaps God's plan for us is simply to be involved in our lives, to have a relationship with us. Hamilton compares this relationship to that of a mother or father, who guides us through our growing-up years, trying to instill common sense and teach us values. After we're grown, that parent surely hopes to still have a relationship with us. We may be off on our own, but hopefully we still ask for advice or share the good and the not-so-good that is happening in our lives. I liked that. God and I "writing the story of my life together," to use Hamilton's words.

"That's where I am with God. All that good stuff we learn from the life and teachings of Jesus gives us a goal to work toward, but we still mess up. A lot. We live in a world filled with abundant blessings and incomprehensible tragedies. For me, having God to talk with about it all makes everything easier. Relying on God's strength and guidance, having it work in my life, is the life-changing faith that keeps me hopeful and gives me courage. Even enough courage to do crazy things like thru-paddling the Northern Forest Canoe Trail alone."

The next morning, it was even chillier than when I had groped for my warm hat in the night. Soon, though, warmed by apple oatmeal and the rising sun, I found the fortitude to leave my sleeping bag. The welcoming spirit of my little campsite kept me journaling until mid-morning. In the distance, I could hear the call of flying loons and, much nearer, the repeated hoarse croaking of a raven. I felt relaxed and hoped today would be an easier day.

My destination tonight was a commercial campground right on the portage between the rivers, just under ten miles away. I paddled slowly through a blue and gold and green world, as the shallow, placid river wound back and forth. I saw my first moose tracks of the trip and a four-inch leech wiggling across the rippled sandy bottom. Once, a coyote shyly disappeared behind the thick branches of a tree blown down beside the river, leaving only his tracks for a photo.

I left the Upper Ammo in West Milan, home of Gord's Corner Store. Gord Roberge is another loyal NFCT supporter, who welcomes paddlers as enthusiastically as he does the area's burgeoning population of ATV and snowmobile riders. Gord has played a role in the stories of quite a few thru-paddlers.

"I've been expecting you," Gord laughed, when I introduced myself. He had recognized me from a "be-on-the-lookout-for" email he'd gotten from the NFCT staff. We didn't visit long, though, because soon he was deep in serious conversation with another customer. The topic was some logistical detail of the vast network of OHRV (off-highway recreational vehicle) trails that crisscrossed the area.

This was a growing business with a growing voice and infrastructure, as evidenced by the brand new OHRV bridge that now connected the store to Route 110A. Constructed on land owned by the Roberge family, it had had its grand opening only the day before. After charging my phone and making quick work of a freshly made roast beef sandwich, I headed out for Cedar Pond Campground, two miles away, my home for the night.

The following evening was very different. Unlike Cedar Pond, there was no hot shower. No spigot dispensing clear, cold, drinkable water. No phone-charging station just steps from my tent. Instead, I was about 12 miles up the much more substantial Androscoggin River, trying to solve a problem that no one could ever have foreseen.

Perched carefully at the top of the steep riverbank, above some serious rapids, I could do nothing but wait in the growing dusk. Colors faded into grayness as I sat, chin resting on my tucked-up knees. At least I was safe, if a little chilled and uncomfortable. The raw blisters on my stomach were hurting and I was hungry. There was at least half an hour left to wait, and I thought back over the day, wondering what I could have done differently.

Many thru-paddlers extend the official portage from the Upper Ammo by putting in at Pontook Reservoir, bypassing the Androscoggin's first couple of quite turbulent miles. I had decided to do the same. *Had the Abenaki really gone up all these rivers?* I asked myself, as I walked on Route 16 beside whitewater that I couldn't envision anyone paddling up. It was, without a doubt, Class II and III. The answer, of course, was yes, and I wondered if they, too, had walked this part.

Sometime after I turned onto Route 16, a pickup pulled firmly to a stop beside me. A long gray beard was the first thing to emerge as the driver leaned out.

"Are you going to the dam?" he wondered.

"Yes I am. And then up the Androscoggin on the Northern Forest Canoe Trail. I'm in the middle of a thru-paddle."

"I could take you down there. We could just throw your canoe in the back of my pickup." People were so kind. Kind, and then incredulous when I said, "No, thanks." And often, too, they seemed to think I hadn't understood the logistics of whatever help they were offering.

"Thank you very much. I really appreciate it. But my goal is to do the whole trail without any help. No rides, no shuttles, not skipping anything."

"But your canoe could fit in the back of my truck. You wouldn't have to walk."

I really didn't know what else to say. I thanked him again and he shook his head, still puzzled, then wished me luck before driving on down the highway.

Sydney and Marji, I soon discovered, had had their own generous offer. Arriving at Gord's three hours after I had, they'd met some friends of Ray and Hildy. After another night of trail angel hospitality, the couple dropped them off at Pontook Reservoir, as I sat studying my map at a picnic table there. We said hello and shared our news, then they went on.

Later, down at the boat launch, a young woman came enthusiastically over to me, after spotting my gypsy boat piled high with gear.

"Are you doing the trail?" she asked with a smile, her tone saying she wished she were going along. "My father and I did it this spring!"

The Androscoggin River in a moment of serenity

Jennie and Steve Caffrey had been two of the names I'd been seeing in trail journals along the way. I hadn't pictured a father and his daughter, though. Now Jennie was guiding an extended Appalachian Mountain Club hiking and whitewater trip for kids. She and her father had completed the trail in just 36 days in a Wenonah Prospector canoe, accompanied in Maine by her younger brother Ben in a kayak. This was my Day 28 and I wasn't even halfway.

The Androscoggin, for the most part, turned out to be deep and broad, with a wild beauty reminiscent of what awaited me in Maine. There were, however, some notable exceptions. The first came just above the reservoir, a mile and a half of adversity and challenge. In fact, is *torture* too strong a word? Wisely, I'd decided to stop for a substantial hot lunch before it got tough, something I didn't often do. I would end up needing the energy.

My journal captured my thoughts on this tough section:

"Stopping now for a rest, I am well into the '1.5 miles of Class I rapids' that lie above the reservoir. Mostly I'm walking, so carefully, on the rounded, water-caressed rocks, thick with slippery, trailing strands of algae. Where the river made a gentle S, I was unable to cross the deep and fast center channel. Here is a time to embrace careful slowness, to celebrate 1/10 mile as progress,

even when 15 of them must be accomplished. I perch now on a rock, feet in the running water, my boat in a tiny harbor. I will survive! By the map, I have now entered Thirteen Mile Woods and am near the last rapids symbol."

The rest of the river lay within Thirteen Mile Woods, where Forest Legacy conservation easements prohibited development, but allowed for multiple-use forest management. From the dam, it was nine miles to Seven Islands Bridge, where I would leave the river to walk five miles to Mollidgewock State Park for another civilized night of camping.

At least that had been the plan.

Just as spring in New England is also mud season, summer is also road repair season, as I'd already experienced multiple times. Route 16, the only artery to where I was going, was being repaved. I started out from the Seven Islands Bridge along the hot and smelly blackness of the pristine pavement, rolling merrily along, until the first car approached, forcing me to maneuver onto the narrow shoulder.

Desperation made me reckless and the canoe teetered dangerously as I wheeled it off the asphalt onto the dirt. There was essentially a four or five-inch cliff along the edge and it didn't get any better as I went a little farther. The shoulder was too narrow and rough for wheeling, with its intermittent guardrails, and there was a lot of traffic. I pulled well off the road when I could, to try to think. I was stumped for the moment. On the river, from here to the state park, the map showed a continuous parade of rapids symbols, ten in all, some Class II or worse.

Ironically, a highway paving project had done what convicts, rapids, and wind had failed to do. Stopped me in my tracks. At first, I couldn't see a way out, short of asking for a ride, which was never really an option. I couldn't go forward, and I certainly couldn't stay here, on the side of busy Route 16, wavering indecisively while the traffic whizzed by.

Sometimes, knowing when to quit is the highest sign of bravery. You can't be too committed to your plan to be flexible. So back to Seven Islands Bridge I went and into the river. I went reluctantly and without much hope of success, upriver into the rapids.

Adrenaline kept me paddling strong past the first of two campsites that showed on my map. Called Osprey, it was full of a large group of young adults unloading a mountain of gear from their canoes. And it wouldn't have done to pause as I passed a pair of gnarled fly fisherman drifting sensibly downstream in a rowboat. Carefully, I tried to compose my face into an expression of confidence, to help explain why I was struggling valiantly upstream into the froth at the edge of dark.

Out of sight of everyone at last, I reached the second campsite, Moose Crossing, and it was empty. I wavered. Was it reserved? Would I wake to find an irate someone with a valid right to camp there? On the other hand, what other choice did I have? What I was facing on the river would have taken concentration to safely navigate even going downstream in daylight.

Finally, a plan came to me. I would try to go a little farther and find a place to stealth camp. Then I could wake up before first light and walk while there was little traffic. By now, I had persevered about a mile past the bridge and was still close to the highway.

So, my search for a site had led me here, to that spot perched on the riverbank, waiting for darkness to fall. Behind me was more than enough space for my tent, but it wasn't up. Busy Route 16 was so close that in daylight a tent would be visible to passing cars. Even worse, after I'd committed to this spot, awkwardly hauling my canoe and gear up and hiding them under some brush, I'd discovered this was a spot to pull off and access the river for fishing.

I cooked supper down by the water, hoping no one would show up to go fishing, and watched for wildlife. At last it grew dark, the tent went up, and I was sound asleep in minutes.

The rest of the plan worked perfectly. I woke at quarter after four and had finished walking to the state park by the time the traffic started picking up. Back on the river, I quickly reached Errol and portaged around the dam, all before breakfast. Where I would continue up the river tomorrow, I sent a SPOT message and went "off duty," though I wheeled my boat back to town with me. Map 7 was in the books.

Errol was a true trail town, its people and businesses obviously oriented toward the outdoor adventurer. At the Northern Exposure restaurant, I wrote for hours, and ended up having breakfast, lunch, and dinner there. The owner of the Errol Motel let me leave my boat there while I waited for Mom and Dad. As it turned out, the motel had been full when Dad called, so he'd made a reservation at Sonja Sheldon's A Peace of Heaven B&B instead.

Sonja had hospitality down to an art after more than twenty years of hosting guests. For breakfast, the food just kept on coming: fruit, zucchini bread, eggs, bacon, and then French toast. And with the food came a surprising story.

"Do you see that ballot box?" Sonja began, pointing to a sturdy wooden box that I hadn't noticed, sitting quietly on her kitchen floor.

Above a large slot in the locked lid, I could see that someone had carved the word *BALLOTS*.

"My house is the town hall for Millsfield. The people vote right here, in my bedrooms. Last year, I even had a visit from our Secretary of State. He came to see how it all worked."

For years, Sonja has baked a cake and invited all 29 residents of Millsfield to her home on Election Day, to vote. The Secretary of State, though, had made that visit for a special reason. The 2016 Presidential primaries were fast approaching, and Millsfield would join two other New Hampshire towns, including famous Dixville Notch, in midnight voting.

In Millsfield, though, this wouldn't be their first midnight vote. For years, the history surrounding this unique tradition was somewhat murky. Until Sonja herself discovered a 1952 *TIME* magazine article, hidden in a time capsule.

"*The seven voters of Millsfield, N.H. (pop. 16),*" the article reported, "*stayed up late on election eve and marked their ballots just as soon as the clock struck midnight. Everybody had gathered in the parlor of Mrs. Genevieve N. Annis's 125-year-old house well ahead of time, and the votes were cast, in the light of kerosene lamps, in a fine conspiratorial atmosphere. Mrs. Annis, the town clerk, collected and counted them quickly, recorded one absentee ballot, and at 12:02 o'clock, proudly reported the nation's first election returns (eight votes for Eisenhower).*"

CHAPTER 11

NO WORRIES

Therefore, I tell you, do not worry about your life, what you will eat or drink; or about your body, what you will wear. Look at the birds of the air; they do not sow or reap or store away in barns, and yet your Heavenly Father feeds them. See how the flowers of the field grow. They do not labor or spin. Yet I tell you that not even Solomon in all his splendor was dressed like one of these.

— Select verses from Matthew, Chapter 6

Heavy rain pounded the river as I finished the last three miles of the Androscoggin into Umbagog Lake the following morning. Then the skies began to clear, and a cheery fisherman yelled that I would have the best part of the day. Memories came flooding back from the start of Paddle for Hope, when I had put in on the Magalloway River, entering the lake from the north, rather than the west. I remembered the immensity of the windy lake and the joy of watching the little triangle that was my boat move across the GPS map screen.

Somewhere, I crossed the invisible state line into Maine. I was home. I was also now, at least unofficially, an NFCT section-paddler, someone who had completed the trail over more than one year. As of the end of the 2016 season, eight people have been officially recognized as NFCT section-paddlers, taking anywhere from two to 20 years to finish.

Around Pine Point, the lake narrowed to meet the Rapid River. The binoculars I'd retrieved in Errol lay close at hand, for this place had the feel of a wild, remote river. A loud crash sounded on the water and

Merganser family on Umbagog Lake

then, from the woods, came the drumming of a pileated woodpecker, close by, but hidden. My senses were on high alert.

Suddenly, something moved in the dark tangled shadows of a fallen tree at the water's edge. A sleek brown body slid smoothly into the water—an otter, the first of the trip. A beaver would have patrolled along the surface or simply disappeared with a mighty tail slap. Otters, though, seem more sociable. Like this one, they usually swim around, their glistening periscope heads popping up curiously again and again. They chatter and squawk, saying hello or perhaps hoping for a quick goodbye. I paddled carefully away. In the distance, I thought I could discern the sound of rapids.

Any feeling of remoteness quickly vanished into ridiculousness as I approached the Cedar Stump campsites at the mouth of the river. A woman paddling a comically overloaded canoe filled with coolers, chairs, and wannigans was the precursor to a bunch of kids in tiny kayak play boats. There were families camping, pontoon boats trailing tethered rafts, and fly fishermen galore. It was a zoo and time to quickly move on.

The Rapid River descends to Umbagog from the Richardson lakes, Upper and Lower. Its entire upstream length must be portaged, with a break in the middle to paddle across one-mile-long Pond in the River.

Beside the river runs a road famous in Maine literary history, simply called the Carry Road. There, in Forest Lodge, overlooking the river, Louise Dickinson Rich wrote about the challenges and humor of life in this remote place in the 1930s and '40s. Her well-loved book, *We Took to the Woods*, is dear to the hearts of generations of readers. On my last trip, I'd had a treasured glimpse into her life.

To reach the Carry Road from Cedar Stump, one follows a half mile of rocky trail, not at all wheelable. In 2011, I'd barely made it with my 48-pound plastic hybrid kayak, dragging it where pine needles carpeted the trail and struggling to carry it the rest of the way. Its detachable seat and my other gear made up two additional loads. This time, my canoe and I, and then the gear, flew quickly over the path in just two trips.

The contrast was remarkable and due mainly to the Kevlar from which my canoe was made. Invented by chemist Stephanie Kwolek, Kevlar was patented by DuPont in 1966. Considered one of the most important organic fibers ever developed, it is five times stronger for its weight than steel and has applications ranging from space travel to bulletproof vests. Over four hundred miles into my journey, I was thankful to have chosen the boat that I had.

Once on the Carry Road itself, I christened it "wheelable with perseverance." Much of the way was uphill. In places, there was no way to avoid bouncing awkwardly over rocks and ruts or dragging desperately through large puddles, hoping to have enough momentum to get through. My kayak cart met the challenges, though, and was, in fact, better than ever. Dad had just made some improvements to it, epoxying PVC conduit into the wheel axle holes to increase the bearing surface. On this first tough test, the modified wheels were doing well.

The Rapid River drops 155 feet over five miles, making it an outstanding whitewater kayaking destination. To put these numbers in perspective, I would be descending only 1,075 feet in the 285 miles from the trail's highest elevation in Maine, ahead near Rangeley, to the end in Fort Kent. This drop after Rangeley, by the way, explains why most of the river travel going forward would be downstream, even though I would be traveling northeast.

As I wandered along one of the well-worn side trails over to the river, a cherry-red backboard leaned nonchalantly against a tree, a silent witness to the river's very real dangers.

Last winter, snuggled up in bed reading about these rapids in the

AMC River Guide: Maine, their names alone had awed me. The Jaws of Death, Cemetery Rapids, and The Devil's Hopyard. Louise wrote about one that she called Cluley's Rips. I tried to figure out which one it was, but never could, and the AMC guide does not mention it. Louise lived here for many years, she knew the river in all its seasons, and she seems to have acquired the forthright speech and realistic attitude of those who must face nature in all its moods.

"Cluley's Rips," she wrote, *"a mile below us, is the most vicious piece of water I have ever seen. It's frightening just to stand on the bank and look at it. The water pours into a narrow gut, overhung by rocks and dripping spruces, with such force that it has no time to level out. The middle of the river humps up, green and white and snarling, almost to the eye-level of the bank-stander. Cluley, whoever he may have been, was drowned there. That's how you get things named after you in this country."*

A couple of miles along, I was surprised to discover Sydney's empty canoe resting there without gear, wheels, or any sign of my friends. Thankfully, I soon found them, discouraged and justifiably exhausted, in the yard of a camp farther up the road. Their new wheels, it turned out, couldn't be delivered to the Errol post office and were now headed for a Rangeley hotel. The rigors of the Carry Road had been the coup de grâce for their old wheels. We agreed that I would try to send back help from up ahead.

The logical place to look would be at Forest Lodge itself, which had been owned for many years by Aldro French, whose father purchased the property in the 1960s. I'd met Aldro last time and was hoping to see him again. I'd heard, though, that he was planning to retire and that Forest Lodge was for sale. I wasn't even sure if he would still be there.

Aldro was a professional fly fishing guide, who also hosted disabled veterans through a volunteer program called Project Healing Waters. Before Paddle for Hope, I'd called him, wanting to visit this place where history and healing met. He'd encouraged me to come. It was the first morning of that trip when I arrived at the large and tidy farmhouse, tan with green shutters, where an American flag flew proudly atop a tall pole. My journal tells the story well:

Forest Lodge at last! I wandered through the surprisingly domestic yard, with its lupines and hummingbird feeder gracing a stump, and around to the wide back porch, which looks out over the river. A quick knock and then I could see through the screen door a man come into sight. He was wearing red swim trunks, a blue T-shirt, and orange Crocs, a black Lab by his side. The dog was Aubrey and the gentleman, with friendly blue eyes and white beard was, of course, Aldro French.

Aldro is a giving person, giving of himself to his fly fishing mission and giving me the first of much North Woods hospitality that I would be blessed with on my journey. He was friendly, gracious, down to earth, and encouraging, never once giving me the impression that he doubted my ability to succeed. Best of all, he was carrying a huge tray of heavenly looking food.

"Go on, go on, open the door," he smiled with a friendly, confident voice, "you're just in time for breakfast." And what a breakfast it was…thick smoked bacon, eggs, giant homemade biscuits with honey, and tasty sweet potato cakes with a hot pepper kick, all washed down with plenty of hot coffee.

I shared the meal with a party of fly fisherman saying farewell to the Rapid River after several days of excellent fishing. They were quick to share their stories, of rising at four to get the best fishing holes, and of the excellent trout and salmon fishing found in the Rapid River. I was surprised to learn that they are encouraged to keep the salmon they catch, to reduce the pressure on the coveted brook trout, whose eggs the salmon devour. All trout, on the other hand, must be released immediately after they are caught. I later learned that the introduction of smallmouth bass into Lake Umbagog in the 1980s poses an even greater threat to the populations of both trout and salmon, as far up as Pond in the River.

Aldro has kept much of Forest Lodge as it was in Louise's day and one could spend a good hour just in the living room, reading and enjoying the décor. All too soon, though, it was time to be on my way. As we said goodbye, Aldro generously handed me a Rapid River Fly Fishing hat for my dad.

This time, though, there was no one around at Forest Lodge. I left, still wondering how Aldro was doing now. I took the slow shortcut through Pond in the River, not wanting to miss another body of water. The portage ended at Middle Dam, which in 1883 had raised the water level, connecting Upper and Lower Richardson lakes.

The owners of Lakewood Camps there kindly promised to send a truck to pick up Syd and Marji. Between Middle Dam and where their wheels waited in Rangeley, they would encounter only one simple road portage. I would be anxious to hear how it all turned out.

"No worries" is an expression that seems to have migrated from my daughter Megan's generation to the rest of the world. It sounded magical to me, an hour after I'd set out on Lower Richardson Lake. A storm was rolling in, heralded by rumbles of distant thunder from the ominous sky, and I didn't have a campsite reserved. Most of the camping on Map 8 requires reservations, making planning difficult for thru-paddlers. I'd gambled on finding an empty site.

Hurrying, I'd almost reached The Narrows between the two lakes when I decided it was time to stop and reconnoiter. At a campsite on the west shore, a young woman was organizing gear beside a bright yellow canoe. Dressed in running shorts, T-shirt, and a tie-dyed bandana, she was about Megan's age, probably not long out of college. She came down to shore, smiling.

"Hello," I said. "I'm looking for a spot to camp, but I don't have a reservation anywhere. I'm thru-paddling the Northern Forest Canoe Trail, so I never know exactly where I'll be at night. Could you tell me which campsite this is?"

She gave me the bad news first. "This one's Spaulding Cove. I think there are two more around the point, but they may be full. And we saw some lightning not long ago." In the same breath, she went on, "No worries, though. If they're full, you can camp with us. We have room."

Looking at the wooded sloping site, I didn't see a lot of room, but that didn't matter. It was a generous, spontaneous offer in the true spirit of North Woods hospitality. I'd seen the lightning, too. I peeked around the point just long enough to spot boats pulled up at both the other sites, then hustled quickly back.

It was Jess who I'd been talking with. She and Becca, friends since college, were on a weekend trip together. Becca was shorter and just as friendly, with an equally cool bandana. Both women seemed athletic and comfortable with camp life. Becca had played field hockey like I did in college, and Jess had been on many wilderness trips, including 30 days canoeing in the Boundary Waters Canoe Area Wilderness, in northern Minnesota.

Gratefully, I squeezed my tent into a small space at the edge of the woods, then sat down at the picnic table to visit over dinner. Jess and Becca were having smoked three-bean chili, from a new Maine company that I'd never heard of. Based in Kittery, Good To-Go makes dehydrated gourmet trail meals that I later tried and found to be delicious.

The next morning, the three of us rose early in hopes of beating the wind. The storms in the night had been intense and right overhead, so we were glad to see the morning sun. As I ate a quick granola bar, I read on the map that the Wabanaki name for Upper Richardson was Mollychunkamunk. That was almost as much fun to say as Mooselookmeguntic (moose-look-mah-GUN-tick), the lake I would portage over to after Upper Richardson.

As we paddled opposite sides of the lake, from across the water came the faint sound of singing from Jess and Becca's yellow canoe. *I bet they're singing camp songs*, I thought, *just like Megan would have been. Megan would have enjoyed them and their enthusiasm for my trip.* On I went, pushed from behind by a gentle wind and awed by the brilliant white and dark chestnut brown of a pair of eagles soaring majestically against the azure sky.

The bald eagle has been America's symbol since June 1782, when Congress adopted the national seal featuring this striking bird. At the top of the food chain, these raptors are also seen as symbolic of healthy ecosystems, particularly since the population has recovered from the drastic effects of the insecticide DDT. In the states along the Northern Forest Canoe Trail, bald eagles have made a miraculous comeback, one in which Maine played a key role.

When DDT was banned in 1972, only 29 pairs of bald eagles were nesting in Maine. Thanks to summer resident Rachel Carson's book *Silent Spring*, the country had woken up just in time. Six years later, when the species was first listed as endangered across the Northeast under the federal Endangered Species Act, the Maine population was already recovering, with 62 occupied nests.

By 1995, when *endangered* changed to *threatened*, Maine had 192 nesting pairs. At that time, New York had the next highest breeding population in the Northeast, with 25 nesting pairs. The bald eagle was removed from the threatened list in 2007. The U.S. Fish & Wildlife Service released its last data in 2006, reporting 414 nesting pairs in Maine and 110 in New York. Today, the sight of an eagle along the NFCT is still breathtaking, but very common.

At Upper Dam, I discovered Jess and Becca, unloading their canoe for the short grassy stroll over to Mooselookmeguntic Lake.

"We wondered if you could hear us," they grinned, when I asked if they'd been singing camp songs. This would be our farewell, as they had a campsite reserved on a different part of the huge lake, which is the fourth largest in the state.

Upper Dam was once home to another celebrated Maine woman, Carrie Gertrude Stevens. She and her husband, guide Wallace Stevens, ran a hotel here for many years, in the early twentieth century. Her fame came from tying flies. Over her lifetime, Carrie pioneered over one hundred patterns that live on today. Their names—Green Hornet, Golden Witch, Blue Charm—have written themselves irrevocably into the lore of trout and salmon fishing for more than a century.

Carrie's fame began with a single cast of a fly she had tied in imitation of a smelt. She called her creation the Gray Ghost. Legend has it that it took but one cast. Fact, in the form of a second-place finish in *Field and Stream*'s 1924 fishing contest, confirms that she caught a 6-pound, 13-ounce brook trout that day, the biggest fish to come out of the huge pool below the dam in many years.

Carrie specialized in tying streamers, melding feathers, fur, and brilliantly colored silk floss into fishing weapons of deadly beauty. The pattern for the Gray Ghost uses an exotic combination of silver tinsel; orange floss; white bucktail; peacock, jungle cock, and silver pheasant feathers; and the crest of a golden pheasant for the wing. In the end, the streamers that she taught herself to tie would be known far beyond Maine for their artistry and precision, elevating the allure of fly fishing in the Rangeley Lakes region.

Mooselookmeguntic Lake can get very windy, so today's weather was a gift. From Upper Dam, I called the friends whose cabin I was headed to that night. With the light wind, I hoped to cross the expansive lake to Haines Landing in Oquossoc, where Paul and Janie would pick me up. The idyllic conditions lasted almost the whole way, although near the end I had to paddle deep into Wildwood Cove to stay safe as the wind began to pick up.

My friends had owned their property north of Toothaker Island for 47 years. They well remembered stories of a different era, when sports arrived by railroad for days of fishing, rowed about by guides in distinctive Rangeley boats. These boats featured small round seats, so fisherman would stay centered during the excitement of battling a large fish.

Their cabin, christened Cup o' Tea, is a place of great traditions. A visit always means a shower, au naturel, with a glorious view of the woods and sun-sparkled lake. Paul created the shower by running hot- and cold-water lines up the hollow insides of a standing tree, where one basks in a cascade of steamy water emerging from a limb. It's the ultimate shower with a view.

Another tradition is signing the wooden stairs that go up to the loft, which still bear the marks that Paul's father made during construc-

Paul and Janie with a Rangeley boat along the Oquossoc portage

tion, almost fifty years before. Among the greetings of generations of visitors, I signed my name once more, beneath the rather crooked letters that read, *"Laurie Chandler, Paddle for Hope, June 21, 2011."*

Having finished Mooselookmeguntic while it was calm, I could relax the next morning. Paul cooked made-to-order omelets, which we ate with toast and Janie's homemade wild raspberry jam. My friends surprised me with the offer to come back for another night, but I carried all my gear with me, in case our plans changed.

We drove to where I'd stopped yesterday and Janie joined me for the walk to Rangeley Lake. Oquossoc, although compact, had a lot to offer. We'd had ice cream yesterday afternoon at The Gingerbread House restaurant, just one of several places in town to eat and shop. The Rangeley Outdoor Sporting Heritage Museum had an authentic Rangeley boat on display beside the road. The portage was easy, but I thought sympathetically of Sydney and Marji, who would either need to find a ride or carry their canoe for a long mile.

I put in and found Rangeley Lake bursting with people on this bright sunny morning. Many were out on the water in brightly colored kayaks or on paddleboards. Some were lounging on their docks, visiting or reading. It was the essence of what summer should be. After a few miles, I came upon an especially friendly woman, who put aside her book to shout hello. She looked as though she wanted to talk, which was fine with me.

"How far have you paddled?" she asked.

The wind had been gradually gusting stronger, and I gripped her dock tightly to steady myself and keep from blowing away. I looked down at my GPS and thought for a minute. This was going to be fun. "Oh, about 445 miles," I said in my most nonchalant tone.

She laughed and I knew she thought I was kidding. After I told her about my journey, though, she was so enthusiastic. We visited for a while, then she started cheering and shouting encouragement as I said goodbye and let go of the dock, immediately digging my paddle in against the wind. I risked a quick glance back and saw her talking excitedly with her husband, who had come down from their cottage with a cup of coffee.

Her joy had given me the extra energy I needed for the last few miles, which I paddled in almost gale conditions. My GPS recorded about seven miles crossing Rangeley Lake, rather than the ten indicated on the map, for which I was supremely grateful. Map 8 ended at the town of Rangeley's Lakeside Park. I celebrated the milestone with coconut shrimp and a salad at the Parkside & Main restaurant, before starting to walk through town.

"Laurie, hello!"

I stopped in surprise, hearing my name as I navigated my rig between the cars parked at an angle along touristy Main Street. Back in June, at the Maine Canoe Symposium, I'd met Beth and Paul Whalon, thru-paddlers from the summer before. They'd sat down with me for an hour, studying maps and telling trail stories. They hadn't had any trouble spotting me, as my appearance simply shouted "thru-paddler."

"We've just been to Ecopelagicon, to thank them for their help last year."

"That's where I'm headed," I replied. When I had passed through Rangeley the last time, the trail had gone a different way. "I'm really looking forward to trying out the new portage. Last time I had to walk on the highway all the way to the logging museum. Now it's been renamed the Maine Forestry Museum, and you can paddle there across Haley Pond."

"Back then, I camped in pouring rain under the museum's pavilion. Now there's a new lean-to there, that NFCT built last year." The place was quickly turning into a paddlers' campus.

"Congratulations on your progress so far," said Beth, who'd been following my blog ever since I left in June. "You have most of the worst of it behind you, for sure. I remember we reached a point in Maine where suddenly we just knew: We were going to do this." Beth and Paul had earned the double asterisks, for finishing the trail unassisted.

After hearty hugs and accosting a stranger to take our picture, we said goodbye.

I walked away slowly, thinking about what Beth had said, about knowing they would finish. I remembered the moment at Grey Gables, when I realized I had a chance of making it all the way. Then, crossing the Maine border had been another huge milestone. Certainly, I now knew I had a good chance of making it all the way. There were still many miles to go, though, and risks and dangers left to face. Being overconfident could have serious consequences.

It was just a short walk to Ecopelagicon, an outdoor outfitter and store with arguably the most creative business name along the trail. From their dock, the portage route crossed Haley Pond to a well-maintained, but non-wheelable, trail with good signage and sturdy bog bridges. It led to the museum, where I discovered two of NFCT's summer interns hard at work. Matt and Evan were there with staff member Noah Pollock, getting ready for a volunteer work trip that would build a new privy near the lean-to.

Vital to NFCT's growth is the development of community partnerships such as the exemplary one unfolding in Rangeley. And vital to the work itself are the people—NFCT's staff, interns, and volunteers—who do the grunt work.

My day ended with a true mountaintop experience. I left my boat in the care of Matt and Evan and went for a ride. Paul and Janie's van climbed and climbed up nearby Quill Hill, 12 winding miles on a gravel road built by a construction contractor just for fun.

We wound our way upward past encouraging signs marking our progress: *QUILL HILL 12 min. to the top*, then *QUILL HILL 9 min. to the top*, then *6*, then *3*, and then we were there. The summit had bright clean picnic tables and a stunning 360-degree view. From high above, I gazed back nostalgically at where I'd been and looked ahead toward where I was going—distant Flagstaff Lake in the shadow of the mighty Bigelows.

In between lay the mysterious and intimidating miles of the South Branch of the Dead River, whose ghosts I would face tomorrow.

CHAPTER 12

PUTTING OLD GHOSTS TO REST

Mottled brown, unseen
trilling notes lift up my heart,
who and where are you?

—Laurie Chandler, "Hermit Thrush"

*I*t's all downhill from here, I thought, as I plopped down early the next morning for some water and a rest. I had climbed Route 16 from the forestry museum to the highest point left on the trail, the divide between the Androscoggin and Kennebec watersheds, elevation 1,685 feet. Not just downhill physically, but mentally, too, although not far ahead lay the section of river where I had pinned my kayak four years earlier.

This time around, in late July, low water levels were likely to be my biggest obstacle. It wasn't raining and the South Branch of the Dead River had a reputation for being "dead" by mid-summer. In fact, Map 9 read, *"After mid-May, this small river may be too shallow to run."* Many past thru-paddlers had not even attempted the river's 19 downstream miles. Noah, though, had encouraged me to try, simply reinforcing what I knew I was going to do.

The first mile of the river was like the Nulhegan. There were alders and runnable beaver dams and yellow swamp candles along the muddy banks. I lifted over one fallen tree and wiggled the canoe under another. It was a good beginning.

Unobtrusively, a few rocks began to break the surface, as the river widened and came to life. Regal fir and spruce gradually replaced the shrubby alder, and my heart lifted at the beauty of this place that many people never saw. *It would have made me sad to miss this,* I reassured myself. *And it's only a mile more to the portage around the falls. How hard can it be?*

Then the current grew serious and the rocks more numerous. Soon, I had to hop out, not particularly surprised. I walked, I pulled, I maneuvered through four boulder gardens, fighting my way along and adding some new scratches to my now well-decorated boat. In places, I could still paddle. The last half mile took half an hour to navigate, but finally the little yellow sign marking the portage around Fansanger Falls came into sight.

Confident of my route this time, I followed the cracked remnants of long-abandoned Old Route 16. The narrow, tattered road did not look wide enough for two cars to pass, but somehow it had worked. For years, it had been all there was. Now it was a restful place to push my boat and let my mind drift. I daydreamed up an antique car and a family, on their way to grandma's house for Sunday dinner. Long ago, back when a drive was an adventure, with a crock of baked beans and an apple pie waiting at the end.

Soon I passed the camp where I'd had my cocoa and then the put-in, where this year I just continued walking. Intermittent glimpses of the river confirmed how low the water was.

Three miles along, a road turned off and crossed the river, en route to a sand and gravel quarry. The bridge wasn't on my map, but it was busy. Kids perched fishing from the steep, rocky banks, and a group was unloading kayaks from the backs of pickups. That looked promising. The water, they told me, was great all the way to the Kennebago Road bridge, where I planned to take out. To me, though, the river still looked very shallow. I decided to walk another mile to the next bridge at Langtown Mill.

Finally, there was enough water and no one around as I put in on river right, upstream of the bridge. In fact, the current grew stronger and the river deeper as I continued downriver. I knew that the place where I capsized must be just a couple of miles ahead and wondered if I would recognize it, or somehow know it.

At the first fast, sweeping turn, I fought the urge to jump out and walk. It took courage to trust myself and remember all the miles that my canoe and I had safely traveled. *Stay in control, don't get pulled to the outside.* I concentrated and shot around that bend and others, too, even some with nasty strainers. The afternoon wore on. In several areas, with less water and more rocks, I was forced to walk what would have been fun rapids at higher water levels.

In the end, I never did spot my tree, but it didn't matter. The memory of that day was simply a part of who I had become. It would be there forever, I knew, somewhere inside me.

Gradually, river conditions improved. I relaxed, weary but delighted that I had been able to paddle a good chunk of the "dead" river. From the bridge not far ahead, I'd walk eight miles along a busy highway to Stratton tomorrow. So, after nine strenuous hours, it was time to find a place to camp, a stealth camp, as there were no established campsites along this section of the South Branch.

Suddenly, above a small gravel beach on the left, the top of the riverbank looked mowed. I pulled over to investigate. Climbing up, I found a farm road. From downriver, it wound along the shore and dead-ended in a large hayfield. Straight across the road was a small, secluded grassy area invisible from the water. There were no buildings in sight and no one to ask for permission. Inspired by a desire for secrecy and a myriad of mosquitoes and black flies, my tent went up as quickly as it ever had. I slept the peaceful sleep of exhaustion.

In the pinkish dawn, I was up, packed, and out to Route 16 early. Far in the distance, a raccoon crossed the road, and then I met Ralph, riding his bicycle to town to get a newspaper. It was a small world. Ralph's son was doing a summer project for college about the Northern Forest Canoe Trail, and we chatted for a while.

I was in a great mood, excited for some upcoming trail magic.

My friend Mary Berger was taking me to Sugarloaf, one of Maine's premier ski mountains, for the night. Mary is the soul of kindness and hospitality. Back home, she often shares her lovely lakefront home with friends and the community. When she lost her husband, an avid supporter of youth athletics, she and fellow Rotarian Mike Hall worked together to found Karl's Kids. This nonprofit honors Karl's spirit by providing financial help for sports-related expenses to many children who otherwise couldn't participate. Today she was going to be my trail angel, making time in her busy schedule to whisk me away for an evening of fun.

By lunchtime, I was at Stratton's White Wolf Inn, one of those quirky places that enthusiastically welcome hikers and paddlers. I'd stayed there on my last trip and discovered delicious food and caring, helpful people, who this time were happy to keep my boat overnight.

Mary arrived just as I was finishing my pecan pie. As we drove to Sugarloaf, she listened intently to all my stories and asked lots of questions. We had a ball together, soaking in the hot tub and sharing news from home while we snuggled in the bathrobes we'd found in our room. Later, eating pulled pork nachos at The Rack, I was surprised to meet the bus drivers from my school, who were there for their annual summer conference.

The next morning, Mary's solid goodbye hug left me almost teary. I lowered my canoe quietly into the stream that ran behind the White Wolf Inn. Thoughtfully, I wound my way through the edge of the village and out onto Flagstaff Lake.

Chris and I had come to Flagstaff together, for a weekend not long after we were married. For the first time on this long journey, I would be where we had been together, see the beauty we had shared and never would again. Chris was very much in my heart that morning.

I hadn't really gone that far when I stopped along the shore and dug out my journal. I wrestled to find words, my mind deep in the past.

The sound of voices brought me back to the present.

It was Sydney and Marji!

I hadn't had any news from them since we'd said goodbye along the Carry Road. I paddled out, pulling my canoe alongside theirs. I couldn't wait to hear everything.

Thankfully, they had gotten rescued in grand style. Not by the folks at Lakewood Camps, but by Aldro French himself. Aldro had been around after all and hosted them in his yurt for two nights. He truly was about to sell most of his property, but would keep a small place for himself. I was happy to think that Aldro would still be there, fishing the Rapid River.

When they arrived in Rangeley, Sydney and Marji had finally caught up with their new wheels, then taken a shuttle to Stratton. *I'm glad they can keep on going*, I thought, as they paddled away into the distance. *They deserve to enjoy Maine.*

Soon the broad expanse of water opened before me. On my right, to the south, the bulk of the Bigelow Range rose in a solid wall, an impressive backdrop on a scale with this far-reaching lake. For Maine, these were serious mountains, including two of the state's fourteen 4,000-footers. The Appalachian Trail ran along the ridge, in its closest proximity to the NFCT, crossing Mount Bigelow's West and Avery peaks at 4,150 and 4,086 feet, respectively.

Dramatic is the word that comes to mind when I think of Flagstaff. The weather, the scenery, and the history that created this place are all dramatic.

Chris and I had camped along the south shore, at Round Barn, once the site of a farm and sawmill. We had been on a mission to see the wild places of Maine, as many as we could. Money had been tight, with four kids at home. Here the camping was free, first-come, first-served, although campers did need a fire permit. Best of all, we could paddle and hike, all from one spot.

Practically from our tent site, the Safford Brook Trail climbed steeply for two or three miles to meet the Appalachian Trail. We left for a hike early one morning, full of energy. Our goal, as usual, was to rest and have lunch at the top, on Mount Bigelow's Avery Peak. Along the way, though, Chris kindly tamed his long legs to match my pace so we could talk.

The summit was well worth the effort. After turning right on the Appalachian Trail, we continued to climb steeply for another mile to the crest of the ridge. Above treeline now, we followed white-blazed rocks in a scramble to the highest point. There, a plaque honored Maine native Myron Avery, who had taken founder Benton MacKaye's AT dream and turned it into reality.

The Northern Forest Canoe Trail, too, had gone from visionary concept to accomplished fact, a tribute to the cooperation and commitment of many people, who brought to the project a broad spectrum of relevant backgrounds and abilities. The trail's evolution is a tale in and of itself.

Remember Mike Krepner, Randy Mardres, and Ron Canter, whose passion was slogging up tiny creeks and toiling over lengthy portages to retrace ancient native routes? In 1997, they approached the Mad River Canoe Company in search of folding canoes for a Belize expedition. This contact would lead to the creation of the NFCT.

In 1999, after selling Mad River Canoe, former Owner Kay Henry and Marketing VP Rob Center agreed to create a nonprofit organization to bring the NFCT route to life, using information from the three original researchers. Their goal was to exponentially increase public access to New England's northern waterways.

From their home in Waitsfield, Vermont, Kay and Rob created a business plan outlining the funding that would be required to divide the proposed trail into sections, each anchored by a host organization with local participation. The key pieces came together from the Federal government and the outdoor industry. Vermont's Senator Patrick Leahy quickly understood the importance that a historically significant water trail could have for economic development in the Northern Forest region. He led an effort of the four states' congressional delegations to find the critical start-up funding through National Park Service-administered federal grants. Meanwhile, The Mountaineers Books agreed to under-write the publication of the 13 section maps.

On National Trails Day 2006, dedication events took place to officially open the NFCT and celebrate the federal, state, and community partners that took a leadership role in its establishment. Today, the Northern Forest Canoe Trail offers 188 public access points, and there is something for everyone—for families, for hardcore whitewater enthusiasts, for those with a day or a week, as well as the relatively few who attempt a thru-paddle.

In describing the trail, Rob likes to say that it offers "a lifetime of adventures." As I was discovering, there was the draw of history, wildlife, and the trail's scenic beauty; the opportunity for remote camping or comfortable, even luxurious, accommodation; and everywhere, people who turn out to be kindred spirits. For me, this year, my NFCT journey was ambitious, challenging, and not even guaranteed to be successful. It had already been more dangerous, strenuous, and involved than anything that most people would want to tackle. However, the appeal of the trail was that it was there, and accessible, to many thousands of people, with a broad range of hopes and expectations for their adventures in the north woods.

From the summit of Avery Peak, Chris and I sat looking down on an incredible vista. The view would have been hard to match from a float plane. Curving arms of green framed blue waters textured with sunlight and dotted with round islands of different shapes and sizes. Behind the lake, and around the lake, stretched hills and mountains as far as the eye could see.

Now, paddling the waters far below, that day did not seem that long ago after all. And remembering it was a good thing, that made me want to smile more than cry.

I thought I knew why. Without a doubt, Chris would have approved of my current adventure. I imagined his spirit there, encouraging me as he often had in life. Our few years together had had as many ups and downs as hiking Avery Peak, but through it all, Chris had believed in me. I remembered the time when my friend Barbara had urged me to apply for the job as youth minister at our church. It was Chris who had seen the vision first, and he'd been right. I'd gone on to have many fulfilling years of ministry, even leading worship a few times.

The woman back on Rangeley Lake was another good example of the power of encouragement. Look how my canoe had conquered the winds after she'd cheered me on. She probably didn't even know what she had done, but that didn't make it any less important. I hoped when I got home I would remember to cheer on others when they could use it.

I must have been feeling poetic, too. I started jotting notes that so far haven't made it into a poem, but probably should: *The cadence of my paddle is the heartbeat of the canoe. The mountains shrug off their stole of clouds to bathe in rays of light. A primeval loon yodels, its striking hues and unearthly voice created for a day like this.*

Much of Flagstaff is surrounded by public land. Maine's Public Reserved Lands total over half a million acres, including more than 36,000 acres in the Bigelow Preserve. These lands are managed for multiple use, for forest products as well as wildlife habitat and recreation. Here, as in the vast forests of northern Maine, responsible timber harvesting supports affordable recreational access to key wilderness areas.

Just as the mountains are layered one on another, in soft shades of blue and green and purple, there are layers within Maine's public land system. The multiple-use philosophy allows for income generation, which in turn protects areas of special ecological significance. Within this larger block, the 10,540-acre Bigelow Ecological Reserve protects 171 acres of heath alpine ridge, home to fragile populations of several rare plant species.

The growing wind was blowing from the northwest and I crossed to the protected northern shore of the long east-west lake. Near the lake's midpoint, Jim Eaton Hill rose sharply from the water, its slopes a blend of shades of green. Here and there, well-hidden cabins peeked shyly out from the forest. Their architecture echoed the colors and beauty of the surrounding hardwoods, reminding me of the Great Camps in the Adirondacks.

What I couldn't see were the other homes, gone now for 65 years. Three small villages lived on only in old photos and cherished memories, their physical remains buried beneath the waters of manmade Flagstaff

Lake. The proposal to create the lake had become a reality in 1927, when the bill authorizing the construction of Long Falls Dam was approved by the Maine state legislature. The Kennebec Reservoir Company now had the right to seize the property it needed along 25 miles of the Dead River, by the right of eminent domain.

Many homes were moved to nearby towns, as was a tablet commemorating Benedict Arnold's famous march to Quebec during the Revolutionary War. During Arnold's march, the colonel reportedly climbed a handmade flagpole in a camp along the Dead River, to hang the flag of the brand-new United States. This event gave Flagstaff its name.

In 1950, the gates of newly constructed Long Falls Dam closed and the water began to rise, filling the narrow river valley. People's homes had been traded for electricity.

I could still sense the lingering ghosts of those villages—Flagstaff, Dead River, and Bigelow. The uncaring water had continued to rise, covering the buildings that were left. Wide front porches where generations of family had gathered to visit and drink lemonade. Rooms where babies were born and pickles were canned and homework done by the light of kerosene lamps. Kerosene, because none of the three villages ever had central electrical service. Residents of Flagstaff Village only had electricity in off-peak hours, when the water-powered generator at the local mill was not needed for manufacturing.

Along Jim Eaton Hill, I found a reminder of those long-gone days. A willow tree grew in the shallows, its leaves still green. Next to it, a rusty iron post leaned wearily with age. Under the wavering water, I discovered the foundation of some long-forgotten structure, a curious pattern of manmade shapes. I beached the canoe and wandered the shore, finding mute fragments of the past. As I held the bits of brick and ceramic in my palm, I thought sadly of those whose lives had once played out beneath the waters we paddled.

At Hurricane Island, I caught up to Sydney and Marji and we ate lunch. It made sense to paddle on together. Terns swooped over the wide water and we flew too, with the wind at our backs. Most of the lake's 21 miles were behind us by the time we made camp on another island near the east end of the lake.

It was a site without many amenities, brushy and buggy. In my journal, I noted the serenading of many loons and not much else. Supper for me was yogurt. All three us were tired and quiet, reading in our tents

Maine's Grand Falls is the highest waterfall on the Northern Forest Canoe Trail

by an early hour. I'd picked up the sequel to *Watership Down* in Stratton and was enjoying the novelty of having a book to read for fun.

Up at 4:30, I was soon gone, motivated by a much-anticipated rendezvous. My son, Taylor, and my parents were meeting me at the Grand Falls Hut for the night.

The "hut," owned by the nonprofit Maine Huts & Trails, was truly a comfortable, eco-friendly backcountry lodge. The organization's ambitious plan, inspired by hut-to-hut trekking in Europe, was to build ten huts in all, connected by an extensive system of trails for cross country skiing, hiking, and even mountain biking. So far, there were four, including one on Flagstaff Lake and one ahead, just a mile beyond where the NFCT would turn north up Spencer Stream toward the Moose River.

The road around Long Falls Dam was mostly wheelable after a short carry. Along the way, a side trail led to an impressive view of the falls. The river raced with abandon down a narrow gorge, spray rising above the froth. Tall conifers kept watch over continuous whitewater in both directions, as far as I could see.

I returned to the road and crossed a bridge to Big Eddy, where several campsites were squeezed in along the edge of the road. At this early hour, it was still quiet, though there were tents everywhere. One young woman slept out in the open. I wheeled carefully and quietly by, just inches from her tousled head. She never stirred.

A bit of moving water started me down the otherwise calm six or seven miles that were left of the Dead River. I drifted gently around the bends in the hopes of finally discovering a moose, but found only eagles, kingfishers, and mergansers.

Majestic Grand Falls was audible well before I reached it. The old portage route around the falls had been confusing and hard to follow. Now, thanks to another thriving partnership, the new and shorter 1.5-mile portage began at the Maine Huts & Trails aluminum dock. I used my portage yoke for the first half mile, then wheeled the rest, passing the first ripe blueberries of the trip and one of Mom's favorite flowers, pearly everlasting.

I climbed up a side trail to view the falls. With its 40-foot drop, Grand Falls was the largest waterfall on the Northern Forest Canoe Trail. The entire width of the river dropped in a curtain of crashing water, cascading over and around the huge boulders within its path. The top of the falls was not protected in any way. I stared at the wall of white, imagining the feeling of approaching the drop from above, unaware. In the relentless grip of the current, seeing nothing but the river dropping away and a spray of mist rising from the mysteries below.

At the Spencer Stream turnoff, I sent a SPOT message and went "off duty." With that, Map 9 was finished, and it was time to celebrate with family. Tomorrow I would take my end-of-map photo with Taylor, before heading north.

I wheeled toward the hut, passing the turnoff for a small fishermen's parking lot with fond memories. During Paddle for Hope, I'd rested there, drying gear, making tea, and waiting for my parents to rescue me. My back had been bothering me after my misadventure on the South Branch and I was going to skip around the upstream section ahead.

It was there that I first remember hearing the sweet notes of the hermit thrush, although back then I didn't know its name. In the margin of my journal, I wrote, "*What is the bird that trills so beautifully?*" Later, I identified the song from the Cornell Lab of Ornithology's website, *All About Birds*, the best resource ever for bird watchers.

To me, the hermit thrush embodies joy and, like the loon, seems to appear when times are tough and I need some uplifting. In the dawn, its lyrical call gently wakes you and in the shadows of the evening, it says

Taylor and Mom on the trail to the Grand Falls Hut

goodnight. Its gift is its music. Shy and unremarkable in appearance, this little brown thrush, with a speckled breast, scratches around the forest floor in search of insects. Its cascade of flutelike notes, though, are like a mountain brook captured in melody. *All About Birds* gives the notes these words—*"Oh, holy, holy, ah, purity, purity, eeh, sweetly, sweetly."* I couldn't have said it better myself.

I hadn't seen Taylor for months. He had driven up from Virginia to join me for a single night. All four of us hiked into the hut, accidentally taking the longer, more rugged way. For Mom, it was a challenge, but with Taylor's help, she made it. Bunchberry, a tiny low-growing member of the dogwood family, was plentiful along the trail. Bunchberry has white flowers, miniature twins of those on flowering dogwood. By mid-summer, the flowers turn to vibrant red berries that are edible when ripe.

Our lodging included dinner, breakfast, and a packed lunch. Caretakers Nate and Sarah fed us steak, rice and beans, salad, roasted vegetables, Cuban bread, and blueberry cobbler. Spending time with Taylor, though, was the best part. After dinner, we walked over to the falls, then stayed up late playing Uno and visiting with some of the other guests. I crawled into my sleeping bag happy and ready for whatever tomorrow might bring.

CHAPTER 13

TAKING THE HIDDEN PATH

Still 'round the corner there may wait
A new road or a secret gate;
And though I oft have passed them by,
A day will come at last when I
Shall take the hidden paths that run
West of the Moon, East of the Sun.

—**J.R.R. Tolkien**, *The Return of the King*

For four years, every time I'd told my story, it was with the addendum, "I paddled all but seven miles of the Northern Forest Canoe Trail in Maine." Hopefully, I would never have to say those words again. Like a monster under the bed, the thought of going up these two elusive streams had pulled me and terrified me. Now I was ready to get it over with. Having Taylor to hug me and start me on my way that morning was the icing on the cake.

The Companion had this to say about the route ahead: *"Regardless of the time of year, heading up Spencer Stream to Little Spencer Stream to Spencer Lake is going to take most of the day, a large part of it poling, tracking, or walking instead of paddling."*

Sydney and Marji had camped in an attractive, roomy site near where Spencer Stream flowed into the Dead River. The three of us started out together, although I soon left them behind, bravely struggling along with their much heavier boat. I had a reservation to camp on Fish Pond, above Spencer Lake, and invited them to share my site that night.

Conditions on Spencer Stream were better than I had anticipated. I could paddle short stretches and decided to keep track of my paddle strokes for an accurate trip report. After two hours, I had gone two miles and reached the confluence with Little Spencer Stream. Eight times I had been able to get in the boat and paddle for short distances. In case you're wondering, I counted 230, 57, 73, 62, 120, 331, 154, and 150 strokes. After months of worrying and wondering about this remote, seldom-paddled water, I was surviving and making progress slowly.

Even my friend Mack Truax, a fast and strong thru-paddler, had gone astray here this past spring. On his GPS, Mack had seen what looked like a network of interconnected roads that seemed far simpler to navigate than dragging his 17-foot sea kayak up these shallow streams. But the roads kept fading away into swamp or forest and leading nowhere.

Bits and pieces of his story came back to me: *"21 miles on logging roads to portage around a seven-mile stretch…maybe the most physically demanding day of my life…crawling on my hands and knees through something that looked like a rabbit trail…best I could find was standing marsh water…I poured it through my camp towel and treated it with chemicals…do not attempt to take logging roads."* And this was the guy who had been training 25 miles a day in icy winter!

In his scariest hour, a tiny road that Mack had been following ended at a streamside picnic area. A bridge that showed clearly on his GPS map wasn't there, so he decided to try following the feeder stream back to Spencer Stream. Here's the story from his trail journal:

The stream immediately became fast water with rapids and I ultimately ditched out on an eddy. The current was so strong it slowly started to pull me over what looked like a Class II rapid that headed towards a canyon with tall cliffs on both sides. I became perched on a rock without my spray skirt on and unprepared to take on what was around the corner. Somehow I managed to exit my kayak and crawl onto the rocks where I was able to back my boat off the rock and stay perched on a dry surface.

I was scared, really scared! This part of my blog is being written after I arrived safely home because I knew that I couldn't tell the real story with my wife and friends reading the journal. Truth be told I do not believe I would have survived going over rapids. When I eventually calmed down I climbed up a very steep bank to see what was ahead of me around the canyon. It dropped off into some nasty looking rapids that on the map are called Spencer Gut. Not good. We talk about trail angels helping us out and in this case I had a real angel keep me from going over. I have a very difficult time even talking about it and thank God that I'm even around today.

Mack was forced to camp as darkness fell. In the morning, using GPS waypoints for guidance, he bushwhacked six-tenths of a mile back to Little Spencer Stream. It took three round trips straight through thick brush and swamp, the last while carrying and dragging his 66-pound sea kayak. From there, it was still several miles upstream to Spencer Lake.

Thinking of Mack's adventure, I turned up Little Spencer Stream and found conditions much the same. I walked with both hands on the boat to steady myself. Carefully, my river shoes stretched for stable footing on the softer, safer pockets of orange sand between the round and slippery rocks. My faithful boat followed. Where I could, I paddled, giving my feet a welcome rest. In the four hours since I'd said goodbye to Taylor, I had been in and out of the boat 24 times.

There was no denying, though, the beauty and the spirit of this wild place. Here was more water that must be earned. Cedar and spruce clung to rocky slopes, and an intense aroma of fir infused the damp air. By now, all that was left of my packed lunch was one of Sarah's no-bake chocolate, peanut butter, and oatmeal cookies. I stopped to eat it, beneath a brownish-gray wall of rock covered with ferns and lichens. Lost in thought, I struggled for words to capture the essence of what I was feeling. Then a sound, a soft squeal, pulled me back.

I looked up and into the eyes of a moose. It was fitting, somehow, that the first moose of my journey would find me here, on this isolated, wild stream that had for so long been an enigma. She was comfortably on the other shore, peeking out from some bushes. First, she sniffed, then turned her head this way and that, trying to puzzle me out. She settled, and stayed. I stayed, too, hardly breathing as I nibbled my cookie.

At last, I told her softly, speaking the words out loud, "I won't hurt you. I'm going to go and leave this place to you." But when I moved, she faded away into the brush, a spirit animal.

Where Parker and Parker Bog brooks entered, one on each side, the stream deepened. Now, in places, I could paddle 500 strokes, rather than 50, before hopping out. And when I walked, now it was on a cleanly washed sand and gravel bottom. Striking yellow-gold Canada lilies brightened the shoreline. I was approaching the deadwaters—Lower, Middle, and Upper—that marked the approach to Spencer Lake.

Lower Deadwater was like a tiny pond, heavenly after the miles that lay behind.

Then came another hurdle. Before Middle Deadwater, I ascended some of the strongest rapids I'd survived so far. A few times, I had to make a breathtaking stretch through racing current to reach an anchor rock. To keep from being swept off my feet, I would immediately sit down for stability and slowly work the boat up against the surging water, one hand at a time. The few deep channels between boulders were invariably found just where the opposing current was the strongest.

Having arrived safely in the second tiny pond, I had to concentrate on navigation.

The traditional portage route began farther upstream, above Upper Deadwater. Approaching Spencer Lake that way was more of an inventive scramble and climb up a cliff than a trail. *The Companion* described the complicated process of ascending the steep gully. *"Tie your vessel to some small, scrubby trees that have taken root in the rocky crevices so you can unload and get everything to the top. You'll need to lift or drag your boat up onto the ledge."*

In 2011, I'd stood on the top of that 30-foot granite cliff at the bottom of Spencer Lake, looking wistfully down at the wild, rugged course of the stream I'd missed.

I dreaded trying to get my boat up that cliff by myself.

I could also see more powerful rapids just above Middle Deadwater, an added incentive to go a different way. On her thru-paddle, Katina had done this section with her daughter Kacia. Late on a weary evening, they had discovered a trail on this second deadwater. It led to a gravel road that conveniently went right to Spencer Lake. Although it was not an official portage, Dan Brown and others had successfully followed this alternative route, avoiding the need to scale the steep cliff. I fervently hoped to do the same.

The clue to finding the start of the trail would be an aluminum rowboat pulled up on shore. Not only was it there, but next to it was a green canoe. I carried up a short trail to a small clearing, turned right on a woods road, and wheeled confidently down to the lake. A loon was waiting to greet me as I emerged victorious near a cabin by the dam. The seven-mile ascent of both streams had taken me six hours and 20 minutes.

Spencer Lake and Fish Pond are hidden gems, undeveloped and pristine. Both offer free camping in small campgrounds, with reservations in advance. I'd been impressed with the clean and spacious sites on my first trip, when Mom and Dad had dropped me off to paddle down the length of the lakes and back. The sturdy outhouse on Spencer Lake had even been equipped for camping. Hanging neatly on the wall were a handsaw, grill, and cast-iron skillet!

Slowly, I covered six more long miles. I stopped to poke along the shore, collecting driftwood, or *dri-ki* as it's called in Maine. In camp, it made a quick campfire, crackling briskly as I set up my tent. Before long, I heard voices and waved to Sydney and Marji. They were continuing to impress me with their strength and stamina. *If Sydney had my boat, I bet she would have already finished, with both asterisks.*

The next morning, I unwittingly gave Sydney and Marji some bad advice. For years, the channel at the top of Fish Pond had been difficult to find for many NFCT paddlers, including me. The alternative was to wheel out along the campground entrance road and around, adding two miles to the six-mile portage along logging roads up to the Moose River.

Sydney and Marji left first, going the longer way by road, while I sat journaling and giving my sore muscles more time to wake up. Soon, though, a motorboat pulled up. Chris, the campground manager, came over to chat. I explained why there had been three names listed on our registration form and where my friends had gone and why.

"Oh, you can almost see the channel from here," was his confident response. "Come down to shore and I'll show you."

Chris was right, I realized sheepishly. The channel was indeed clearly visible today. I felt badly for my friends and even worse later, when I glimpsed a startled moose along the short paddle to Hardscrabble Road. There were a couple of beaver dams to lift over and a new wildflower, like a tiny blue-purple orchid, called Allegheny monkey flower.

The day was already turning hot and humid as I started slowly up the dusty road. Not far along, a small road led off to the right, by a sign that read *POW MEMORIAL*. I left my boat and walked through a campsite to a small clearing. There, a granite marker stood in front of a crumbling brick structure covered with olive-green moss. A few pieces of rusty metal lay scattered on top. This was the most tangible evidence of a surprising time in Jackman's history.

Back in 1944, in just eight weeks, the U.S. Army had built a prisoner of war camp here, its buildings rising like a phoenix from the endless forest. A mess hall, washroom with laundry, hospital, post exchange, chapel, and five large barracks where 250 German POW's lived under the command of their own officers.

The *Waterville Morning Sentinel* described the arrival of the first prisoners that summer: *"A few citizens…went to the railroad station, and stood in the darkness watching the prisoners of war in the lighted cars. They were just an average group of young men ranging from 18 to 27 years of age, blond and blue-eyed, all looking older than their years. Dressed in clothing like the U.S. soldiers, they wore white caps with visors and had the letters W.P. in red on the back of their shirts or jackets."*

For work, the men harvested pulpwood for the Hollingsworth and Whitney Company. The logs were transported by water, floated down to the Dead River and on to markets along the Kennebec. Surprisingly, their journey followed the same narrow way I'd just travelled.

There were four main POW camps in the state, the largest attached to the Army airbase in Houlton, northwest up near Canada. The 3,000 prisoners housed there between July 1944 and May 1946 worked on local farms, picking potatoes and harvesting other crops.

It was sad to think of so much history just sinking into the forest floor, gone and forgotten, a piece of a foreign war that had come to distant Maine. One local resident remembered the time when three prisoners escaped on homemade snowshoes and were soon captured with just eleven cents in their pockets. These were stories that shouldn't be lost.

For those men, World War II had not just meant the terror of battle in the muddy fields of distant France, but cutting pulpwood, and even making friends, here in Maine. In 2009, the town of Houlton had invited all surviving POW's who had been imprisoned there to return for a visit and to be made honorary residents of the town. Four came, rekindling friendships with townspeople they had known and worked with sixty years before.

The granite marker hadn't been here long. With the help of community grants, it was erected by the Forest Hills eighth grade class of 2007, as part of a service learning project. When teacher Deborah Achey first brought her class here from nearby Jackman, there wasn't much to see. A rusty saw blade, an ancient can of meat, and this square of bricks with an opening clearly meant for baking bread. It had been the camp oven. The students researched local POW history and then worked to fulfill the dream of commemorating "their" camp with a memorial like the one they'd seen while visiting Houlton.

Back on the road again and tackling a long uphill, I was having trouble making progress. Large patches of ripe, red raspberries grew along the sunny roadside, in easy reach. I kept pausing to pick and eat them by the handful. Judging by the scat along the road, the bears shared my enthusiasm. As I dawdled, my mind drifted back four years, to the night when events had forced me to stealth camp for the very first time.

I'd planned to camp at the POW site. I was walking slowly that late afternoon, too, and anticipating the fun of exploring the old camp. Not far from the turnoff, though, I paused. The smell of wood smoke is usually cheery, but not when you are tired in every muscle and heading for the only campsite around. Drawing closer, I heard men's voices, talking and laughing, confirming my fears. The site was taken and I slipped quietly past, thinking that there was no need to advertise my presence. I would, though, need somewhere to sleep.

A gravel pit on the right had plenty of space, but my tent would have been visible from the road. I kept on going. A little farther on, an inviting road curved away into open woods, behind a substantial barricade of sturdy boulders. No one would be driving in there, and a quick survey revealed several flat, gravelly spots out of sight of the main road.

Quickly, hoping no one would notice me, I did what I needed to do, with a surprising sense of urgency. I almost ran back and forth with my gear, hiding everything temporarily behind the boulders. Stealth camping had sounded adventurous in theory, but now I felt unsettled and nervous. I'm not sure why. Perhaps it was the thought of the loud, rowdy voices around the campfire back at the POW campsite.

So far, no one had passed me during the whole portage and my luck held. With the wheels still attached, I hauled my kayak up into the woods and covered it with ferns and brush. The yellow of the boat still showed, so I piled on more, until it lay safe and hidden. Just as I finished, inspected my work, and hustled out of sight around the bend, I heard one, two, then three vehicles pass by.

That turned out to be a beautiful place to camp, on a knoll where I looked out my tent window down the peaceful road. In the evening, though, I heard gunshots three different times from the direction of my POW neighbors. The rest of the night passed quietly and uneventfully.

Later, I learned that my parents had come to the POW camp looking for me and talked to the guys there, who seemed friendly after all. They said a German girl had visited that day with her grandfather, who had been a prisoner there so many years before. To meet the pair would have been an unforgettable experience. Nonetheless, I was glad that I had trusted my instincts and knew that I would continue to do so.

A mile or two up the road, I was pulled abruptly back to the present. There were Sydney and Marji, sitting quietly by their unmoving canoe, drinking some water. They were remarkably calm, considering that their brand-new wheels had broken, after just a few miles of use. Sydney was certainly learning the lessons in patience and perseverance that she would need for leading expeditions one day.

We ate raspberries while we talked through what to do. A solution presented itself when the faint sound of a motor grew louder. It was a young man on a motorcycle, who pulled up with a smile and a rueful shake of his curly light brown hair. Scotty was headed home to Jackman, which he hoped to reach before the last of his gas ran out. It would be close, he thought, but he promised to return with his pickup to get Sydney and Marji. So, we said farewell once more, with hopes of meeting that night at the Jackman Landing Campground.

The last few miles to the put-in were punishingly hot and I stopped often. That day, I drank an entire gallon of water. After launching my boat, though, my energy returned. The wild river featured a parade of giant boulders, a testament to the vast power of the glacier that had moved them. "*Glacial erratics,*" I wrote, "*God's punctuation on a river of immense beauty.*"

*My daughter Megan and I paddled the Moose River
and camped at Attean Falls in 2011*

I would follow the Moose River for 46 miles to Moosehead Lake, through Attean Pond, Big Wood Pond, and the town of Jackman, then Long Pond, Little Brassua (BRASS-aw) Lake, and Brassua Lake. This would be my third time over most of this route and I expected to see more wildlife than people.

Although generally calm, there were two short sections of white-water, after about seven miles. Both Attean Rips and adjacent Attean Falls, a Class II rapid, had portage trails for the cautious. I'd first come here in 2010, choosing the Moose River Bow Trip for my first short solo wilderness kayaking adventure. This 34-mile loop partly overlaps the NFCT and is a great choice for families or beginners.

That first time, I smoothly ran Attean Rips, emerging in a large pool of sunshine and reflections, where blue flag bloomed. Along the left side of the pool stretched an enormous beaver lodge. On the right, a small creek dotted with lily pads came curving around a bend and entered the pool. The second portage trail began beside the stream, ran through several campsites on a small bluff, and ended below Attean Falls.

It was mid-June and the river was deserted. I landed my kayak and climbed the steep bank to investigate the campsites and scout the rapids. As my eyes drew level with the top of the bank, I realized I was looking at a moose. She was just standing there, right in the middle of the campsite, very close. After glancing at me, she calmly ambled away into the woods. After that, I had to camp there!

Late in the afternoon, camp was set up and I was squatting by the fire. Suddenly, on the far side of the creek, quite close, I noticed movement in the weeds. Right across from me, a beaver came sliding down the bank, his mouth full of a tangle of plants. I froze. This was by far the best look I had ever had at a beaver.

As the evening went on, I sat by my fire quietly enjoying an amazing experience. The pool was alive with beaver. Over and over, one would appear on that slick muddy path across the creek, sliding down or climbing up, glossy brown fur matted with water, wide tail dragging behind. Quietly, another would swim down the creek from places unknown, trailing ribbons of bright green. Others calmly patrolled the pool, back and forth, only occasionally doing a tail slap and dive. My moose returned, too, to feed at the falls, silhouetted against the sunset sky.

The following morning, I ran Attean Falls with an empty boat, then loaded my gear at the end of the portage trail. The description of this Class II rapid in the official NFCT guidebook is concise and accurate: *"Boulders funnel the current right and push a lot of water against a large rock. Canoes are often pinned here."* During Paddle for Hope, my daughter Megan was with me overnight and we both had fun running Attean Falls.

Four years later, I was more exhausted and there was less water. With no regrets, I listened to my aching body and didn't run it. I also knew that I wasn't going to get to Jackman that night. My left elbow was bothering me, a shooting pain with every paddle stroke, and my shoulders hurt, too. When an intense line of storms came through in the night, I was safely camped on Attean Pond's Sally Mountain beach.

I did my laundry the next morning at the campground where I'd hoped to meet Sydney and Marji. There was no sign of them. I wasn't worried, exactly, but wished I knew whether Scotty had come back and where they were. I had lunch, then found the Mountain Country Supermarket and carefully stocked up. This was it. The last grocery store before the end of the trail, almost 200 miles away.

Dad often says that the easy parts of the trail make the shortest stories. For seven miles, I drifted down the Moose River, aided by a gentle current and a friendly wind, until the last riverbend faded away into the shallow, marshy west end of Long Pond. Deep blue skies and wispy clouds stretched into the distance above the gently waving grass. The stark skeleton of a weathered old tree jutted from the water. As I paddled closer, I saw that it was covered with birds, but only as they flew did I realize they were osprey.

Long Pond is long, almost nine miles long. *Enough is enough,* I thought, after making it about halfway. I hated to lose the benefit of the strong tail wind, but my aching left elbow was begging to stop. Fighting to keep the canoe on a straight course is surprisingly difficult when the boat is being pushed so hard from behind.

"Tonight is what camping should be, well-earned and peacefully beautiful." That journal entry summed it up well. Though it lacked a proper sign, this sandy beach campsite was a good one. A sturdy handmade bench sat beside the campfire and an ancient gnarled white cedar became my clothesline. I could relax. The sun left in a shimmer of color and the haunting call of loons reverberated across the water. *An evening to remember when the cold of winter comes.* The skies were clear and I lingered by the fire beneath the stars and a growing moon.

The cry of a loon woke me in the dawn. I stretched, thinking that I had just one more night before reaching Moosehead, where I would take a rest day. My hurting body needed it, although the blisters on my stomach had finally healed, leaving behind bright pink tender scars.

The wind moved gently across the water, creating ever-changing patterns of ripples, but no waves yet. I followed the glittering path of the climbing sun. It was hot already. By a rocky island, I left my canoe drifting in the shallows and swam in the comfortably warm water.

The river exited Long Pond for an energetic two-mile run to the Demo Road bridge. There were three or four rapids along the way, the last two the most challenging that I had run so far with my new canoe. At the third one, a moose stood in a grassy cove on the right, head buried in the water. I tried to paddle unobtrusively, not a wise choice in white-water. Soon, the canoe was hung on a rock and the moose, probably a small bull, was gone. At the fourth rapid, I lined the canoe past some ledges on river left, then ran the rest.

The concrete bridge was visible from far upriver. A spot of yellow on the left was a painted depth gauge, the markings on the huge rock all far above the water. The quiet river was saving its strength for the churning Class III+ water below the bridge. John Mautner, who I hadn't heard from since Vermont, had signed the kiosk here on July 20, nine days before. He would be finishing his thru-paddle soon.

The portage was four miles that seemed longer. I was grateful for good signage, as there were several turns. Yellow and blue blazes marked the route, with NFCT signs and arrows at every junction and even some for encouragement on the straight sections. Gravel logging roads gave way to a brushy, muddy woods road. I saw several flickers, then a snowshoe hare melted into the underbrush. The last half mile of woods trail had to be carried. When the first glimpses of water appeared through the trees, I felt like cheering.

Little Brassua Lake was austere, a place of deep bays and rocky islands, dark fir and wild hills. If there were dwellings, they were well hidden. I felt the solitude that must have greeted the first people to reach these shores.

I was heading for one of the few NFCT campsites in Maine, Poplar Hill Island, on the far side of Brassua. Above me, bald eagles wheeled and screeched, then dove for fish among the waves. The wind, strong from the northwest, forced me to paddle up the lee shore quite a distance to cross more safely at the narrowest spot.

The island gradually separated itself from the wooded shore. The campsite was in a cove on the far side of the island. Surprisingly, the old trail journal from my previous visits was still there. In it, I discovered a few warped and stained Paddle for Hope cards. In its wooden box and plastic bag, the ancient composition book had survived seven long Maine winters.

The dark campsite was more cheerful in the morning sun, and I was up and away early. I found the start of the portage around Brassua Dam marked by a towering pile of dri-ki. After a short walk, I returned to the river, ready for the final run to Moosehead, Maine's largest lake. Some fastwater and one fun Class II rapid with standing waves pushed me along. Above the river's rumble, a fly fisherman in waders shouted his success with "brookies."

As I neared Moosehead, the river resembled a crowded marina more and more. Docks and sleek, expensive boats crowded the shore, along with an occasional floatplane. It took some getting used to after days of solitude. Then the first view of Mount Kineo appeared and I knew that I was close. The channel, marked with red and green buoys, entered on the lake's western shore, about halfway up its nearly 40-mile length.

I resisted the temptation to be lazy and just go north. Instead, I paddled south into strong winds to sign in at the Rockwood kiosk. A stranger took my picture with Kineo rising in the background and it was done. Map 10 could be put away.

Then I turned, sailing with the wind at my back, past the river and up to The Birches Resort. Our family loved this place, which had plenty of old-fashioned charm. Owner John Willard had been an early member of NFCT's board and was always interested in my adventures. Tomorrow I would take my rest day, to recharge and reorganize before the wilderness journey ahead.

CHAPTER 14

ONCE IN A BLUE MOON

If you see a few white crests they appear nearly level with the rest of the lake, but when you get out so far, you may find quite a sea running and erelong, before you think of it, a wave will gently creep up the side of the canoe and fill your lap, like a monster deliberately covering you with its slime before it swallows you.

—Henry David Thoreau, *The Maine Woods*

The blue moon rose bold and shimmering beside Kineo, throwing a path of ethereal light to where I stood among the shoreline birches. The second full moon in any calendar month is a blue moon, and today was July 31. I'd had my rest day, and tomorrow I would journey on, with my father's younger sister Sue joining me across the northern half of Moosehead.

Sue was here with my parents, but they'd driven up separately. In two days, Mom and Dad would drive to the top of the lake, for one last goodbye before I entered the most remote section of the trail alone. Then they'd drive home and return to see me finish. Sue would paddle back to The Birches from there, camping along the way. For Sue and me, the next two days would retrace the miles that we had paddled together during Paddle for Hope.

I'd needed the day off. Dad, Sue, and I had done a bit of early morning exploring, paddling up a nearby brook to look for moose. We'd ended the day by driving down to Greenville, at the south end of the lake, where our pastor Ken and his wife Kathy treated us to dinner. They had a camp on a pond not far from there and were up for a couple of days. Mostly, though, I'd just enjoyed the restful atmosphere and doing not too much.

When logging contractor Oz Faye used his unemployed loggers to build The Birches during the early years of the Great Depression, he was fulfilling his dream—to create a place where guests could hunt and fish, swim and canoe, and where nature could renew the spirit.

John still carried on that tradition, offering a wide variety of outdoor activities on his thousands of forested acres. My favorite had been the time that Dad and I went up with John for a floatplane ride. We'd flown north, seeing the waters that I'd be paddling during the next few days. Far below, we'd watched moose run along an intricate web of trails in the bright green marshes and searched in vain for the dark black spots of bear.

Staying in the lodge was like a journey back in time. On the rustic pine walls, trophy fish mingled with vintage photos and tools once used for harvesting ice and logs.

In the dining room, large windows framed the lake and the meals rivaled those of days gone by, in quality and quantity. Hungry from our morning explorations, we ate thick slices of French toast with maple syrup beneath a true work of art. The finely crafted wooden canoe that hung above us had been made by Fred Reckards, in whose memory the Moose River Canoe Race is run each spring. Looking around, there was always something new to discover, like the shelf fungi that still clung to a wooden post near our table.

I loved the massive fireplace. On the mantel, Oz posed in an old framed photo with his happy young family, and a tall silver cup recorded for posterity the largest salmon caught each year. On the side of the stone chimney, cast-iron fish swam in an open grate. Called a heatilator, the device was used to circulate the warm air.

The next morning, the forecast for midday thunderstorms was on our minds as we waved a quick goodbye to John and Mom. For now, the lake was calm. Dad decided to come with us for a while and we paddled east, passing between Farm Island on the left and Mt. Kineo on the right. Then Dad turned away, to continue around the island and back to The Birches. Sue and I hurried toward the welcoming shelter of the far shore. The distant mountains rose in layers, their slowly lightening shades of blue like colors ascending a paint sample card.

From our angle, Kineo sloped to the lake in classic mountain fashion. On the far side, hidden from view, a sheer cliff dropped over 700 feet straight to the water. This odd shape, mirrored on mountains throughout Maine, can be explained by the flow of ancient glaciers across the landscape. Thoreau had written, *"Mount Kineo, and two other mountains ranging with it north-easterly, presented a very strong family likeness, as if all cast in one mould."* The mountain's spiritual and economic value to the native people had been as dramatic as its contours.

"We never have climbed Kineo," Sue reminded me, as we stopped for a quick drink.

"I know. One of these days we will. I'm curious to see the rock that it's made of."

"I remember reading about that," she continued. "It was excellent for tool-making."

"That's right. Kineo gave the native people one of their most valuable resources, a volcanic rock called rhyolite. It fractures perfectly, creating very sharp edges. And Kineo's rhyolite is a unique shade of green. Tools made from this specific stone have been traced to sites throughout New England and maritime Canada. There was a lot of trading going on. And tools of Kineo rhyolite have been found dating back to the arrival of the first people here."

"How long ago was that?" Sue wanted to know.

"Around 11,000 years ago, not long after the last glacier retreated. Known today as Paleoindians, they made beautiful, finely shaped stone tools. It's hard to imagine, but back then there were wooly mammoths and mastodons here, even giant beaver. Small bands of people roamed the land, hunting with spears and spear-throwers. Their main prey was caribou, but most likely they hunted those other animals, too."

"The land must have been very different back then," Sue added. "Wooly mammoths must have needed lots of open space."

"It was incredibly different," I agreed. "The glacier was almost a mile thick and completely covered most of our mountains. As it retreated, it left behind a changed landscape, scraped, rocky, and wet. Vegetation returned gradually. Those first humans probably discovered a grassy tundra, with lots of bogs and trees just starting to regrow."

Lost in thought, I hardly noticed when the wind began, a helpful nudge at first. We had reached the far shore and turned north, hoping to find one of the roomy campsites in Big Duck Cove available. If we did, Sue planned to camp there for a few days. She was a strong paddler, confident about returning solo across Moosehead after saying her goodbyes to me tomorrow. Chatting together, the miles went quickly and we began to hope for a quiet afternoon in camp.

As we rounded the last point, my binoculars were already out, checking for an empty site. It was a summer weekend, so there was no guarantee that we would find a spot. The wind pushed us toward the tiny pebble beach where we'd camped last time. To the left, I could see one group's gear and tents, and ahead, a young couple fishing by our beach.

They had good news, though. The site behind theirs on the same small point was open. The thunderstorms held off as we gratefully set up camp. Just as I finished organizing the stuff in my tent, a red squirrel ran past and I called to Sue.

"There's something in its mouth," she noticed. "I think it's a baby." Gently carrying the tiny bundle, the squirrel scampered off on her maternal errand.

Weak sun struggled out eventually and we tried to convince ourselves that it was warm enough to swim. We may have lasted three minutes, then sat on rocks to thaw while minnows nibbled on our toes and a tiny crayfish explored the bottom. Out on the cove, the wind churned up whitecaps until the surface resembled a racing river.

Sue's dinner made me wish I'd brought a frying pan. I gathered firewood, while she melted butter and sautéed a bunch of fresh vegetables from her garden with turkey sausage. After dinner, I tossed a rope up over a branch to hang my food bag. I struggled to lift it, bit by bit, hoping the branch wouldn't come crashing down on my head. All my food for the next nine or ten days was crammed into the bulging yellow dry bag. The heaviest would have to be eaten before I reached the long, challenging portage across Mud Pond Carry, three days ahead.

In the morning, Sue cooked and I packed. Full of pancakes, bacon, fresh peaches, and morning energy, we paddled briskly out of the cove. I wondered what Moosehead had in store for us today. To be safe, we followed the shore. Not like the last time, when I'd gotten us lost.

The northern end of Moosehead divides into two upreaching arms, which end in the historic canoe portages of Northwest Carry and Northeast Carry. Both are part of the NFCT, and paddlers can reach the West Branch of the Penobscot River either way.

Four years ago, Sue and I had been aiming for Northwest Carry, to camp with my parents. We left Big Duck Cove in the early morning calm, as bright sun sparkled across the water. Gambling, and with a careful eye on the weather, we angled northwest up and across the lake.

Soon, on every side, the sky touched the thin dark line that was the shore. Our whole world became a bowl of blue, and we were two small dots. Our progress seemed inconsequential against the vastness of the lake, but the calm held. The wind had just begun to whisper in the trees when Sue raised her paddle in victory on the far shore. The open water crossing of five miles had taken more than two hours.

We continued up toward Northwest Carry, poking into little coves, until the wind got serious. Knowing what I know now, I would have paddled farther out, but we stayed close to shore. Waves pounded our kayaks as we struggled to keep from being turned sideways, while dodging hidden rocks. Near us, a pair of loons also rode the wild water.

The top of the arm drew closer, though, and we tried to guess which buildings might be Seboomook Wilderness Campground. We decided to aim for a dock where an American flag snapped briskly in the wind. Amid the crashing waves, I beached the boat and went to check.

At a nearby house, a man was working in his garden.

"Hi. Can you tell me where the campground is?" I asked.

His answer was a shock.

"What campground? Seboomook Wilderness Campground is miles from here."

A few moments passed before I understood. We would not be relaxing by a campfire anytime soon. Somehow, against all my intuition and sense of direction, we were at Northeast Carry. Five dangerous, windy miles from our intended destination. We had paddled up the wrong arm of the lake. Thinking back, I realized that I hadn't been looking at the GPS coordinates or map, just the growing miles. We must have angled too far north and landed between the arms, rather than below them.

"And there's a bad storm headed this way," the man added, as we both looked out where whitecaps already crowned the growing waves. There was no way we could head back out under those conditions. It was time for a change of plan and a trip to Raymonds Country Store, just up the road.

Now, four years later, we planned to go to Northeast Carry, where I would portage two miles to the West Branch. With the wind behind us, seven miles went fast. Soon, the buildings began to take shape, then color, until crashing surf again deposited us on shore.

Sue and I were hoping for another visit with Ed and Shirley Raymond, who are anchors in this remote corner of Maine. It was Shirley who had taught me the North Woods ethic that kept me squatting on a log for hours with a boy from Brooklyn, back on the Raquette River.

"Up here it doesn't matter," she had said in a matter of fact voice. "Even if it's your worst enemy, if someone needs help, you help."

When they aren't rescuing misplaced paddlers, Shirley and Ed serve fresh doughnuts and grill heavenly cheeseburgers. Their store carries a small selection of groceries, but visitors may find it closed as often as two days a week when Ed and Shirley have medical appointments.

Back in 2011, they had certainly helped us. We used Shirley's phone to call Mom and Dad, who were just sitting down to lunch in Greenville. We had lots of time to wait, lots of time for stories of life at Northeast Carry.

Once there were two men, out for a last fishing trip before one was having surgery. When they returned to their truck, it wouldn't start and no one was around. They tried sleeping, but it was too cold. There was nothing left to do but walk 17 long miles. Only one person passed, a "cutter" who was headed to work and refused to help.

"No one up here does that," Shirley said, her eyes grim and her tone carrying a depth of conviction that came from years of living where there was no backup plan.

A broken arm was set by someone with no medical training. Two EpiPens were shared to save a life, against the advice of a distant doctor. Often Shirley and Ed were the only people there to help. There was no one else, and decisions needed to be made. Lives hung in the balance.

One particularly gruesome morning, an older man was ice fishing when a thread from his glove caught in his ice auger and ripped off his thumb. At Shirley's urgent insistence, the first medevac flight to Northeast Carry arrived to rescue him. Rescue personnel had been there not long before to locate a helicopter landing spot, and it was time to try it out. She didn't tell me if they saved his thumb, though.

This avalanche of tales all started when I asked Shirley and Ed if they had to rescue people often, given that there was no one else around to help.

"Not like we used to," was their simple reply, but their stories said otherwise.

This year, I began the portage across Northeast Carry before Mom and Dad arrived to check on us and say goodbye. I wheeled the almost-flat road at a good pace, crossing the imperceptible divide between the Kennebec and Penobscot watersheds.

Near the end, the portage turned off on a short, muddy, rutted road down to the river. As I muscled the canoe on its wheels through the worst of the puddles, I thought of others who had come this way before. Shirley had told me the story of two ingenious young men who used to come up to paddle Moosehead and the West Branch. To portage, they would bring a homemade set of wooden wheels, use them to cross Northeast Carry, then burn them in their first campfire. Next time, they'd have built a new set.

Then there were Thoreau and Withee, who had no wheels.

Everyone knows Henry David Thoreau, naturalist, philosopher and author of *The Maine Woods*, his classic account of three trips through the Maine wilderness. Thoreau crossed Northeast Carry twice, on his second and third trips. In 1853, he arrived by steamboat and had his canoe and gear transported on "a truck drawn by an ox and a horse over a rude log-railway through the woods." In 1857, when Thoreau and a friend arrived in a birchbark canoe with their Penobscot guide, Joe Polis, they carried everything across in two trips.

Few people know Henry L. Withee, a lawyer from Rockland, Maine, whose 1911 journal, *Down the Allagash*, I'd discovered in the collections of the Maine Historical Society.

Withee's account impacted me as much as Thoreau's. I enjoyed his humorous writing and descriptions of a far busier river, dedicated to transporting a vast quantity of logs. He inspired me, too, with the legacy he'd left behind. He was someone like me, not famous, whose stories had lived on long after he was gone. Withee, traveling with his friend Horace Bailey, covered far more than Thoreau of what would one day become the Northern Forest Canoe Trail. From Northeast Carry, the pair had gone to the trail's end in Fort Kent without a guide.

When the two friends climbed off the steamboat at the start of the carry, they tackled the challenge much as I would have. They toted their "dunnage" in the first load, and then the canoe. Back then, there was also a store, and hence an audience, as they set off with the canoe:

"Our gait was brisk until we got into the woods out of sight of the store— then, with perfect accord, we cast the canoe from us and sat down by the road. That craft was scheduled to weigh sixty-five pounds. It deserved excess baggage charge of two hundred pounds more, in our opinion. It was now pretty dark, so we picked up our burden and staggered ahead, at every step a new muscle we had never known about before, waking up to register a protest."

I sure had it a lot easier with my featherweight Kevlar canoe. Before saying goodbye to my family, we all drove back to the store for a visit. Ed and Shirley looked the same as ever and were still as busy. Just that day, a stroke victim had been medevaced out. As we left, I looked back once more at the store's colorful sign. At the bottom were the words, *"Real Maine for Real People."* Nothing could be truer. In Northeast Carry, life was real and trail magic was a tradition that was lived out every day.

Ten minutes later, I was alone, truly alone. Sue had started back down the lake. Mom, Dad, and my cell phone were gone. My wheels, too, were riding away in the back of Dad's truck. I would carry my boat and gear across the few remaining portages, all unwheelable. It was somber and it was thrilling. Short of a true emergency requiring the 911 button on my SPOT, I was on my own. For the first time, I would paddle the Allagash solo.

I set off with the strength of new beginnings. The West Branch, like the Allagash ahead, was an iconic northern river. The shores were an unbroken green and yet ever-changing. Each tree had its own unique shape—the spruce, the fir, the cedar, their colors and textures blending to create a tapestry of exquisite beauty. In the clear water, vast beds of water plants waved in the gentle current. Around bend after bend, the wide river carried me onward.

A joy flowed through me that was beyond mere words. Born of a kinship with nature, the simplicity of the wild, and the closeness of God. Here, I could remember that this journey was about something more than me. It was a chance to share the gift of this place with others. The shroud of civilization and its demands, even those that had followed me along the trail, could fade for a time. I was filled with purpose.

After a couple of miles, Lobster Stream entered on the right near a grassy island. I had just passed a canoe where a lone man sat hunched among piles of gear. He barely returned my greeting with a curt nod, and I was glad when he turned off toward Lobster Lake.

Two miles farther along was a bridge where the Golden Road crossed the river. This was the main thoroughfare in these parts, even paved in places. It was the last link to civilization. Floating beneath it and on down the river felt like crossing the threshold of the wilderness. Not into virgin forest, but into land much wilder than it had been a century earlier.

A nonprofit corporation called North Maine Woods, Inc. (NMW) manages access to over 3.5 million acres of land in northern Maine, including the Penobscot River Corridor and the Allagash Wilderness Waterway. This partnership between forest landowners of all sizes and Maine's natural resource agencies has simplified recreational use of these lands.

Before Maine became a state with the Missouri Compromise of 1820, it was part of Massachusetts. Much earlier, way back in the 1780s, a lot of what is now northern Maine was auctioned off in 6-mile-square townships. Often, several people jointly purchased large tracts. As time and generations passed, ownership was divided among their many heirs. Later, large corporations, mainly in the forest products industry, purchased some of this acreage. The resulting multitude of landowners had different rules for access and recreational use, causing confusion for visitors.

DeLorme's *The Maine Atlas and Gazetteer* (an invaluable resource for poking around the Maine woods) still shows many townships known only by the grid numbers assigned so long ago. These unnamed townships are part of Maine's Unorganized Territory, where about 9,000 residents live in an area that covers half the state. Tonight, I would be camping in T4 R14 WELS. The "WELS" stands for "West of the Easterly Line of the State," because the grid system used the eastern border of Maine as its baseline.

Today, most people enter the vast NMW management area by vehicle, through gated checkpoints on perimeter roads. This has allowed many interior gates to be removed. There are now uniform regulations and user fees across the property of all these different landowners. On the Penobscot and Allagash, the state of Maine owns the river corridors and manages and patrols the waterways, while NMW collects the camping fees.

The 100,000 visitors who annually enjoy these woods and waters owe forest landowners a huge thank you for sharing their lands. The vibrant working forest supports all that we love to do, whether it's paddling, fishing, snowmobiling, or camping.

Some people are saddened when they see a forest being harvested. Logging, though, is simply the last step in farming the old forest and the first step in regenerating a new one. To afford to own farmland, farmers must pick and sell their crops. Timber is a renewable resource, one that can and will regrow. To quote NMW, by working together we can take forest products, fish, wildlife, and pleasure from this great region, while taking nothing that will make it any less in the future than it is today.

Just past the Golden Road bridge was an island where Thoreau had camped on a chilly night in September 1853. After returning from moose hunting with Penobscot guide Joe Attean, he slept in the open under a blanket, on a bed of fir, in front of a massive campfire:

"We had first rolled up a large log some eighteen inches through and ten feet long, for a back-log, to last all night, and then piled on the trees to a height of three or four feet, no matter how green or damp. In fact, we burned enough wood that night as would, with economy and an air-tight stove, last a poor family in one of our cities all winter."

From Thoreau's island, it was seven miles to the first of a cluster of campsites scattered along the West Branch above and below a large island called Big Island. I kept track of my progress by counting the streams that entered on both sides of the river. Near Moosehorn Stream, where the river bent slightly northwest, the current quickened. In the lowering light of evening, the surface of the river was alive with swirls, ripples, and the occasional menacing waves of a submerged rock. An eagle flew from a tall spruce, so close that I could hear a squeak with every powerful wingbeat.

Smith's Halfway House, with bright new picnic tables at its two sites, came first, on river right. This was a place that a century ago had been bustling, its past remembered now only in old photos, stories, and the name of a couple of remote campsites.

Withee and his friend had arrived here at dinnertime, on foot, after battling their way around five log jams. I tried to imagine the turmoil and danger, the sheer noise, of what they'd struggled past. The longest jam they'd encountered had stretched for four miles. Carrying along the tote-road that paralleled the river, they'd met river-drivers, a horse-drawn supply wagon whose driver grudgingly squeezed their canoe in for a few miles, and even a mail carrier walking his 40-mile route.

At Smith's, they discovered a large working farm, with a dining room where a hearty dinner "extended their belt lines to the very frontier." Refreshed, they walked a mile back upriver to where they'd left their canoe, near rapids that today no longer exist.

"Just as we arrived at the canoe, the men working on the jam at the rips opened a channel down which the logs rushed. We shoved in and a moment later were shooting the rapids with the speed of a race-horse. With every nerve alert to escape being rammed by the logs, dodging boulders with quick paddle-strokes and yelling at the excitement, we ploughed through the chop at the foot of the falls, ran a few rods below Half-way House and when

an opening presented itself between the glancing timber, we swung in the opposite shore and drew up for the night."

For me, too, it was time to find camp for the night.

One of Big Ragmuff's two sites, next to a bustling stream on river left, was occupied by a friendly-looking group who waved to me energetically, but I wanted solitude.

The next possibility, Lone Pine on river right, was empty. It wasn't the roomiest, but it would do. Several huge trees had blown down around the grassy edges of the site and the work of clearing them up was still in process.

The rhythm of camp was comfort at the end of a weary day. Squatting quietly on shore, filtering water, with always the hope of a moose appearing. Gathering firewood, in a friendly race against the falling dusk. Effortlessly hanging my food bag from the sturdy horizontal pole over the picnic table, put there to provide the ridgeline for a tarp. Hiking to the outhouse on a board bridge beside a highway of moose tracks in the mud.

All the campsites along the Penobscot and Allagash would have the same civilized amenities. The wooden outhouses were clean and in good repair, and the newer models had translucent plastic corrugated roofs, to let in much-needed light. Often there would be mown grassy areas around the picnic tables, which all had those convenient ridgepoles.

Afterwards, I sat mesmerized by the flickering dance of the campfire, the moon a brilliant white in the darkness beyond the firs. My soul felt at peace. The challenge of Mud Pond Carry still lay ahead, but the rest of the trip should be simple. In Greenville, my friend Kathy had asked me how the journey was changing me and I hadn't known the answer. Bits and pieces, maybe, but I had come away determined to use the quiet days ahead for reflection.

I woke in the morning to the song of the white-throated sparrow. Its high, whistling notes sang out, "My sweet Canada, Canada, Canada." In late July 1857, Thoreau had written, *"The note of the white-throated sparrow, a very inspiriting but wiry sound, was the first heard in the morning, and with this all the woods rang."*

The sun's glow hit the highest treetops across the river. In the stillness, a fish broke the surface and the throaty croak of a raven came again and again. I caught up on journaling as I ate my oatmeal. Once on the water, I paused midstream to write: *"The slow drifting of surface bubbles contrasts with the swift darting of the swallows, as they skim just inches from the water. It is the last of that shadowed time before the bright sun illuminates all."*

The river gained energy as it approached Big Island. There were riffles to navigate and several spacious, inviting campsites. Only one was occupied, by a family with two small children. The river was shallow and the outside of the curves held the most water. I bottomed out once after stopping to photograph a magnificent bank of Joe Pye weed.

I'd pulled over for a snack when the family I'd seen at Big Island paddled past, in a canoe and a kayak.

"I hope you see a moose," I shouted, glad they would go down the river first.

"If we see an animal, we get ice cream!" the little boy called back.

I wanted to play that game. That's just the sort of thing I would have done when my kids were younger and we'd spent so many days hiking and camping in Shenandoah.

Later, when they stopped on a sandy beach to swim, I passed them again. I decided to stop, though, if I saw a moose and let them win their ice cream. Sadly, the extent of the wildlife that morning was a bald eagle circling magnificently in the growing wind.

Gradually, the river slowed and widened and the shores became marshy. Any help from the current evaporated just as the wind began to get serious. I fought my way southeast straight into it, toward where Pine Stream entered on the right. There the river would make its last turn north toward Chesuncook Lake.

I took the turn too tightly and found myself in shallow flats. It felt good, though, to walk my boat for a while and stretch my back. After I turned the corner, the wind became a friend, a ferocious friend. I stopped at the Boom House campsite on the right. It was time to batten down the hatches. The family with the kids had done well in the wind and pulled in near me. I wished them well on their journey down the lake.

"We're in for a wild ride," were my last prophetic words.

CHAPTER 15

INTO THE ALLAGASH ALONE

There is magic in the feel of a paddle and the movement of a canoe, a magic compounded of distance, adventure, solitude, and peace.

—**Sigurd F. Olson,** *The Singing Wilderness*

Chesuncook is Maine's third largest lake, but the NFCT paddler sees little of it. The trail crosses the lake's northwest end, above the huge bulk of Gero Island. Today that was a good thing, as the winds surpassed even what I'd experienced on Lake Champlain. If my route had taken me down the lake, I wouldn't have been going anywhere.

After making sure that every item in the boat was secure and my PFD tightly buckled, I left the Boom House campsite. The river turned east and widened as it met the lake. I hugged the south shore, temporarily sheltered from the brutal wind. I would miss visiting Chesuncook Village, just down the lake, but it was too rough to venture down there. The village was best known among paddlers for its store, which sold just two items: homemade root beer and fudge.

Studying the map, I decided to follow the west shore of the lake northward, then cross to find calmer waters in the lee of the island. Soon, the long length of the lake stretched away to the southeast, to a clear view of the peaks of Katahdin and its neighbors. After a quick glance, I focused on the waves, which were driving up the lake with great force. Surf battered the rocks near shore, and I was forced to stay farther out. Passing the mouth of Caucomgomoc Stream, the waves were at their most confused. It was time to fight for the shelter of Gero Island.

Concentrating, I tried to hit the waves at a 45-degree angle. I quartered into them for a while, then away. Surprisingly, it was harder to stay on course with the waves behind me.

The winds whipped ever more strongly. Pure adrenaline filled me as the swells lifted me and flung me forward in a giant surge. Then I would sluggishly wallow back and turn sideways. I could feel my shoulders and forearms losing strength.

Only once, though, did the boat feel unstable. Frantically flipping in tons of water, I dug in my paddle like a rudder to turn to a safer angle.

The waves were fighting me for control and I was losing. By now, I was comfortably near the island, or it would have been terrifying. Again and again, I was turned sideways and pushed up the lake. Luckily, this was the direction that I wanted to go.

Finally, I simply surrendered. The wind turned my boat broadside and scooted me along, parallel to shore. It felt relatively safe, if a bit funny, to be simply along for the ride. Going almost two miles per hour, I was at the mercy of the lake. The waves were carrying me to safety, around the curving shoreline to calmer water.

I floated over one last shallow sandbar into tranquility. I beached the boat, grabbed a snack, and collapsed on a large driftwood log. The water bottle trembled as I lifted it to my mouth. Around me on the quiet beach, all was still, while offshore, whitecaps raced along.

I allowed myself an hour's rest. I'd stopped shaking by the time I hopped in and started up the broad arm of Umbazooksus Stream, which stretches to the north above Chesuncook.

There would be no crossing back and forth across this wide, wind-whipped arm. I stayed firmly to the left, where far in the distance I could see a clump of RV's at the North Maine Woods campsites that marked the end of Map 11. If I could only get there safely. Using my paddle far back as a rudder, I kept myself on course.

At one point, a giant wave lifted me and I surged forward, surfing. For a moment, the GPS speed measured 7.3 miles per hour. I imagined the RV's full of people, watching my perilous journey to join them. They would be amazed that I had braved these conditions and awed by my paddling skill. But when I got there, the campground was deserted.

A small sandbar jutted out into the lake and I pulled my canoe up behind it. There was one empty campsite, my home for the night. I piled my gear on the sand, then hauled the empty boat up on the beach while the SPOT message finished transmitting.

I was carrying the last awkward armload of bags and paddles up to my site when I heard a sound. I whirled around, to see that my boat had been lifted off the solid beach and plunked into the water. Rapidly, it began skidding up the lake. I dropped everything and tore down the sand and into the water. I was waist deep when my hand stretched out and just grasped the gunwale. With a sigh of relief, I carried the canoe far from the water and flipped it over on the grass for the night.

Later, a car drove in, backing in between my campsite and the water. An older woman got out with a smile and introduced herself as Nancy. She was dressed practically, in jeans and sneakers, and her car was packed with gear. Nancy was on a journey of rediscovery, visiting places where she'd camped with her family in the 1960s and '70s. Later, she went far down the beach to swim and had just returned when the winds blew in the rain.

Nancy and I quickly retreated, to car and tent. When pea-sized hail began bouncing up like crazy from the grass outside, I was comfortably stretched out reading, dry and cozy. Later, more thunderstorms rolled through, one after the other. Then, at the last, a rainbow curved across the water, toward where I would go tomorrow. This day had given new meaning to the words "unsettled weather."

Nancy took my end-of-map photo in the early light of morning, then stood waving until the curve of the shore hid her from view. The wide part of Umbazooksus Stream ended as it passed under a bridge, where I was forced to paddle hard against the storm-strengthened current.

The stream meandered on through a grassy marsh, where yellow water lilies were mirrored in the still waters. Across this landscape were scattered immense twisted, tortured stumps of dark weathered brown. They seemed surreal in this peaceful scene of space and light, where swallows swooped and red-winged blackbirds flashed their brilliant spots of color.

I followed the stream up to where it flowed out from Umbazooksus Lake through the gaping metal mouth of an abandoned dam, painted a dull red. I pulled myself cautiously up through the opening on a scary roller coaster of waves.

Umbazooksus Lake itself was unremarkable, at least the part I saw.

Everybody knows how many times they've done it. Usually it's once, or not at all. Although I once met an Allagash ranger whose count was seven.

"Done it once, don't need to do it again," was one thru-paddler's assessment.

For me, after today, hopefully it would be twice. Mud Pond Carry has been the traditional route into the Allagash for thousands of years. As a legendary gateway, it leaves a lot to be desired. It would be hard to invent a more arduous route. I wasn't exactly scared. I had been through there four years before, with no one for miles around. Dad and Taylor had met me later, on Chamberlain Lake. The hazards of Mud Pond Carry, though, remained very real. It was isolated and long—carrying everything in two trips would mean six miles of fighting the bugs, navigating fallen trees, and trudging through thick mud with only frogs for company.

On the far shore, I spotted the start of the carry. It was marked by a large rock cairn that had been rebuilt during the summer of 2011 by my friends, thru-paddlers Justine Jarvis and T.K. Kiernan. Their brave but tiny dog, Moxie, a four-pound Yorkshire Terrier, had the honor of being the first dog to thru-paddle the Northern Forest Canoe Trail.

The feet of generations have worn the path so deep that most of Mud Pond Carry is now a stream. With the portage yoke firmly on my shoulders, I took my first steps up through the clear water, which bubbled down over a bed of rocks. I was ready to do this. There was relief in being here, in tackling the challenge that would carry me through to the prize of the Allagash.

Gradually, the water turned cocoa brown, hiding the slimy, slippery rocks below. Across the trail, trees had fallen. Each had to be carefully lifted over or maneuvered around. After a half mile, the carry crossed a wide logging road, and I went back to get the rest of my gear. The SPOT went with me, just in case.

Surprisingly, from the road I managed to float my canoe almost another half mile, with my gear inside. All those storms the evening before must have raised the water level, giving me an unexpected reprieve. Where the trail climbed further into dry and open woods, I stopped for lunch. For a short way, I walked on dry ground. It was a welcome contrast. For much of the carry, it was difficult to find even a small dry spot to pile my gear.

After that, conditions worsened. Back to slogging through murky water, no longer deep enough to float the boat. Carefully, thoughtfully, I planted my feet. The ankle-deep slurry hid countless rocks and a bottom that might be solid for your left foot and a sucking vortex for your right.

The perils were invisible and unpredictable. Carrying the boat, high and balanced, was easier than lugging the heavy bags, held awkwardly above the mud.

"Mud is demoralizing, creepy, and uncomfortable, packing itself painfully into every crevice of your shoes," I later wrote. And while we're talking shoes—why do they lie abandoned along the trail? Three orphans, expensive brands in different sizes and colors. Flung to the side or buried in mud, as if the wearer had just slogged on, unaware that he or she was now barefoot.

Parts of an old corduroy road remained, a silent witness to the days when this was the primary route into the Allagash. Native peoples had long come this way to reach Chamberlain Lake, which they named A'pmoojenegamook, meaning "lake that is crossed."

When Thoreau arrived in 1857, he found a Canadian, Jules Thurlotte, living in a log hut with his family, near the start of the carry. A "toter," he carried lumbermen's gear across on his back. Thoreau and his companion ended up lost, following a dubious supply road to Chamberlain Lake, but his description of the start of the carry attests to its wetness then as well: *"After a slight ascent from the lake through the springy soil of the Canadian's clearing, we entered on a level and very wet and rocky path through the universal dense evergreen forest, a loosely paved gutter merely, where we went leaping from rock to rock and from side to side, in the vain attempt to keep out of the water and mud."*

At times in the years that followed, teams of oxen pulling sleds and wagons provided transportation across the carry. Sporting camps were built and the clearing grew ever larger. Withee, having survived the rigors of portaging the log drives, simply wrote of Mud Pond Carry: *"Toting a carry is not an easy matter under any circumstances, but our hard experience on the West Branch had taught us something. After we had crossed (Umbazooksus Lake) the following morning and had landed at Colby's Camps, where the twomile carry to Mud Pond begins, we carefully upholstered the thwarts and gunwales of the canoe with our blankets and made the trip across with comparative ease. It was such an improvement that we almost regretted that this was the last long carry of the trip."*

My scariest moment came when my right foot suddenly slipped between two of those ancient logs, wedging at an awkward angle. Thankfully, I was slowly maneuvering bags at the time. As I wiggled my foot free, I shuddered, imagining if I had been carrying the canoe, with a lot of forward momentum.

Near the end, five hours in, the bottom firmed up and the water grew clearer. By now, I had crossed the high point separating the Penobscot and Allagash watersheds. The water, now running in my direction, was once again deep enough to float the boat. I had survived. With a smile, I summed it up—*Did it twice, don't need to do it again!*

Thunder was rumbling by the time my canoe and gear were finally reunited at the edge of broad, shallow Mud Pond. A bank of ominous clouds filled the far sky, casting an eerie light across the water. My skin tingled, sensing the hushed anticipation of the approaching storm. Out on the pond floated long, curving fingers of grass, a bright green in the strange lighting. I waited, hoping the storm would pass to the north.

I knew that across the pond was short, vigorous Mud Brook, a tiny, rushing stream full of rocks that would take me to Chamberlain Lake. I'd probably have to walk the boat and didn't want to be navigating that with lightning around.

I got lucky. The storm moved away, and I scrambled down the stream, holding onto my boat for dear life. Along the banks, the first goldenrods of summer were just coming into bloom. It was August now, and only a week was left before my journey's end.

In camp, too, I noticed that the darkness came a little earlier. It was chilly and I ate close to the crackling campfire, where a friendly chipmunk kept popping out to visit.

The prevailing winds on the large Allagash lakes have been known to hold paddlers captive, windbound for days. The next morning, I willingly rose at a very early hour to be sure that didn't happen to me. From the Mud Brook campsite, I would paddle up the west shore for several miles before crossing to the far side of Chamberlain Lake.

The lake was hushed and mine alone, beneath a glorious sky. Layers of clouds, in delicate pastels, glowed with the promise of dawn. From this luminescent beauty, rays of light reached down to touch the distant shore.

The dip of the paddle created an endless pattern of tiny eddies. Their gentle ripples were colored blue and brown and white, a kaleidoscope of sky and water. Into my quiet mind came words of scripture, though I didn't remember them perfectly: *"For now we see in a mirror dimly, but then face to face. Now I know in part; then I shall know fully."*

The sky, those words, brought a longing to my soul. A longing to do something worthy of the beauty that surrounded me. Like ripples from a tiny eddy, we catch glimpses, reflections of something so much greater than ourselves. On a journey like mine, this was especially true. Day after day, all around me, I witnessed the drama, the intricacy, the colors and patterns of nature. Its glory demanded a response, a growing within myself to become something more.

I would continue to simplify, to focus on the parts of life that were truly important. What I wanted most, I knew, was to share my journey through my writing. But would it be good enough? Could I find the words I needed?

Part of faith, though, was to carry on without all the answers, just as I'd been doing on the river. To meet each new day with confidence and believe that I would find the way, even when the path ahead was only dimly seen. In the rhythms of the trail, I had found an assurance in myself that I hoped would come home with me and help me with my writing.

The lake stayed peaceful and calm for the six miles up and across Chamberlain.

There was so much history along the waterway. I would have liked to explore the site of 600-acre Chamberlain Farm, but it was across on the east shore and I was paddling up the west. For eighty years, the farm's cattle, sheep, apple orchards, and fields of potatoes, grain, and vegetables had fueled hungry river workers and lumbermen throughout the Allagash.

Farther up, I angled diagonally across the still water, straight for Lock Dam. This was one of two possible portage routes to the next lake. For me, the choice was simple. The other alternative, the Tramway Carry at the upper end of Chamberlain, was three-fourths of a mile long, and I had sent my wheels away. Lock Dam was just a short carry up and over to a stream that would lead to Martin Cove on Eagle Lake.

Many dams had been constructed over the years to control the flow of the Allagash waters, which naturally went north. Gil Gilpatrick's well-researched book, *Allagash: A Journey Through Time on Maine's Legendary Wilderness Waterway*, helped me understand how they worked. The book has three parts: a route description filled with stories, a history of the logging era, and a fictional narrative woven around the seasonal rhythms of the Wabanaki.

Gilpatrick's diagrams showing the progression of Allagash dams explain the clever engineering that allowed so much timber to float south to hungry mills. Lock Dam was once the upper of two dams with gates, that functioned as locks. Logs were moved from Eagle into Chamberlain just as we'd traversed the locks into and out of Lower Saranac Lake.

I usually didn't bother with hot food during the day. This morning, though, I still felt drained from the rigors of Mud Pond Carry. I was craving something salty. At the dam, I made potato soup with bacon. The hot food warmed me, body and soul, while my tent dried in the weak sun. Once again, there had been rain during the night.

After crossing Lock Dam, I carefully reloaded my canoe at the start of the rushing stream. It was a sparkling half mile of fun, barely paddleable all the way to Martin Cove.

Withee wrote with the heart of a poet about emerging here: *"We were unprepared for the view which presented itself on our entrance to the lake. The water, clear as crystal, lies above a bottom of white sand. A narrow, beveled bank of smooth, clean rocks surrounds the edge, above which is a narrow fringe of white birch, then the unbroken forest of various hardwoods slopes up into low hills. Here and there are islands, covered with maple, birch and poplar which stand so near the water as to give the islands the appearance of having precipitous sides... The cloudless sky, the sparkling water, and the clean, silent shores gave us the feeling that we had, unawares, paddled straight into the land of magic."*

It wasn't quite as magical today. I had caught up to a large group of other people and was following a parade of red and green canoes. We paddled along between the shore and a large island. Pillsbury Island marked the farthest point north that Thoreau had reached on the NFCT, before returning home along the East Branch of the Penobscot.

A steel-gray cloud was also rapidly overtaking the blue sky, although the sun still shone on distant Farm Island. Then, just like that, the canoes ahead were obliterated by sheets of rain.

As the squall descended, the wind changed. Now it was in my face, challenging me. The rain hammered the lake, and giant drops cratered the surface. It was too late for raingear. I shivered in my soaked clothes. Already, though, the storm was moving on. To the west, the sky turned lapis blue with dots of puffy white. I toughed it out and paddled hard, my head tucked down. Then I watched the line of sunshine along the shore ripple closer, tree by tree, until my goosebump skin felt the rays, and instant warmth.

I pushed into the wind to the Eagle Lake end of the Tramway Carry. This day of paddling was like a journey through time, a whirlwind tour of historical logging milestones.

Visiting the locomotives on Eagle Lake during Paddle for Hope

The story began in the late 1830s, when the search for large white pine brought early timber barons north, where they found what they were looking for along the Allagash. One by one, the dams were constructed, allowing the large rafts of logs called "booms" to be floated downriver from farther and farther north.

But not all logs were moved by water. By the start of the twentieth century, men were dreaming of even faster, higher-volume solutions to the eternal problem of sending timber south. By then, it was not just white pine, but spruce and fir, too. Not just sawlogs, but smaller pulpwood for making paper. Along this carry, wood had been moved in two ways.

The tramway, which put Lock Dam out of business, was in operation from 1903 to 1908. The heart of the system was a 6,000-foot cable, weighing 14 tons, that stretched in a giant loop the length of the carry and back. Attached to the looped cable were small 2-wheeled trucks, each of which carried one log. The truck would move its log from Eagle to Chamberlain, drop it into the water, and then ride back on the bottom of the loop, upside down.

What came next made the tramway seem like a ghost of the past. I knew what was here, but still I was awed. I beached my canoe and walked up through the woods, past a graveyard of metal, rusted and overgrown. Just a messy jumble, until I looked up. There, abandoned in the forest, stood two towering locomotives, side by side on twin tracks that went nowhere.

The lumber industry bred big men. They didn't come any bigger, in vision and sheer impact, than Edouard Lacroix, the man who built the Eagle Lake & West Branch Railroad. Setting aside judgment on whether it is ethical to change the direction a river flows or turn deep forest into an industrial site, one cannot help but be awed by the story of "King" Lacroix. He began as a wagon boy and ended up a major landowner and logging contractor. As a member of the Quebec House of Commons, it was his legislation that defined the "cord" as a standard unit of measurement for wood volume, bringing greater equity for the average woodcutter.

The railroad operated from 1927 to 1933, transporting 6,500 cords of pulpwood per week in open railcars. From Eagle Lake, the tracks crossed Chamberlain Lake on a 1,500-foot trestle to Umbazooksus Lake. To maximize production, the operation ran day and night. The railroad stretched 13 miles, then abruptly ended 600 feet out in the middle of a remote lake. To facilitate unloading, both the floor of the cars and the tracks were tilted. This allowed some of the wood to fall out easily when the pins holding the hinged sides of the cars were pulled.

Gray skies blew in again, and a feeling of sadness came over the little clearing. Someone had scrawled graffiti on the engines, which made me angry. I remembered how much fun we'd had when I visited with Dad and Taylor, climbing up inside to play conductor, and I missed them. Rain was sputtering as I set out again across the windy lake.

At Priestly Point, well up the lake, I discovered two empty campsites. One was grassy and dry, the other darker and muddy. Not many people were around, so I took the more attractive site.

When two canoes pulled in an hour later, I felt badly and offered to switch campsites, but my offer was declined. These were more instantly comfortable friends. All from Vermont, there were Heidi and Mary in one canoe and Amy and Chris with their two children in the other. Three of them were science teachers, and Amy had hiked the Long Trail and most of the Appalachian Trail. They invited me to bring my dinner over later and eat with them.

Zayda and Zeb were kids after my own heart. With help from their yellow Lab Ziggy, they built a fort down in the woods below my campsite. It was just what we would have done growing up. After hours of construction, the pair was ready to start giving tours. There were all the comforts of home, plus custom features like a s'more toaster with a rack to hold it and a candy dish, a hollowed rock filled with ferns.

Later, we talked into the darkening evening, as their large tarp kept another round of showers at bay. Water levels would be great along the river, we decided.

"You have to eat the weight," Amy laughed, as they gave me a hot dog and some home-grown green beans. By now, we'd seen more canoes and the lake felt busier. Tomorrow, if the sites up around Churchill Dam were full, I invited them to share my campsite.

I could have, maybe should have, gone farther the next day. Then again, maybe not.

The day had been windy from the start. Wind in the treetops had woken me before dawn. I'd packed my dry tent, grabbed a few handfuls of granola with my morning coffee, and gotten on the water. It was ten miles to where I planned to camp.

Soon, I heard the call of a loon, close by, and then a perfect echo from the darkly wooded shore. Again and again came the haunting tremolo, then the voice from the woods. I was so enjoying the loon—his wing stretching, the closeness, the echoes—that I didn't give any thought to the why of the scene. Until I spotted a small dot near the mother, a chick. I carefully angled away to leave the little family in peace.

I made steady progress, finishing Eagle Lake, then Round Pond and Churchill Lake. Along the way, nature gave me some breaks from the nonstop wind. There were patches of water smartweed, whose small pink spiky head is much different from the more common white and yellow water lilies. A yellow-bellied sapsucker, and then a cow that was Moose #4.

By late morning, my tent was set up in the middle site at Jaws, in the narrows below tiny Heron Lake. I was just where I wanted to be, a mile below Churchill Dam, poised to tackle the most difficult stretch on the Allagash the following morning. Chase Rapids must be run between eight and noon, while water is released from the dam to create four or five miles of steady Class I and II whitewater. I wanted to be first in line for the excitement.

Churchill Dam has a small museum, the Churchill Depot History Center, in what used to be the old boarding house. I paddled over there in the afternoon and spent an hour looking at old photos and artifacts, imagining life in places that are now so wild.

The courage of the river drivers and the women who had come here to teach school, in tiny log cabins where classes were held in French and English. The mountains of biscuits and pies that a "cookee" had baked in the huge and battered reflector oven, using heat from his campfire. The workers who had pumped energetically along the railroad tracks, delivering supplies on the brightly painted red-and-yellow velocipede.

Still daydreaming about the olden days, I paddled back toward camp, hugging the shoreline against the steady wind. The afternoon was growing late. I wondered if my Vermont friends had arrived while I was gone and found the note I'd left for them.

I was pulled back to the scene around me by a flash of light near shore, far ahead. It was sunlight, reflecting off a rushing cascade of water. Puzzled at first, I couldn't figure out what had disturbed the tranquil waters of the protected cove.

Then I realized—it was a large bull moose. As he raised his antlers, still in velvet, water streamed down around his huge head. From his mouth trailed long strands of green. I was far away and he hadn't noticed me. Slowly, I worked toward the shelter of a small point, where I would be hidden from view. Paddling like crazy when his head was submerged and freezing when his head came up. I gathered camera and binoculars, then pulled myself stealthily forward among the bushes to a great vantage point.

Bull moose in velvet near Churchill Dam in the Allagash

The bull never sensed my presence, and I must have watched him for over half an hour.

It was a special, sacred time. I thought of Chris and how he would have loved this and felt his presence there beside me. At least, I hoped that, somehow, he was there in spirit. If life had worked out differently, today would have been our tenth anniversary.

I hadn't planned it, hadn't even realized it at first. But tomorrow, when I reached Umsaskis Bridge, would be ten years to the day since I had first seen the Allagash, in that same spot, at the start of our honeymoon. This summer, this journey, had chosen its own timing. This was the first summer I could have gone, and I'd left just as school was finishing. And now, here I was and it felt very right. There were tears in my eyes and a prayer in my heart as I gently paddled away and left the bull still feeding.

CHAPTER 16

FROM THE PAST
WILL COME THE FUTURE

Stand at the crossroads and look, and ask for the ancient paths, where the good way lies; and walk in it, and find rest for your souls.

—Jeremiah 6:16

When I got back to camp, full of my encounter with the bull moose, my friends were there. They'd discovered my note and made themselves at home. Chris had a pot of chili cooking, and Heidi's cornbread was browning by the campfire, in a modern-day reflector oven. She promised to share the recipe, which she'd gotten from a famous New Orleans chef.

Solitude is priceless, I thought, *but sometimes so is companionship.*

Tomorrow I would run Chase Rapids with my gear, and I was nervous. The rangers at Churchill Dam offer a shuttle around the worst four miles, hauling gear, or even reluctant paddlers, for just ten dollars. I'd made it safely through before, but with an empty kayak.

I was wide awake by four, anxious and excited. Soon Ziggy came over exploring, and Amy and Heidi followed, encouraging me with the reminder of all that I'd already been through to get this far. Together, they walked down to see me off.

"Look at that!" Heidi exclaimed, pointing across the misty narrows.

A cow moose stood knee-deep in the water, beside a great blue heron and a family of Canada geese. If that was a good omen, I hadn't paddled far before I got two more. Where the bull had been yesterday, a small calf trailed behind its mother through the shoreline grasses. There were moose everywhere. Mist danced on the water and the aroma of fir was intense in the dampness. Even the colors of the kingfisher seemed more brilliant in the early light. Nature was working her magic, calming my jitters.

At the dam, Josh was the ranger on duty. He collected $25.92 for my six nights camping along the Penobscot and Allagash, and I carefully folded away my paperwork. On the well-staffed waterway, a ranger might ask to see it at any time. Josh thought I would do fine keeping my gear, and I carried it down to the put-in, still with butterflies in my stomach. He was releasing 1,000 cubic feet per second from the dam, bringing the flow to a vigorous 2,000.

Only a tantalizing glimpse of whitewater could be seen before the river curved away out of sight. The first time we'd come here, Dad, Taylor, and I had watched intently as a group of Boy Scouts went first. On the dark banks, towering spruce and fir had dwarfed the slow drift of the small red canoes toward the unknown that waited around the bend. Now I knew what to expect, miles of adrenaline that started as soon as you committed to the river.

My gear was secure. My paddle dug in and I was off. Around that first curve, I could see whitewater churning among a sea of rocks, but I could also see the line that I would take—straight down the middle— and my canoe was responding well. The standing waves were higher than I remembered, and I took on water before pulling safely over to the calm on river right.

The release of water from the dam was designed to create a steady series of Class II rapids, and the first four or five were the hardest. After each, there was quiet water or an eddy where you could catch your breath. After the second set, I bailed five gallons of water from my boat, thanks to the huge standing waves that Josh was creating. *"My boat is forgiving and tough and brought me through quite confidently,"* I later journaled.

When we ran Chase Rapids in 2011, it was more about survival than style. Dad and Taylor were together in Chris's old blue canoe, and I was in my kayak. The rangers had our gear. We made it safely through the first two rapids, then it was their turn to go first.

They took their time, reading the rocks, trying to decipher the safest path. The canoe, though, was slow to respond. They had been paddling lakes, not rivers, and certainly nothing like this. The current was strong and the river in control. I hung back, giving them space. Suddenly, they hung on a rock and the canoe was pulled sideways. Time stood still for a moment, then the canoe tipped and they were both in the water. After a struggle that I could only partly see, they righted the boat and scrambled back in, minus the beautiful 40-year-old wooden canoe paddle that Taylor had been using. He grabbed the spare.

Before long, they dumped again. I will never forget the vision of Dad calmly bobbing down the river, feet up for safety, Indiana Jones hat still firmly on his head. In his hand, he calmly held his paddle. Suddenly, though, the tip of the paddle wedged in a rock. It was torn from his grasp by the force of the current, the handle standing straight up like a flagpole. Dad, however, was fine and soon swam safely to shore.

He's probably loving this, I thought to myself.

Seventeen-year-old Taylor had earned a river nickname that trip. *Sackett,* inspired by the larger-than-life family in the Louis L'Amour book he was reading. At that moment, Sackett came into his own. Unyielding as a river rock, he stood strong, holding the canoe, half-full of water. The river strained to rip it away. I watched, impressed, as he slowly worked it over to the bank and dumped it out.

It was obvious they were in for a challenge, but the only direction to go was forward.

In my kayak, I was faring much better. Having no gear gave me a sense of freedom and confidence. The boat was responding well in the current and my movements came naturally, although I hit my share of rocks, too. It was a moment of great satisfaction when the rushing water delivered me to the spot I had been aiming for, and I snatched Dad's paddle from the river. Later, Dad's keen eyes discovered Taylor's lost paddle drifting in an eddy.

Dad and Taylor ran the rest of Chase Rapids much better, and later acquitted themselves well together on the surprisingly strong rapids of the St. John River.

Alone, four years later, there was less drama. The Saranac River in flood stage had been much more powerful and the rapids on the Moose River trickier, with less water. I was glad that I had kept my gear, which gave my boat the feel it had had for hundreds of miles.

The rapids didn't stop after Bissonnette Bridge, where the rangers' shuttle ends, but the worst was over. The current whisked me downriver, past banks of glorious Joe Pye weed, and an osprey soared overhead.

Several miles past the bridge, I met two young men with a canoe full of rocks. Jared and Paul, NFCT interns, kept on lugging while we talked. It was their last day of work for the summer, and they were just completing new steps for the Meadows campsite. I thanked them, saying what a difference trail improvements had made in my journey.

We traded stories for a while. They'd met Sydney Aveson and John Mautner in their travels and seen two bears. As I was saying goodbye, their moose count reached 45 and mine nine when Paul calmly said, "There's a moose now," as a cow emerged from some bushes.

Past Chisholm Brook, islands began to appear, and the broad river split into channels and quiet backwaters. The marsh was without a breath of air. In the hushed stillness, I was the only thing that moved. Along the shore of a low island, I found the body of a great blue heron. It had caught underwater on a branch, and one foot at the end of a long leg moved gently beneath the wavering water. Its long beak was vivid yellow and its feathers gray and matted. I felt sad, yet knew this was but a part of nature, a cost of having lived.

A little farther on, the river quietly entered the lower end of Umsaskis Lake.

The stillness on the lake was uncanny that afternoon. I paddled in silence, slicing a path across a mirror. Billowing clouds on a blanket of blue were repeated on the shiny surface of the lake, in all directions, from shore to shore. It was amazing, powerful, and my heart was full of emotions. Since I'd realized when I would arrive here, I'd wondered what it would be like. Would I feel Chris's spirit in some special way? Now, I had my answer.

The canoe drifted to a stop. I put the paddle gently down. Where could I begin to try to unravel the thoughts swirling inside me? There were treasured memories, regrets, and a large dose of guilt. I hoped Chris knew that I was sorry and that I still thought of him so often and that it was the good times, like our honeymoon, that I remembered most.

Chris and I had driven in on the American Realty Road, to the far end of Umsaskis Lake. There's a ranger's cabin there and several campsites. We'd set up our roomy tent for the first night, then left our vehicle to be shuttled ahead 34 miles to Michaud Farm.

For five wonderful days, we explored and fished and cooked over the campfire, winding our way downriver. I could have stayed forever. The flow of the current, the march of the fir and spruce, the misty morning moose, and the stars of the ebony-dark nights sank into my soul and I promised I'd return. Chris never had the chance to.

Today, I felt at home here. I had come alone and it had been alright. I had discovered within myself unexpected strength, courage, and endurance. My body had hardened. At times, it moved with a confidence and assurance, a fluidity that surprised me. The rhythms of life on the river came naturally—the canoe and I moved as one and we thought together.

I thought of the words from "Hymn of Promise," the song that had helped me through my grief. From the past had come the future, perhaps one that God alone had seen.

Under this incredible sky, God was affirming the path my life would take when I got home. I would strive to live simply, embracing the essence of wild places. I would try to live gently and deeply and appreciatively. I would take time to just be, to know myself, to continue to reflect on the path my life was taking. I would write, and in that sharing, I prayed that there would be something greater than myself.

My hands reached for the paddle and I started northward once more.

Floating under the American Realty Road at the north end of Umsaskis marked the end of Map 12. I almost forgot to take a photo, then snapped a selfie in the narrow thoroughfare that led to Long Lake, with the bridge in the background. I unfolded Map 13, the last of the trip.

Only one more map to go!

In the curve of the lakeshore, a heron stood solemnly, a statue among the spiky sedges. He let me paddle far closer than herons usually do. His reflection in the water was clear and still. Slowly, the living image began to banish the memory of that foot waving in the current, the dead and matted feathers, the yellow beak and lifeless eye. I was glad.

Farther along was yet another moose, this one feeding in deep water. As I had with the bull in velvet, I eased closer to her, unseen at first. I thought how happy she must be. She was up to her neck in water, protected from the swarming bugs. Down she would go for another mouthful of food, and almost disappear, emerging later with a vast mouthful of plants.

She wouldn't let me go quietly, though, once she spotted me. She stampeded far up the shore, splashing mightily through the shallows. Once on the sand, she shook herself like a dog. For a moment, a halo of water droplets enclosed her, then she slipped into the brush.

I set up camp at Sams, well up Long Lake, a spacious site with evidence of a history in the dumped debris scattered through the woods. I ate bean soup with tortillas, cheese and olives, then sat reading by the campfire through the dry and sunny evening. In the depths of the night, I woke once more to the sound of rain pounding the tent.

The following day, I had an ambitious goal in mind, a favorite campsite called Deadwater North, 24 miles away. It would be a long day. There was a strong headwind right from the start, as I got on the water just before eight. My mind went back and forth between being glad I went as far as Sams and wishing I had gone farther.

I was very grateful to reach the end of Harvey Pond, the little pond above Long Lake that announced the return to the river proper. Immediately, riffles embraced my boat, their speed quicker than I remembered from other trips.

That should have warned me, I suppose.

Not even a mile farther, I came to the spot where Long Lake Dam had once stood. This far downriver, logs were still being driven north into the St. John River. After the first attempt at a dam washed out in its first season, another was finished in 1911. Constructed of huge pine logs at a cost of $50,000, the timber crib structure measured 700 feet across. Its 18 gates, each eight feet wide, impounded 15 feet of water. According to the Maine Bureau of Parks and Lands, *"When the gates were opened, the force was felt more than one hundred miles away at Van Buren."*

Now, high banks of earth and stone on either side marked the spot, and the river boiled over the remains of the washed-out dam. Underwater, metal spikes lurked, a danger that prevented most paddlers from even attempting to run the old dam remains. Rather, boats were usually lined through on river left or more commonly portaged on river right, where a trail climbed up through the two closest campsites.

Here, Dad and I had camped in the chill of late August 2009 and discovered our fireplace birds. That late in the summer, the mornings had been frigid. I rose early, wishing that I had brought gloves. I was rewarded by the sight of a distant moose, just a dark silhouette far down the misty, barely-pink river. She lingered long enough for Dad to see her, too.

It was so cold that our pancakes wouldn't cook over the campfire, and coffee turned icy almost as soon as it was poured. A real taste of fall. Later, I climbed back to the top of the earthenworks to take some pictures in the morning light. To get the proper angle, I squatted down above a hole in the ground, among a jumble of rocks. The opening must have led into the interior of the old dam supports, for out of the hole came the most delicious, wonderful warm air. On that crisp wilderness morning, it was like sitting on top of a heating vent!

Even though I'd been through here several times before, this time I

Great blue heron on Long Lake in the Allagash

decided to do something stupid. On our honeymoon, with Chris's long legs and strong decision-making, we had successfully lined our boat through on river left, but I'd never tried it again. Now, though, perhaps in memory of Chris, I decided to go for it, with my boat full of gear.

Lazily, I didn't take the time to attach a stern line. I inched forward slowly, holding the boat by just the slender bow line. The high water was a help at first, making it deeper than usual near shore. I worked the canoe along the shallow edge, far from the brutal metal spikes, my feet dry and secure. At the last swift drop, though, the shallow edge evaporated.

Now I was scrambling across wet rocks, tightly grasping the thin rope. Quickly, with no time for me to react, the churning river snatched at the boat. It was almost a disaster. For a moment, the canoe tipped and began to take on water. Luckily, my footing was steady enough. With all my strength, I wrestled it back upright and maneuvered it into the calmer pool below. My heart hammered as I bailed a couple of gallons of water and tried not to picture my gear being sucked into the turmoil of the dam ruins.

I had almost paid dearly for my complacency, just a few days from the end of the trip.

For the ten miles from there to Round Pond, the river's current trumped the wind. I flew along, until, in the distance, I could see a single tree standing sentinel on the marshy bank. A well-known landmark for paddlers, it was a lucky survivor of a horticultural disaster.

The first U.S. epidemic of Dutch elm disease began in Ohio in 1930. From there, the disease spread relentlessly across the country. The deadly fungus, spread by root grafting as well as bark beetles, was particularly devastating in towns and cities, where it felled the tall, beautifully shaped American elm that shaded street after street.

Here in the Allagash, isolation had saved a few elm trees. They were scattered throughout the marshy delta approaching Round Pond. As I neared the first of them, dark clouds created a dramatic background behind the bright green crown.

Choosing the leftmost of three possible channels, I hurried toward the lake, wondering if I was going to get wet again. The answer was yes. As I entered Round Pond, the rain started, then intensified into a deluge like the one on Eagle Lake. At the first campsite on the left, Inlet, two canoes, one red, one green, waited patiently while their occupants huddled under a large tarp. As usual, I was in my bathing suit, a thin T-shirt, and shorts, and I probably looked crazy.

Oh, well; once you're wet, you're wet, I thought, remembering our day on Lake Champlain. Paddling oblivious to downpours had become a trademark. Rain pelted my arms with a feeling that was part pain, part excitement. The temperature plummeted and the rain quickly iced my skin. Once again, it was too late for a rain jacket. Burning calories with vigorous paddling would have to warm me instead.

Not far past Inlet was a ranger's cabin where I stopped at the small beach to bail out my boat. The ranger called out from his door to come in and warm up.

His name was Kale and he looked familiar. It turned out that he had been the intern at Michaud Farm for the past two years, and I must have met him there. As usual, I asked about bears, as I was always hoping that someday I would see one along the water. He hadn't seen any and he'd been in the Allagash all summer.

When I think of bears on the Allagash, an encounter that Gil Gilpatrick had right here on Round Pond often comes to mind. His group had made camp early that day. Having an afternoon of freedom, he'd taken one of the canoes out alone. After a while, he ended up in the outhouse at an empty campsite called Back Channel, at the south end of the lake.

"With no one around," goes Gil's story, *"I left the door open to enjoy the view. Within a minute or so the view included a good size bear strolling leisurely down the hill about 5 yards in front of me. While I know bears are shy and avoid human contact whenever possible, it is still a little unsettling to be that close to one in such a compromising position. A little later, as I made my way back down the hill, the bear was there feeding on some berries in the empty campsite. He quickly disappeared as I approached."*

As Kale and I were talking, a float plane landed, then took off again. It had brought the woman who owns Jalbert Camps, one of two grand-fathered commercial camps that remain along the waterway. Four of the lakes along the waterway allow float plane use.

I didn't stay until the rain ended. It was just as warm moving, especially since I'd put a dry thermal top underneath my PFD. I still had a long way to go. Kale thought it was more like 30 miles from Sams to Deadwater North, although I hoped that his calculations were wrong.

So far, I hadn't seen any moose today. Kale had confirmed a sad story that I'd heard along the trail. The moose population was in decline, and the main culprit was winter ticks. Biologists believed this species of tick was faring better as Maine's winters grew shorter and warmer. Exploding numbers of winter ticks were killing moose, their preferred host, and rangers had been finding dead calves along logging roads in the Allagash region. It was somewhat comforting to learn later that they rarely fed on humans.

A single moose could be infested with as many as 100,000 winter ticks. The parasites took so much blood that affected animals became anemic and sometimes died. If they survived, they would scratch themselves bare in large patches and then die from hypothermia or fall prey to other parasites like lungworm.

With that in my mind, it was magnificent when I rounded a bend to see a huge bull in command of the river. He was close to shore and never ran, perhaps too secure in his monarchy to worry about a mere human. I searched him carefully for signs of ticks, but he looked strong and healthy. He stayed put, but kept an eye on me to be sure I behaved as I floated past.

Then there was the crazy loon. What a show he put on—preening, splashing, and dancing across the water, flapping his outstretched wings and doing somersaults. His mate's response to all those acrobatics was a soft "coo" or two.

A garter snake living among the fireplace rocks at Deadwater North

Later, I passed two more cows, bringing my moose count to a lucky thirteen.

My GPS read 27 miles when Deadwater North came into sight, beneath clouds tinged all the colors of the rainbow. Somewhere it must still have been raining. Part of me was so exhausted that I wondered why I hadn't stopped sooner. With difficulty, I got out and stood, staggering up the steep bank with a bag or two. I had snacked and lunched on the water and only stopped once, to warm up in the ranger's cabin.

By now, you've probably gotten the idea that no place is ever the same when you come back. The landscape may be unchanged, but there are so many other ingredients—the season, the weather, the company, and the chance meetings with wildlife.

Deadwater North was our favorite "Mike" campsite. Dad and I had met Mike on Umbazooksus Stream one summer, when he'd come from Kansas to spend a month camping and exploring Maine. Impulsively, we invited him to meet us at Umsaskis Bridge a few days later, with a rented canoe, for a short trip down the Allagash. Mike, who was around Dad's age and a skilled paddler, found us as planned. We ended up here one magical evening.

This time just wasn't the same. Dad and his reflector oven weren't there to bake peach cobbler. The berries we'd picked last time were out of season, and blueberry pancakes with bacon were just a dream. There were no huge bucks wading the river and no moose standing and watching Mike wash his dishes down by the river.

However, a garter snake had taken up residence in the fire pit and gazed at me intently with bright black eyes. The intricate mosaic of colors on his body curled perfectly into a miniature cave in the rocks. For supper, I had Good To-Go's herbed mushroom risotto with basil pesto, the first meal I'd tried from the Maine company that Jess and Becca had told me about back on Richardson. The food looked fresh and colorful and tasted delicious. Plus, as the package proclaimed, I could pronounce all the words on the list of ingredients.

The struggle to get here just might have been worth it after all.

CHAPTER 17

SO WORTH IT

When the point is reached where the rhythm of each stroke is as poised as the movement of the canoe itself, weariness is forgotten and there is time to watch the sky and shores without thought of distance or effort.

—**Sigurd F. Olson,** *The Singing Wilderness*

Shimmering sunlight bathed my tent with warmth. It was Sunday once more, and I dawdled, enjoying a quiet morning in camp. The garter snake came out and three cedar waxwings claimed the cherry tree on the edge of the small clearing.

Then a gray jay came, branch-hopping always closer to the picnic table, and breakfast. This dapper uncrested relative of the blue jay can be found across most of Maine, but to me they symbolize the north woods and embody the friendliness that you find among the region's human residents. A bird of many names—Canada jay, camp robber, whiskey jack—the gray jay may boldly visit camp as this one did or follow you companionably down a woods road.

Remarkably well-suited to the boreal forest, gray jays store food for the winter in an unusual way. Using saliva, they stick small clumps of food among pine needles, under lichen, or behind loose bark, high above the snow line, to eat later. Omnivores, these resourceful birds eat everything from fungi and berries to amphibians and baby birds. Strangely, they nest in late winter, in February or March, when temperatures are still dropping well below zero.

My next visitor was one of those friendly humans. A green canoe with a small motor putted upriver, and in it was a ranger. When Matthew heard that I was thru-paddling the trail, he came up to visit. His family was originally from the village of Allagash, where they'd lived a half mile up the St. John River at Dickey Plantation, home to a Revolutionary War-era settler. Matthew had moved home to the family farm not long ago. His enthusiasm for reviving it shone through as he told me about his plans.

"I hope to build a life around it, working on the Allagash and bringing the farm back to life. I'm going to start with some chickens and go from there."

As he left to work on leveling tent spots in the adjacent campsite, I packed up. It would only be a short way to the Cunliffe Depot campsite and two relics of true Yankee ingenuity.

Timber harvesting in the Allagash was a winter endeavor, and wheeled vehicles were of little use in the snowy, icy Maine woods. One night in 1900, A.O. Lombard of Waterville, son of a blacksmith, suddenly had a brainstorm and rushed home to draw out his idea. Instead of wheels, he would use articulated tracks on a machine to haul sleds of logs through the winter forest. He patented his track design, one day destined for use around the world.

The Lombard Log Hauler, built in Maine, resembled a small locomotive, with tracks on the back and skis on the front. It handled the terrain well, hauling as many as 15 log sleds along roads sprayed with water to create a smooth and icy path. On the downhills, in fact, maintaining control of the chain of careening sleds was often problematic.

In his book *The Allagash*, Lew Dietz gives one old-timer's memory of a Lombard at work, *"To meet one on a still, bitter night deep in the woods, the head lamp cutting through the darkness, chugging and rocking as it towed a train some five hundred feet long—blowing steam and smoke and fire to the treetops, was something indeed to remember."*

Chronologically, the heyday of the Lombard Hauler fell between the tramway, which it put out of business, and the railroad. The original steam-powered models were followed by ones with internal combustion gasoline engines. Back in the woods at Cunliffe Depot rested one of each, fenced to keep visitors from exposure to asbestos. Although parts of both machines had been removed over the years, the moss-shrouded tracks remained, clearly recognizable as the grandfather of the caterpillar tread on modern bulldozers and military tanks.

All paddlers departing the waterway must check out at the Michaud

Farm ranger station. Although I found no one in the office, I signed out on the self-service porch clipboard. The posted river flow was still very high for August—1,900 cubic feet per second.

In 1911, Withee and his friend Horace had stopped here, too. Back then, the main house on the prosperous farm was dubbed the "Allagash House." The pair had come away with milk fresh from the cow, a bag of potatoes, and a batch of biscuits baked while they waited.

Several miles downriver, they pitched their tent by Allagash Falls. *"At that place of surpassing beauty…baked potatoes, trout rolled in corn meal and fried in bacon fat, fresh biscuit, cake and blueberries, tea and milk made up the menu…that camp was as nearly perfect as a camp could ever be…(with) a rousing fire to toast our feet by and the orchestra of the falls to lull us to sleep."*

I was headed to the falls next. Climbing back into my canoe, a memory came back, from the year we'd said goodbye to Mike here. He and Dad had shared a farewell drink, then I'd hugged Mike goodbye and Dad had led us off downriver. From ahead, his voice drifted back to me and I realized he was singing a song from my childhood, *"Alouette, gentille Alouette, Alouette, je te plumerai. Je te plumerai la tête, je te plumerai la tête. Et la tête, et la tête. Alouette, Alouette."*

Then a long, drawn-out "oh" and on he went, doing justice to the French voyagers of long ago, his blue boat drifting merrily down the wide river. I smiled, remembering, and was glad that in two days Dad and I would be reunited on the river.

Below Michaud Farm, the character of the river began to change. The heavy woods receded, and airy, grassy shores took over. The river widened, splitting around midstream islands, where silver maple stretched far out over the water. At typically lower summer water levels, I would have had to be vigilant to avoid the shallows, but this trip I had no problems.

It was truly bittersweet when, all too soon, my faithful canoe sat at the start of its last portage. On other trips, with heavier boats, the one-third of a mile carry around the falls had seemed a monumental challenge. Today it was a breeze. I had Allagash Falls to myself and sat for a time, eating a PB&J wrap and contemplating life. The grandeur of the 30-foot falls on a blue-and-gold day encompasses the entire world around. Turbulent waters drop through a chute of enfolding ledge, framed by the spires of the ever-present conifers.

Beyond being an aesthetic gem, the falls now serves as a critically important barrier to another nonnative species, the muskellunge or "muskie."This large, voracious game fish has made its way from Quebec, where it was introduced into Lac Frontiere by a biologist, throughout the St. John watershed to the brink of the falls. So far, the Allagash River above the falls is free of muskies, as well as yellow perch and small and largemouth bass, all of which would threaten the native brook trout fishery.

Just an hour and a half for the portage and I was back on the river and contemplating where to camp. I was in the mood to try somewhere new. As I passed Big Brook entering on river right, I checked the map. There were three campsites not far ahead that would leave me about ten miles to paddle tomorrow to meet Mom and Dad.

Clusters of clean, white-skinned birch brightened the forest and the shore in places was a mass of grass and wildflowers. Some easy riffles and scattered rocks made for fast and fun progress. I didn't want to be going so quickly that I missed the campsites, though, so I stayed vigilant. I came to Big Brook South first, on the left. Above a steep and slippery scramble, the roomy campsite was dry and empty. I took it.

When I could, I tried to stack some firewood, often tucked up underneath the picnic table, for whoever camped after me. This seemed to be another admirable north woods tradition. At this site, some kind soul had split kindling to leave beside the tidy stack of birch logs. A pair of red squirrels chased each other around while I settled in.

Not surprisingly, the evening felt profound—it was my last night of wilderness solitude. Tomorrow I would be in a cabin in Allagash village, trading nature for companionship. I stayed up late writing. One by one, the stars emerged, as I wrote my thoughts under their watchful gaze. I never wanted the night to end.

One thread that wove its way into my reflections was simple gratitude that this waterway existed in its present form and was being allowed to return to a wilder state. Established in 1966, the Allagash Wilderness Waterway was designated a National Wild and Scenic River in 1970, under the stewardship of the Maine Department of Agriculture, Conservation, and Forestry. Its value to the public should not be taken for granted.

In December 2012, the state published a new management plan, to shepherd the waterway through its next fifteen years. Within it lie truths and insights that go beyond what I would have expected to find in a dry government document.

Of the four zones delineated in the management plan, the innermost is the Restricted Zone, a ribbon of land along the waterway, 500 feet in width and totaling almost 23,000 acres. As defined in the Allagash statute, this state-owned and managed zone *"shall preserve, protect, and develop the maximum wilderness character of the watercourse."*

Surrounded as it is by a working forest, this narrow border must be carefully managed for both conservation and recreational use, while maintaining its wilderness character. *"Wilderness character can be thought of as a mix of physical, social, managerial, and even symbolic conditions coming together to create a setting with specific traits experienced by visitors."*

For each of these four components, the plan lists actions and attitudes that together strive to preserve this wilderness character. Many are what you would expect and hope to find—rustic design, protection of native plants and animals, screening of campsites and structures, limited access points, and fewer signs. However, there are surprises, too.

The section on the social aspect of wilderness begins, *"Natural views, sounds, and smells dominate. Solitude, freedom, adventure, self-reliance, relaxation, appreciation for nature and history, and a sense of connectedness with something larger than one's self are predominant values. Pristine environments, primitive campsites, and minimized evidence of modern human activity...provide opportunities for inspiration and contemplation."*

Another bullet point addresses the symbolic aspect of wilderness: *"Intangible Waterway values such as heritage and pride, freedom, conservation, the interconnectedness of nature, mystery, restraint and humility, etc. will be emphasized in Waterway information with the intention of enriching visitor experiences. Visitor experiences are enriched and wilderness character is enhanced by forging intellectual and emotional connections between visitors and the natural and cultural resource stories unique to the Waterway."*

This lengthy management plan voices the spiritual reasons that I come to the Allagash and other wild places. It honors the values that abide in wilderness and are revealed to us when the blur of civilization falls away. Wilderness helps us find meaning in our lives. It gives us a place, a breadth of space in which to do so that can never be overvalued. Acknowledging that and preserving it should be a guiding principle for natural areas everywhere. That the plan's writers expressed these ideas is a key to understanding why the Allagash is such a special place.

The next morning, the crackling campfire made a circle of warmth in the crisp air. Perched on a fireside rock, I ate the last of my oatmeal, then sadly packed up.

I had forgotten how beautiful the final miles of the waterway were. Many tree trunks, though, had been ravaged by the savage power of the spring ice breakup. The scars, high above the level of the river, reminded me what a different world this was in winter. The strength of the rain-swelled river had created a Class II rapid that didn't show up on the map, about halfway between two landmarks with haunting names. McGargle Rocks and Ghost Bar Landing both commemorated fatalities of the logging era. I ran the unmarked rapid safely.

At Twin Brooks Rapids, also Class II, the official waterway ended, although the river would continue for another six miles to the village. I thought that I'd finish with a count of thirteen moose, but spotted a young bull just past the sign that marked the end of the waterway. Moose #14 had small velvet antlers and very long legs and browsed unconcerned among a patch of bright pink spiky fireweed. He was the last moose of the trip.

I had a good friend I was looking forward to seeing in Allagash village. When Dad, Taylor, and I had gotten off the river back in 2011, Sue Kelly had given us the warmest welcome imaginable. We rented one of her cabins, and she brought us homemade brownies and the little items we'd run out of and let me use her computer for hours. We have since come to know the rest of the folks at Two Rivers Lunch and Tylor Kelly Camps.

The first sign of the approaching village was a backhoe working on the left, where a road now ran along the river. Then came a house high on the bank and I knew there was just a curve or two to go. After pulling up on the gravel shore, I carried all my gear and the boat up to the restaurant yard. Sue was away doing a river shuttle, so I ordered lunch and wrote.

John Mautner had signed the guestbook, but hadn't dated his entry. I wondered if he, too, had suddenly felt a desire to be finished, to wrap things up, and the certainty of success.

Mom and Dad soon arrived, bringing a cooler with pork chops for dinner, and it was so good to see them. Then Sue returned from her shuttle, got us our key, and there were hugs and congratulations and lots of news to catch up on. We headed to bed early, as Dad and I were contemplating trying to finish tomorrow. We'd originally planned to take two days to cover the 28 miles to Fort Kent, but there was nothing appealing about camping in the forecast rain.

Our final day was not fun. Dad capsized and lost his GPS. I

destroyed my camera by dropping it in the water. Not a promising start for what would turn into a grueling marathon.

After a hearty breakfast, we had said goodbye to Mom about nine o'clock. From the put-in, it was less than a mile until the Allagash would meet the St. John River. In this short section lay straightforward Casey Rapids, barely worthy of a name. Dad suggested that I go first today, to find a good line through any whitewater.

Once through, I swiveled around to check Dad's progress. He was just threading his way between two rocks when he hung up on a third. His canoe began to tip away, upriver, and took on water. Within a minute, he was in the river taking a chilly swim. I scooped up his hat and water bottle as they floated by. Dad was fine and walked his canoe to shore, still with a solid grip on his double-bladed paddle. Trying to be helpful, I hauled his boat up on the pebbly beach and dumped out the water.

It was the next day, driving home, when Dad suddenly realized that his lost GPS was most likely on that beach, not in the river!

Back on the water, we passed under a bridge and turned right on the St. John, still going northeast and downstream. This would be my last river, but there wasn't time to dwell on that. We were searching for Dad's cherry canoe paddle, which had floated away when he dumped. Luckily, it had also made the turn, and Dad spotted it washed up on a gravel bar.

The St. John seemed huge after the Allagash. Along its length, it was fed by one brook after another, adding to the considerable current. The first 11 miles to the town of Saint Francis contained several Class II rapids, including an unmarked one where Pelletier Brook entered on river right, only a mile along. It was a sea of rocks that came at lightning speed. Committing myself to the center of the river, I ended up with enough water and ran it safely, just barely.

Dad, nearer shore, was forced to get out and line his boat through, crossing the mouth of the brook on foot. I pulled over below the rapids and walked back to bring him a makeshift walking stick I'd found. With my other hand, I tried to take his picture. This was not a smart idea. I ended up dropping the camera in the water, the end of the action shots.

After that, we fared better. By lunchtime, we were nearing Saint Francis, where we would rendezvous with Mom. She had gotten comfortable driving Dad's truck just for this trip and was meeting us for lunch. At the general store, we packed in the calories, wolfing down cheeseburgers, sodas, and candy bars. We heard it would be another four or five hours to reach Fort Kent.

So far, the rain had held off and we decided to go for it. As much as I had wanted to dawdle on the Allagash, I wanted to hurry now. Soon it started to rain in earnest, but at least all the difficult rapids, four of them, had been before lunch. Dad had run the last ones fine, including Cross Rock Rapids and the huge standing waves of Rankin Rapids. The fast-moving current helped us, and we averaged about four miles per hour.

Soon we passed the mouth of the St. Francis River and the land on our left became the Canadian province of New Brunswick. This was an area of rolling hills and agricultural fields, where here and there a white church spire hinted at a town. In the rain, there wasn't any wildlife and we amused ourselves instead by guessing how soon we'd finish, and later, *whether* we'd finish. The map indicated it was 17 miles from St. Francis to the trail's end.

In his book, *The Lonely Land*, Sigurd Olson writes, *"We were often cold, wet and weary, but this was the price we expected to pay and the paying itself was good."*

On other rainy days, I probably would have agreed, but not today. Sheer determination, at which I was now an expert, was barely enough to keep me going. I can't imagine how Dad made it, but he never mentioned giving up.

It was late afternoon, and we were spent, when a large bridge came

Raising my paddle in victory on Day 53, Fort Kent, Maine

into sight. This was the International Bridge, a border crossing into Canada, and a sign that we were almost there.

First Dad, then I, slipped under the bridge. Near the mouth of the Fish River, on river right, I backpaddled and drifted, waiting while Dad went slowly up to the truck to get his phone. When he returned, I paddled the short distance that remained to come into Fort Kent's Riverside Park, raising my paddle high for a victory photo.

"My numb, white fingers and shivering self tempered some of the emotion of the moment, but I still felt ready to cry. So many days of beauty, danger, kindness, and endurance were coming to an end. A dream, that once seemed beyond all reach, would now become a treasured memory."

Just before six in the evening, I stood at the kiosk marking the Eastern Terminus of the Northern Forest Canoe Trail. I was finished. My GPS had recorded roughly 750 miles in 53 days, and I had covered every mile unassisted. It felt unbelievable.

Behind me stretched a journey of faith, trailing back across four states and one province. That it had unfolded roughly as planned was due only in part to me. I had brought an unwavering goal, to earn the two asterisks, unless injury or a boat catastrophe intervened. In my mind, anything less would have been quitting. The rest came from those who helped me and believed in me and from God who went beside me.

I wish I could say that I dropped to my knees in prayer or uttered some memorable words, but mostly I just wanted some hot soup. The rest would come later.

EPILOGUE

In time of sorrow…may you see God's light on the path ahead
When the road you walk is dark,
May you always hear, even in your hour of sorrow,
The gentle singing of the lark.
When times are hard may hardness never turn your heart to stone—
May you always remember when the shadows fall—
You do not walk alone.

—A Celtic blessing

There was still a bit of summer left to savor when we got home, then life grabbed me, with back-to-school and the-world-goes-on demands. It wasn't until January that I returned to the book with the focus and discipline this project needed. My room downstairs in my parents' home became my haven, simple living by necessity, with a woodstove for heat. The quiet writing, especially in the early mornings, fed my soul in the absence of the river.

My two waterproof journals filled with tiny, neat writing helped immensely. In researching, I favored historic sources and authors whose works had influenced me before the trip. What I found interesting, I shared. The names of a few characters, including the students from the Brooklyn school, were changed because their permission was impossible to obtain.

The community of paddlers is a wonderful, caring, far-flung group. In August 2016, when my parents and I arrived in the Netherlands on a cruise of a different kind, there was some NFCT trail magic waiting for me. Geoff and Valerie Welch, 2014 thru-paddlers, took me kayaking. It was the day before they left for an expedition in Mongolia, but off we went to Delft to explore the town's quaint, flowery canals and ramble up church towers.

I signed the trail register in Fort Kent below John Mautner, the thru-paddler we had met on Raquette Lake. He had gradually pulled ahead and finished the trail 17 days before me, on July 25. When *The NFCT List* was updated for 2015, there was my name, between John

*Kayaking the Delft canals in The Netherlands with
2014 thru-paddlers Geoff and Valerie Welch (Valerie Welch photo)*

Mautner and Mack Truax, my friend who had gotten lost around Spencer Stream. All three of us had earned the double asterisks.

As it turned out, Sydney and Marji Aveson were done for 2015 when their rescuer, Scotty, returned as promised and drove them to Jackman. Friends with a cottage on Moosehead Lake picked them up, after they couldn't find new wheels at any of the outfitters. Marji had to get back for the start of the school year and Sydney didn't have the equipment to finish alone.

The following summer, though, they returned together in "Old Green." Their adventures paddling from Kineo to Fort Kent included the good, the bad, and the ugly. Mud Pond Carry was tough, but they were tougher. Sydney finally saw her moose, a bunch of them, including a baby. An Allagash ranger gave them a blueberry pie. And then there was that swim in Chase Rapids, the day that the bear barrel floated away. But in the end, it all made for a great story, and Marji says they bonded in ways they'd never imagined.

Mack, too, came back to the NFCT in 2016, becoming the first person to thru-paddle the trail twice. He didn't get lost, although he did damage his kayak on the Saranac River and left the trail for a day on Lake

Champlain to go and buy another one. He holds the current thru-paddler speed record of 21 days, including his day of unexpected shopping.

Katina Daanen switched gears in 2016, put on a backpack, and set off from the south end of Shenandoah National Park in Virginia for a flip-flop thru-hike of the Appalachian Trail. We hiked together one day there and again for three days as she crossed from Vermont into New Hampshire. After summiting Katahdin, she went home. In 2017, she started anew at Springer Mountain, Georgia and hiked north to her original starting point, finishing her two-year, 2,150-mile section hike of the AT on June 30.

When I wrote to Ed and Shirley, from Raymonds Country Store on Northeast Carry, for permission to use their stories, it was by snail mail. They pick up their mail once a week far down the lake in Rockwood. Shirley answered right away.

"As for the fellow who lost his thumb," she wrote, *"a year or so after the accident on a busy Saturday, a fellow comes rushing into the store, comes right up into my space and starts waving his thumb in my face. He was so close that I was cross-eyed looking at the thumb. He was very excited and saying, 'They saved it, look, look!' When the accident occurred, he was all bundled up from shock and the cold so we never really got to see his face and now some man is in my space. Once he calmed down and we saw his brother in the background we realized who he was. It was fantastic!!!! Everyone involved did a great job. His thumb was reattached and usable. Now we see him every winter with a working thumb. Great to see happy endings."*

The Northern Forest Canoe Trail will continue to gather paddlers, for a day or a season. The NFCT community of towns, traditions, and especially people will grow, building on the foundation laid by those in my story and many others, just as dedicated.

Soon, other women will take to their boats alone for an NFCT thru-paddle…in fact, one already has. Some will go far faster than me, or run more of the difficult rapids, or even travel in boats they have crafted with their own hands. More writers will share their journeys and their stories will be new and yet the same. To help this come to pass, I would urge you to consider NFCT membership, a gift of stewardship, education, and preservation of this timeless way.

I have one last story, though I've blurred some details on purpose. I was walking my canoe along a road, muddy and bleak from a morning of steady rain. *I wish I had some ice*, I thought, wiping my sweaty face on my shirt and thinking of the last of my white wine in its little paper box. There wasn't a store for miles, though, so it was just wishful thinking.

Late in the afternoon, a couple of guys in a red pickup truck stopped to chat. The driver could have been a logger or a farmer and was the one who did the talking, while his passenger slouched silently in the other seat. He was younger, a lot skinnier and a little rough looking, with tattoos and a grimy baseball cap. Like folks everywhere, they were intrigued by my trip.

"Not a good day for canoeing," the driver pointed out and I told him how windy and rough it had been out on the water that morning.

Then I glanced into the bed of the pickup. Along with a bunch of other stuff, there was a worn blue and white cooler, no doubt containing ice. After what seemed like a respectable amount of friendly conversation, I decided to ask.

"You don't have any ice, do you?"

Still without a word, the younger guy hopped out, opened the cooler lid, and pulled out a clean bag, full of ice. He opened it, shaking ice cubes into my empty Nalgene bottle. When it was halfway full, I tried to stop him.

"That should be plenty. I don't want to take all your ice."

At last, he spoke. "We're headed out past the store. We can get more." As he carefully filled my water bottle to the brim, I thanked him. Somehow, that act of kindness was all the more meaningful for being rather surprising.

The tale doesn't end there, though. Not long afterward, a car came along. It looked shiny and expensive and too new to be driving these rugged roads. The older couple inside also stopped to say hello. They often drove this road at dusk to look for moose, they said.

Soon they brought up religion, sharing how involved they were in their church. They talked at length about the importance of the Spirit in their lives and congregation, like they wanted to convince me. Then, a minute later, the conversation changed direction.

"Did you see two men come past earlier in a red pickup?" they asked.

Before I could do more than nod my head, they continued, "We didn't like the looks of them. They're probably drinking or doing drugs. The high school kids around here are always coming out here to party. Leaving trash, getting high. Of course, the Mexicans were even worse. Did you know they used to camp right near here when they were planting trees? You can never trust a Mexican. They'll slit your throat for twenty dollars down in Mexico."

By now I was speechless.

Later, after they'd wound down and driven off, I thought of the contrast between the two vehicles that had stopped to visit. What can I say? I can hear Jesus telling the guys in the pickup, "Well done, my good and faithful servants!"

I will choose to believe the best of people.

In the mornings, when I remember, I ask God to make me a blessing to others that day, a simple prayer that works out better some days than others. I believe that in people, in their compassion and enthusiasm, generosity and smiles, we can catch a glimpse of God. And give one, too. The trail angels I had found along the way certainly proved that true.

On my last morning in camp, Gil, I remember leaving the outhouse door propped open wide. No bear came along, but I did see the ebony winging of a raven and a dainty cluster of perfectly formed mushrooms. That spirit of hopefulness, of discovering what adventures the day would bring, kept me moving, always upwards. Back home now, I try to cherish the promise of each new dawn and remember, always remember, that every day is a gift.

Henry Withee ended his account with these words, about coming home:

"We had sound, hard bodies, clear, alert eyes and minds and thoroughly alert appetites. After our return, so our folks tell us, it was some time before the spell of the wood left us. We were quiet, serene, and the voice of the river seemed to be still with us. At night we were shooting rapids, or struggling over log-jams, or catching thousands of trout. The spell gradually wore away, but the memory of that trip will remain for many years. And if we live, we shall go again, for the enchantment which falls upon those who have gone into the woodland is never broken."

Twice now, I've landed in special places on dates heavy with meaning. Umsaskis ten years after our honeymoon. And another time, during Paddle for Hope, when I brought Withee's journal with me to read along the way. Do you recall his race through the river of logs to a campsite just below Smith's Halfway House? The date was July 7, 1911. Precisely one hundred years later, on July 7, 2011, I sat reading his story at the Big Ragmuff campsite along the West Branch, realizing with astonishment that I was in almost the same spot.

September 2053 will be the bicentennial of Thoreau's second trip through the Maine woods. I'll be ninety-one then, if I'm still around. Perhaps I will paddle the West Branch of the Penobscot that fall, following Thoreau one last time. I like to believe it's possible.

My friend Arne Aho honored my expedition in a truly memorable way

ACKNOWLEDGMENTS

For many of us, family is our foundation. We don't get to choose them, but if I could, I would choose mine all over again. Every single incredible, unique, and caring one of them. Mom and Dad, you nurtured my true self through the years and gave me the gift of time together, outdoors, where it all began. Greg, everyone should have a little brother. I was lucky to get one who loved exploring nature as much as I did! Grandma Jan, you gave me books and wildflowers, birds and writing—I hope you know that *Upwards* came in part from you. Grandma Grace, you told me to go have fun, and I did—you were always utterly enthusiastic about our adventures and set us a fine example (for 101 years) of living our days to the fullest. Megan and Taylor, you were the greatest gifts that God ever gave me and still are, every day.

Putting your manuscript in the hands of others takes courage. Once you do, though, their thoughts become changes, adding clarity, accuracy, depth, and character to the pages that you have read so many times. Katina, from the moment you told me that a blog would bring me lots of love, through the finest detail of your countless editing hours, words cannot express my gratitude.

Dan (my editor at Maine Authors Publishing), you brought the book to a new level of professionalism and, in the process, taught me the fine art of the comma. Wendy, you patiently crafted my vision for the book design into a beautiful reality. The rest of the folks at MAP—Kristine, Jane, Nikki, Amy, and Kelly—cheerfully and expertly guided me through the publishing maze to the magic moment when I held the first copy of *Upwards* in my hands.

Sandy, Karrie, Kay, and Rob, you gently helped me do justice to the NFCT story. Dad, you kept me honest and tried to tame my superlatives. And to everyone else who encouraged me, prayed for me, read bits and pieces, or answered my eternal questions, every kind word kept me at my computer longer.

Words flow best for me in the serenity of the natural world. I deeply appreciate the friends—Steve and Jo, Ed and Carol, and Bill and Mary—who kept my boat by the lake and my soul in the woods by sharing their corners of Maine. For all the quiet places to write and the wise dogs (and one cat) who knew when to pull me away to the woods—thank you—especially to Jon, Cyndy, Lily, and Moxie the walking cat; Steve, Kathy, Indy, and Kit; Dave, Sheila, and Emma; and Don, Betsy, and Bella.

Much of the year, my weekdays are spent in middle school, helping students with special needs thrive in regular classrooms. Anne and John, you proved that 7th and 8th graders can cover a lot of ground in two years. While teaching and inspiring them, you nourished a budding author, too.

Naturally, if your name appears within this story, you were a part of my journey and a key to my safe completion of the trail. Not only was every day a gift, but so were all the people who made my days comfortable, memorable, delightful, or just plain endurable. I am thankful that you were where you were, when you were, and hope that you have enjoyed reading our tale as much as I have enjoyed writing it.

REFERENCES

Allington, A. (2009, October 29). *German POWs return to Maine in friendship.* Retrieved from the Voice of America website: http://www.voanews.com/ a/a-13-2005-05-06-voa46-67389482/275278.html

Allyn, A. (1877). *Vermont Historical Magazine: Indian history of "Long Pond."* Retrieved from The US GenWeb Project website: http://www.rootsweb.ancestry.com/~vtwindha/vhg3/0105_charleston.htm

ANS Task Force. (n.d.). *Harmful aquatic hitchhikers: Crustaceans: Spiny water flea and fishhook water flea.* Retrieved from the Protect Your Waters website: http://protectyourwaters.net/hitchhikers/ crustaceans_spiny_water_flea

Appalachian Mountain Club. (2008). *AMC river guide: Maine.* (J. Fiske, Ed.) Boston: Appalachian Mountain Club Books.

Barker, A. (n.d.). *Lacroix's legacy.* Retrieved from the North Maine Woods, Inc. website: http://www.northmainewoods.org/images/pdf/lacroix.pdf

Burnell, A. L. (2010). *Images of America: Lost villages of Flagstaff Lake.* Charleston, SC: Arcadia Publishing.

Cook, D. S. (1985). *Above the gravel bar: The Indian canoe routes of Maine.* Milo, Maine: Milo Printing Co.

Cornell Lab of Ornithology. (2015). *Belted kingfisher, Hermit thrush, Gray jay.* Retrieved from the All About Birds website: http://www.allaboutbirds.org

Daanen, K. (2014). *The Northern Forest Canoe Trail through-paddler's companion.* Self-published.

Dell'Amore, C. (2015, June 1). *What's a ghost moose? How ticks are killing an iconic animal.* Retrieved from the National Geographic website: http://news.nationalgeographic.com/2015/06/ 150601-ghost-moose-animals-science-new-england-environment/

DeLorme. (2011). *The Maine atlas and gazetteer.* Yarmouth, Maine: DeLorme.

Dietz, L. (1968). *The Allagash.* Camden, Maine: Down East Books.

Duquette, J. J. (1985, April 2). Evolution of the locks joining the Saranac River. *Adirondack Daily Enterprise Weekender.*

German war prisoners quartered at Spencer Pond lumber operation. (1944, August 2). *Waterville Morning Sentinel.* p. 8.

Gilpatrick, G. (2003). *Allagash: A journey through time on Maine's legendary wilderness waterway.* Skowhegan, Maine: Self-published.

Great Lakes Research and Education Center and the Great Lakes Restoration Initiative. (2010). *Spiny water flea (Bythotrephes longimanus)*. Isle Royale National Park: National Park Service, U.S. Department of the Interior.

Hamilton, A. (2011). *Why? Making sense of God's will*. Nashville: Abington Press.

Hilyard, G. R. (2000). *Carrie Stevens: Maker of Rangeley favorite trout and salmon flies*. Mechanicsburg, PA: Stackpole Books.

Jerome, C. (1994). *An Adirondack passage: The cruise of the canoe Sairy Gamp*. New York: HarperCollins Publishers.

Lake Champlain Basin Program. (2014, August 28). *Spiny water flea confirmed in Lake Champlain*. Retrieved from the Lake Champlain Basin Program website: http://www.lcbp.org/2014/08/spiny-water-flea-confirmed-lake-champlain

Maine Bureau of Parks and Lands. (2013). *Allagash history, The Eagle Lake & West Branch Railroad, The Eagle Lake Tramway*. Retrieved from the Department of Agriculture, Conservation, and Forestry website: http://www.maine.gov/dacf/parks/discover_history_explore_nature/history/allagash

Maine Division of Parks and Public Lands. (2012, December). *Allagash Wilderness Waterway management plan*. Retrieved from the Department of Agriculture, Conservation, and Forestry website: http://www.maine.gov/dacf/parks/get_involved/planning_and_acquisition/management_plans/docs/AWW_Final_mgt_plan_2012.pdf

Maine Historical Society. (2010). *To 1500: People of the dawn*. Retrieved from the Maine History Online website: http://www.mainememory.net/sitebuilder/site/893/page/1304/display

Maine Natural Areas Program. (2013). *Bigelow Preserve: Ecological reserve fact sheet*. Retrieved from the Department of Agriculture, Conservation, and Forestry website: http://www.maine.gov/dacf/mnap/reservesys/bigelow.htm

MDIFW Commissioner and Advisory Council. (2004, September 23). *Bald eagle management goals and objectives 2004–2019*. Retrieved from the Maine Department of Inland Fisheries & Wildlife website: https://www1.maine.gov/ifw/pdfs/species_planning/birds/baldeagle/baldeagle.pdf

Mielke, B. (2016, February 3). *Meet the voters who will cast the first primary ballots of 2016*. Retrieved from the ABC News website: http://abcnews.go.com/Politics/meet-voters-cast-primary-ballots-2016/story?id=36647998

North Maine Woods, Inc. (n.d.). *History of the North Maine Woods (NMW)*. Retrieved from the North Maine Woods, Inc. website: http://www.northmainewoods.org/aboutus/history.html

Northern Forest Canoe Trail. (Dates vary). NFCT Maps 1 to 13. Seattle: The Mountaineers Books.

The Northern Forest Canoe Trail, Inc. (2010). *The Northern Forest Canoe Trail.* Seattle: The Mountaineers Books.

Northwest Regional Planning Commission & Vermont Agency of Transportation. (2013). *Guide to the Missisquoi Valley Rail Trail.* St. Albans, Vermont: Northwest Regional Planning Commission.

Novotney, A. (2008, March). Getting back to the great outdoors. *Monitor on Psychology*, p. 52.

Olson, Sigurd F. (1976). *The lonely land.* Mineola, NY: Alfred A. Knopf.

POW camp discovery provides history lesson. (2006, November 26). *Maine Sun Journal.*

Rich, L. D. (1942). *We took to the woods.* Camden, Maine: Down East Books.

Sears, G. W. (1963). *Woodcraft and camping.* Mineola, NY: Dover Publications.

Skow, J. (1997, September). Big dreams in the big woods. *AMC Outdoors*, pp. 22–27.

Thoreau, H. D. (1864). *The Maine woods.* Boston: Ticknor and Fields.

TIME. (1952, November 10). The nation: Election day. *TIME*, p. 22.

Turner, J. L. (2015, April). Sundews, butterworts, and bladderworts, oh my! *New York State Conservationist*, pp. 6–9.

The University of Maine. (n.d.). *Tick species of Maine—Winter tick or moose tick.* Retrieved from the UMaine Cooperative Extension: Insect Pests, Ticks, and Plant Diseases website: http://extension.umaine.edu/ipm/tickid/maine-tick-species/winter-tick-or-moose-tick

U.S. Fish & Wildlife Service. (2015). *Bald Eagle.* Retrieved from the U.S. Fish & Wildlife Service website: http://www.fws.gov/midwest/eagle/index.html

Vermont Department of Environmental Conservation's Watershed Management Division. (2015, May 6). *Stop the spread of spiny water flea!* Retrieved from flow: http://vtwatershedblog.com/2015/05/06/stop-the-spread-of-spiny-water-flea

Withee, H. L. (1911). *Down the Allagash.* Retrieved from the Maine Historical Society: Maine Memory Network website: http://www.mainememory.net/media/pdf/17311.pdf

CAMPING, LODGING AND
MILEAGE STATISTICS

Day 1—June 20—to lean-to on Seventh Lake, NY (14.7/14.7 mi.)

Day 2—June 21—to Tioga Point SP on Raquette Lake, NY (11.7/26.4 mi.)

Day 3—June 22—to Deerland Carry lean-to on the Raquette River, NY (13.1/39.5 mi.)

Day 4—June 23—to Hidden Cove lean-to on Long Lake, NY (7.5/47.0 mi.)

Day 5—June 24—to lean-to on the Raquette River, NY (15.4/62.4 mi.)

Day 6—June 25—to island campsite on Middle Saranac Lake, NY (14.3/76.7 mi.)

Day 7—June 26—to Dave and Patti's home in Saranac Lake, NY (13.8/90.5 mi.)

Day 8—June 27—to Bear Point campsite on Union Falls Pond, NY (20.1/110.6 mi.)

Day 9—June 28—to Baker's Acres Campground on the Saranac River, NY (21.3/131.9 mi.)

Day 10—June 29—to the Comfort Inn in Plattsburgh, NY (20.0/151.9 mi.)

Day 11—June 30—to Knight Island SP on Lake Champlain, VT (17.9/169.8 mi.)

Day 12—July 1—to the Swanton Motel in Swanton, VT (26.1/195.9 mi.)

Day 13—July 2—to stealth campsite on the Missisquoi River, VT (12.3/208.2 mi.)

Day 14—July 3—to the Abbey Restaurant on the Missisquoi River, VT (8.7/216.9 mi.)

Day 15—July 4—to stealth campsite on the Missisquoi River, VT (16.3/233.1 mi.)

Day 16—July 5—to Grey Gables Mansion B&B in Richford, VT (5.4/238.5 mi.)

Day 17—July 6—to Canoe & Co. on the Missisquoi River, QC (12.1/250.6 mi.)

Day 18—July 7—to Perkins Landing on Lake Memphremagog, QC (18.8/269.4 mi.)

Day 19—July 8—to the Derby Four Seasons Inn in Derby, VT (15.9/285.3 mi.)

Day 20—July 9—to Great Falls NFCT campsite on West Charleston Pond, VT (10.3/295.6 mi.)

Day 21—July 10—to the Ten Mile Square NFCT Farmstand on the Clyde River, VT (11.1/306.7 mi.)

Day 22—July 11—to Brighton SP on Spectacle Pond, VT (12.8/319.5 mi.)

Day 23—July 12—to Vermont River Conservancy campsite on the East Branch of the Nulhegan River, VT (16.0/335.5 mi.)

Day 24—July 13—to Samuel Benton NFCT campsite on the Connecticut River, VT (16.6 miles/352.1 mi.)

Day 25—July 14—to Weston Dam in Groveton, NH and Ray and Hildy's home (10.1/362.2 mi.)

Day 26—July 15—to stealth campsite on the Upper Ammonoosuc River, NH (14.1/376.3 mi.)

Day 27—July 16—to Cedar Pond Campground in Milan, NH (9.8/386.1 mi.)

Day 28—July 17—to stealth campsite on the Androscoggin River, NH (15.3/401.4 mi.)

Day 29—July 18—to Errol, NH and the Peace of Heaven B&B (7.9/409.3 mi.)

Day 30—July 19—to Spaulding Cove campsite on The Narrows, Richardson Lakes, ME (15.8/425.1 mi.)

Day 31—July 20—to Oquossoc, ME and Cup o'Tea cabin (14.8/ 439.9 mi.)

Day 32—July 21—to the Maine Forestry Museum in Rangeley, ME and Cup o'Tea cabin (10.1/450.0 mi.)

Day 33—July 22—to stealth campsite on the South Branch of the Dead River, ME (15.9/465.9 mi.)

Day 34—July 23—to Stratton, ME and Sugarloaf (9.1/475.0 mi.)

Day 35—July 24—to island campsite on Flagstaff Lake, ME (18.2/493.2 mi.)

Day 36—July 25—to Spencer Stream and Grand Falls Hut, ME (9.8/503.0 mi.)

Day 37—July 26—to Fish Pond campground, ME (13.8/516.8 mi.)

Day 38—July 27—to Sally Mountain Beach campsite on Attean Pond, ME (18.1/534.9 mi.)

Day 39—July 28—to Lower Narrows campsite on Long Pond, ME (15.9/550.8 mi.)

Day 40—July 29—to NFCT island campsite on Brassua Lake, ME (16.4/567.2 mi.)

Day 41—July 30—to The Birches Resort on Moosehead Lake, ME (10.0/577.2 mi.)

Day 42—July 31—The Birches Resort on Moosehead Lake, ME (0/577.2mi.)

Day 43—August 1—to Big Duck Cove campsite on Moosehead Lake, ME (9.3/586.5 mi.)

Day 44—August 2—to Lone Pine campsite on the West Branch of the Penobscot River, ME (20.6/607.1 mi.)

Day 45—August 3—to Umbazooksus Stream West campsite, ME (14.4/621.5 mi.)

Day 46—August 4—to Mud Brook campsite on Chamberlain Lake, ME (7.9/629.4 mi.)

Day 47—August 5—to Priestly Point campsite on Eagle Lake, ME (14.0/643.4 mi.)

Day 48—August 6—to Jaws campsite on Churchill Lake, ME (9.4/652.8 mi.)

Day 49—August 7—to Sams campsite on Long Lake, ME (17.3/670.1 mi.)

Day 50—August 8—to Deadwater North campsite on the Allagash River, ME (27.0/697.1 mi.)

Day 51—August 9—to Big Brook South campsite on the Allagash River, ME (12.0/709.1 mi.)

Day 52—August 10—to Tylor Kelly Camps cabin in Allagash, ME (9.8/718.9 mi.)

Day 53—August 11—to the NFCT kiosk in Fort Kent, ME (30.8/749.7 mi.)